Steve Austin is sought out by environmental agencies, law enforcement authorities and border protection forces around the world for his expertise in working with creatures great and small, particularly dogs. He has trained these remarkable animals for an extraordinary variety of tasks including protection of many different types of threatened wildlife and habitats in Australia and elsewhere – his involvement in the world-first environmental rescue of Macquarie Island is a particular highlight. He lives with his wife, Vicki, on the outskirts of Sydney with ample room for their menagerie.

Working Dog
HEROES

Steve Austin
with Hazel Flynn

ABC
Books

The ABC 'Wave' device is a trademark of the Australian Broadcasting Corporation and is used under licence by HarperCollinsPublishers Australia.

First published in 2016
by HarperCollins*Publishers* Australia Pty Limited
ABN 36 009 913 517
harpercollins.com.au

Copyright © Steve Austin 2016

The right of Steve Austin to be identified as the author of this work has been asserted by him in accordance with the *Copyright Amendment (Moral Rights) Act 2000*.

This work is copyright. Apart from any use as permitted under the *Copyright Act 1968*, no part may be reproduced, copied, scanned, stored in a retrieval system, recorded, or transmitted, in any form or by any means, without the prior written permission of the publisher.

HarperCollins*Publishers*
Level 13, 201 Elizabeth Street, Sydney, NSW 2000, Australia
Unit D1, 63 Apollo Drive, Rosedale, Auckland 0632, New Zealand
A 53, Sector 57, Noida, UP, India
1 London Bridge Street, London SE1 9GF, United Kingdom
2 Bloor Street East, 20th floor, Toronto, Ontario M4W 1A8, Canada
195 Broadway, New York, NY 10007, USA

National Library of Australia Cataloguing-in-Publication data:

Austin, Steven, author.
   Working dog heroes: how one man gives shelter dogs new life and purpose / Steve Austin with Hazel Flynn.
   978 0 7333 3439 9 (paperback)
   978 1 4607 0514 8 (ebook)
   Dog trainers – Australia – Anecdotes.
   Working dogs – Australia – Anecdotes.
   Animal shelters – Australia.
   Other Creators/Contributors: Flynn, Hazel, author.
636.70886

Cover design by Christa Moffitt, Christabella Designs
Cover image by Dwayne Sprigg/EyeEm/Getty Images
Typeset in Bembo Std by Kirby Jones

To Vicki, who has taught me more about dog training than anyone else, and to all the dogs I've worked with — they've taught me much more than I ever taught them.

CONTENTS

Foreword by Dr Harry Cooper ix
Prologue: Never a dull moment with dogs xiii

1. Runt of the litter — 1
2. Sooty: The happy-hour dog — 18
3. Sweet Sally and big ambition — 31
4. Sunny: A born champion — 40
5. TV stars and cool Hot Dog — 66
6. A tricky pig and one clever cat — 87
7. 'Can I have a volunteer from the audience?' — 103
8. Airport detectives: Dogs keeping Australia safe — 120
9. Hunting the world's ugliest treasure: Truffle hounds — 146
10. Conservation detectives — 174
11. Bristlebirds, cheetahs and rabbits, oh my — 191
12. Miracle on Macca: Adventures at the world's end — 214
13. Dangerous dogs and a scary sea lion — 233
14. Life-changing dogs: The Young Diggers and more — 254

Epilogue: Gifts beyond measure — 265
Appendix: My top tips for dog owners — 268
Acknowledgements — 287
About the co-author — 289

Foreword
by Dr Harry Cooper B.V.Sc. OAM

There is an old saying, often used, and very true: 'Some people have it, and some people will never have it as long as their rear end points to the ground.' Over the years it has been applied to many, but within the pages of this book it refers to one man who certainly has 'it' in spades.

Steve Austin is not only a friend but a superb animal trainer. It has been my pleasure to know and work with Steve for over three decades – on the small screen in episodes of *Talk to the Animals*, *Harry's Practice*, and of late *Better Homes and Gardens*; as well as in front of live audiences at shopping centres, fun days, veterinary clinic open days and, oh, so many other events that it would take forever to retell the tales. I especially remember working with Batman, an unbelievable moggy cat with attitude to burn, and with one of the best border collies ever, Bobby. Sadly neither are with us these days, but who could forget that outrageous cat, walking the plank and leaping effortlessly over Bobby, who would be crouched with his head and both front paws on the timber. Sometimes we added my noggin in there too, just for a challenge. Nothing was a problem for that very special cat.

And no animal is a problem for Steve. He has trained rats and mice to run mazes and cope with other obstacles. He has trained chickens to play the piano. He has even trained cockroaches for television!

Sometimes, though, it's possible to train an animal *too* well. You probably would recognise a cheeky little rough-coated Jack Russell called Tony from many TV commercials. Tony's very easy to train, and does everything on command from hand signals and cues given off-camera. He's a great dog. On one filming, we wanted him to show interest in a snake that we had let loose. Most dogs would not be too happy about being around a snake, but even though he'd never done it before, we managed to train Tony to chase it in no time. The only problem is now he wants to chase every snake he sees! A not-so-good outcome for dog training that time.

As well as the many events we've done together, Steve and I also have spent cold wet mornings out on a Tasmanian hillside watching and judging Retrieving Trials, where the competitors included everything from labradors to German shorthaired pointers, and those recently developed dogs commonly known as working springers, who are about as far removed from the show springer as a dachshund is from a beagle. Nevertheless, they have proved very adept at their work and Steve has truly taken the breed on board and bred and trained many, some of whose exploits you will read in these pages. They have even found their way into the country's police force as explosive-detection dogs.

Training dogs for specific purposes takes great skill. Anyone of us with enough time and knowledge can train our dogs

FOREWORD

in the basics of obedience, such as Sit, Stay, Drop etc, but to train a dog to tell the difference between an avocado and a jar of avocado face cream takes expertise. In his work with the Australian Quarantine Inspection Service (AQIS), Steve has been responsible for training not only the dogs and their handlers, but the dog trainers themselves, in working to protect our borders from many infectious diseases. I remember hearing one story about a beagle on its first day out at an international airport. In spite of a novice handler and all the noise of the passengers and baggage carousels, this little protégé managed to locate a traveller with two disease-ridden queen bees hidden in two ink pens, which were in the inside pocket of a suit coat. Wow! How did she do that? Simple – she had a great teacher.

Steve also does much work in the area of conservation, and was strongly instrumental in the program to eliminate rabbits from Macquarie Island. It's not easy to teach a natural hunting dog to leave all the native wildlife alone and just concentrate on the rabbits. He did it. Eventually the dogs were successful in completely eradicating every single rabbit from the island.

As president of the Pet Industry Association of Australia (PIAA), Steve saw the need for a body that acted in the best interests of animal welfare, and worked towards setting standards for pet shops throughout Australia. In addition, courses were established to update the knowledge of those employed in the pet trade. Although no longer in the chair, he still plays an active role in the organisation and continues to strive for improvements in pet industry standards.

Teaching at technological colleges and travelling all over the globe as a keynote speaker at animal-training conferences takes up much of his valuable time, and he is recognised by his peers both here and internationally as being at the very forefront of animal training. How many people would he have trained over the years? Far too many to count I would suggest, and I can personally attest to having been one of his pupils from time to time. Yes, there have been many occasions when quite frankly I have been stumped by a dog's behavioural problem, and have decided to call Steve rather than resort to the drug cupboard to try to sort it out. His advice and suggestions, often adopting a different perspective, have always brought about a successful conclusion.

Steve and I have shared many wonderful times together, and some sad ones too. When he lost his beloved Rottweiler, King, there was no consoling him. I believe it is his genuine love not just for dogs but for all animals that makes him such a great trainer. Dogs can certainly sense this love – they read it in body language (Steve is always smiling), and it's even been shown that they can smell it through pheromones. It's this love that makes dogs like him and want to please him. As I said at the beginning, Steve has it, and he has it in truckloads.

Yet as busy as Steve is, he remains at his core a family man. He and his lovely wife, Vicki, live in the semi-rural area west of Sydney, where they share their home with a number of dogs, a couple of cats, and an amazing array of parrots! Yes, he also has a passion for birds – though he will admit that most birds are not on the same intelligence level as dogs.

My partner and I are privileged to call both Vicki and Steve our friends. He has many, and yet he makes time for each and every one of us. This is the mark of a man.

As someone once said, 'If a dog likes you, you've gotta be okay.'

PROLOGUE

NEVER A DULL MOMENT WITH DOGS

October 2009, Macquarie Island, halfway between New Zealand and Antarctica. I was alone and my dog Gus was in big trouble. In the brief time – no more than a minute or two – it took me to reach the deadly, quicksand-like seal wallow in which he was trapped, he had used up almost all his strength. When I spotted him he was going down for the last time.

I threw myself down onto my stomach, reached back to grab a grass tussock, praying it would be strong enough, and stretched my other arm out to grab his collar. I was leaning far over the muck, and I had just managed to get hold of his collar when suddenly my backpack shifted, tipping me forward. It wasn't looking good for either of us ...

* * *

I love my life. One week I'll be on a freezing Victorian mountain top with Missy, Australia's only weed-hunting dog, the next I'll be in balmy Queensland while my clever but ugly spaniel Bolt makes sure cane toads haven't snuck back onto an island that's free of them. Or I'll be in the remote mining camps of Western Australia hoping no-one's been silly enough to bring in drugs, because if they have they won't be able to hide them from Pippa's keen nose. Or out on a tiny rock in the middle of the Southern Ocean.

I've trained pigs and chooks and one damned fine cat. I've used the training techniques I've developed to teach zookeepers how to convince crocodiles to obey instructions and how to conduct scent experiments with sea lions. But it's dogs I know best, dogs I have learned so much from, and dogs that have taken me on adventures all around the world, from hand-feeding a baby cheetah in Namibia to going behind the scenes with the LAPD in America, from the Czech Republic to halfway to Antarctica.

I've had truly wonderful dogs of my own – Sunny and Hot Dog and King among them – and known and trained many more. I've donned full protective gear to get control of dogs that would have ripped out my throat if they could have, and I've stood defenceless in my shirt sleeves in front of a man-killing attack dog.

My life is never dull, that's for sure, and I might never have experienced any of it if it hadn't been for an unwanted black puppy in the right place at the right time many years ago ...

1

RUNT OF THE LITTER

In their own ways, both school and home contributed enormously to my life, because they showed me what *not* to do. You always have a choice: repeat the pattern or change it.

I'm not one for dwelling on the past. I'd much rather focus on what's happening right now and what might happen in the future. That attitude partly comes from the fact that until I was an adult there wasn't a lot I could look back on that didn't have a shadow of loss and loneliness, at least where my family was concerned. In many ways, my deepest and most rewarding relationships in childhood were with animals.

I was born four days into 1953 at the maternity hospital in Camperdown, just a short tram ride from my family's home in the inner-west working-class suburb of Tempe. My dad, Albert, was a heavy smoker who managed a timber yard not too far away from the hospital, in what's now part of the grounds of

Sydney University. My mother, Irene, was a housewife, as they were known in those days.

It's not exaggerating to say I wasn't wanted, at least by her. By the time she was forty-six, Irene had had four children, the eldest of whom, my brother Ray, was twenty-one and already married with a child of his own. She'd also had two miscarriages. She thought her child-rearing days were well and truly over when she went to the doctor about the abdominal pain she was having. 'Don't worry,' he said to her, 'it's a bit of wind. It'll pass.' That 'wind' was me: a textbook change-of-life baby.

Some people get a bit softer as they age. The things that got them riled up in younger years just don't seem so important any more and they develop more patience. That certainly didn't happen with my mother. She was as hard as nails, and nothing I could do was ever good enough for her, even when I was little. She didn't scoop me up and cuddle me if I fell over, and she would never say 'I love you' or praise my achievements or talk to me about my interests.

The front lawn of our place wasn't huge, maybe four metres by five. When I became old enough it was my job to cut the grass. We didn't own a lawnmower so I used to get down on my knees and cut it with hand shears. When I'd finished my mother would come out to inspect it. There was no 'Thanks' or 'Good job'. She'd take a look and her only comment would be 'You missed that bit.' The way I dealt with this was by deciding, 'Right, I'm going to shut her up. I'm going to get it perfect so she will have nothing to complain about.' And that's how it went from then on. It was like an unspoken battle between us, and those occasions when she couldn't find fault about something were victories for me: 'Ha, I got you!' What a way to raise a child.

My three sisters were living at home, but they had lives of their own. I've heard that in families where there is a big age gap the older girls can take the new baby under their wing, almost like a second mum. That didn't happen for me. Yvonne and Elaine were already in their teens when I was born and Aileen was twelve. They would correct me if they thought I was doing something wrong or naughty, but we didn't really spend much time together. They had their friends and they pretty much left me to my own devices. I never met any of my grandparents; they were all dead by the time I came along. I had cousins and aunts and uncles but we rarely saw them. I had food enough and I was clothed – I wasn't deprived in any material sense – but there was not a lot of loving warmth in my life.

Looking back now, I think my dad tried to be there for me, but he was always constrained by my mother's domination of the household. When I was about five he got me my first pet, a terrapin whom I named Tommy Tortoise. (The simplest way to think about the differences between turtles, tortoises and terrapins is that turtles have webbed feet or flippers and live in the water; tortoises live on land; and terrapins divide their time between water and land.) I loved that animal, and it might sound strange, given that he hibernated for months at a time in the winter, but he was a great companion for me. I would save bits of meat for him and hand-feed him and, with Dad's help and encouragement, I made him his own little section in the backyard. I built a low fence to keep him in and Dad made him a small concrete pond. I would spend hours and hours with Tommy, either out the back or in my room, talking to him and observing his behaviour.

Dad and I had a daily ritual that I loved. As well as working around timber all day, he did woodwork and carpentry as a hobby, making furniture and other things for the house. He had a work shed for this purpose at the rear of our yard. The shed backed onto a laneway, and just across from it was a set of tennis courts, surrounded by the usual very high wire fences. Early in the mornings, before Dad went to work and I went to school, we would go out there together and he would feed the wild pigeons. They'd be lined up on the tennis-court fence, waiting, and we would climb up onto the shed roof. Dad would scatter crumbs and the birds would come over to the roof and eat.

I became more and more captivated by the pigeons' behaviour. I badly wanted to get some of our own to keep, as lots of people in the neighbourhood did, including some of my mates from school. Dad would have been quite happy with that kind of set-up – we shared a love for creatures great and small. But my mother wouldn't have a bar of it. The best I could do in the years that followed was to spend some time with a bloke down the street called Ray Halright. He would have been in his fifties and he was a cranky old bugger much of the time, but he used to breed and race pigeons and even at an early age I could tell he really understood those birds.

Racing pigeons was a classic working-man's sport in those days. The people who did it, invariably men, were known as pigeon-fanciers. The trained homing pigeons would be put into cages early on a Saturday morning and driven to the race's starting point, usually hundreds of miles away. The birds would be released and the winner was the first to make it back home (with their finish times adjusted for the difference in distance to their various home lofts). Even today debate persists about how exactly the birds' internal navigation systems work, but their feats of endurance and their ability to find their way back from any direction are simply astonishing.

I guess Ray could tell that I was genuinely fascinated, so he tolerated my hanging around watching him train and care for the birds. In the end I was going down to his place every Saturday to wait for the birds to come home and help him when they did. Back then the way the birds' times were recorded was that each one had a uniquely numbered rubber tag around its leg, and when the bird landed at the loft the owner had to scoop it up, take off the tag, put that into a manual clock and print out a record showing the precise time down to the nearest hundredth of a second. Races were often won or lost on these tiny fractions of time, so it was really important to get the birds in and registered as quickly as possible.

As time went by, Ray trusted me enough to open up and share some of his training secrets, including the fact that on race day he fed the birds a special seed mixture – one that was a real treat for them. This gave them the incentive to come into the roost nice and quickly and stay calm and patient while he got their tags off, because they knew they would then be rewarded with this special feed. I was so impressed with this simple but effective idea. It really started me thinking.

As much as he could, Dad encouraged my fascination with animals. He came home one day with a lovely little brown-and-white rabbit for me. He must have known my mother would blow up, and she did, but he weathered that one, telling her that he and I would keep the rabbit out in the yard and care for it and she wouldn't have to have anything to do with it. I suppose a rabbit was a funny pet to have in a way – it wasn't too many years since the hawkers known as 'rabbitohs' had walked these very streets selling rabbit meat to people who couldn't afford much else, and the meat was still stocked in every butcher shop. Well, no-one was going to eat Bugs, as I named him.

Dad and I made him an enclosure in the backyard, with a little shelter against the shed wall. There were a lot of things to like about Tommy Tortoise, but terrapins aren't known for their cuddles, so it was lovely to be able to pat and hold Bugs. (Little did I know that decades into the future one of the great triumphs of my professional life would involve eradicating rabbits.)

But one morning Bugs was nowhere to be found. Dad told me that he must somehow have escaped from the enclosure and hopped away. I couldn't quite see how that was possible, but I didn't have any reason to disbelieve it. In hindsight, though, I suspect that my mother just put Dad under too much pressure and he finally gave in and spirited the rabbit away in the night. Bugs caused her no extra work or worry, so why she couldn't have just let me be happy in his company I don't know.

I've got to give Dad credit: he kept trying. The next time it was fish. He built me a cement pond, about a metre by a metre-and-a-half, and got some goldfish to put in it. I would watch those fish for hours. I found being with them soothing and I liked to try to detect the patterns in their behaviour. Initially almost by accident, then following a deliberate plan, I began to train them. I would tap my fingers on the side of the pond and they would come up to the surface, where I would reward them with food. In time I had them eating right out of my hand. To this day I love having fish around me, and I keep stocked ponds throughout my garden and tanks around the house.

RUNT OF THE LITTER

* * *

When I was nine life got bleaker. My father died. Even at the best of times he hadn't been robust, and he had often been unwell. Whenever we spent time together it was quietly, at home. He would never take me to the park for a kick-around or anything like that. He'd had the physical presence of an old, old man and he would wake in the night racked by coughing. He'd always seemed to have a smoke in his mouth – mostly a handmade rollie but occasionally a more expensive filtered cigarette. Technically what killed him was cancer of the stomach, not the lungs, but I have absolutely no doubt that the smoking contributed to his premature death. I knew little about what was going on until it was all over. I was told he was going into hospital for an operation. I found out later they basically opened him up, saw how bad things were and closed him back up again. He died in hospital soon afterwards.

Nobody sat me down and really helped me through it. Dad's death was barely discussed in my presence and my mother and sisters didn't allow me to go to the funeral. Perhaps they thought that was for the best, but it was the worst thing they could have done. Although Dad hadn't been a perfect father by any means, he had loved me and had reached out to me in his own way. Then suddenly, almost from one day to the next, he was gone. I was expected to shrug it off, act like nothing had happened and just get on with things. So I did. I spent even more time out of the house, helping Ray with the pigeons, and doing anything else I could find to do. I knew that whatever learning, friendship and stimulation there were to be had wouldn't come from within my family.

They wouldn't come from school, either. Some teachers were better than others, but their general philosophy seemed to be that mistakes were to be pointed out and punished, whereas right answers barely merited a response. And anything that wasn't 100 per cent correct was a mistake. I learned early on in primary school that the safest option was to keep your mouth shut. If you put your hand up in response to a teacher's question and said anything other than the complete, correct answer you were told off, sometimes ridiculed and occasionally even given a clout. There was never, ever a 'Good effort, Steven, but that's not quite what I'm after.' So, along with lots of my classmates, I became afraid to try. If I didn't say anything I couldn't make a mistake, and if I didn't make a mistake I'd stay under the radar. As a consequence, the only part of school I really enjoyed was sport. I'd have been out there playing it all day, every day, if they'd let me.

In their own ways both school and home contributed enormously to my life, because each showed me what *not* to do. As a direct result of those experiences, when I reached adulthood I consciously set about doing things differently, both with the animals I trained and in my role as a father. But that was still far into the future.

In 1965, at age twelve, I started at Enmore Boys' High School. It did nothing to change my view of school, but something else happened that year that opened my eyes in a different way. It began with a simple notice in the window of the local newsagency: 'Paperboy needed'. My mother was on the widow's pension, which covered the basics, but I knew that if I wanted anything extra I would have to pay for it myself, and that meant getting a job. I spoke to the newsagent and he agreed to give me a try as a barrow boy, pushing newspapers and magazines through the streets, every afternoon from Monday to Saturday. Those were the days when newspapers had huge circulations and Sydney supported two competing afternoon papers.

I would blow the silver whistle I'd been given and people would come out of their houses to make their purchases. I quickly got to know who read what and I'd have their paper ready and waiting for them. The newsagent paid me a cent or two for each paper I sold, but I also carried the most popular magazines – *Woman's Day*, *The Australian Women's Weekly*, *TV Week* and *TV Times* – and I made good money from them, something like five cents each.

When I'd been a barrow boy for a few months and proved myself a hard worker who was honest with the takings, I got promoted to a coveted stand job. Each afternoon paper stands would be set up at railway stations, on busy corners and outside pubs to serve all the workers who'd knocked off for the day. A mate from the neighbourhood had the stand outside Sydenham's General Gordon Hotel, a classic Aussie pub on a busy intersection opposite the suburb's train station. I was entrusted with the stand across the road.

I'd go straight there after school. A truck would bring around the tied-up bundles of papers, I'd get them up on the stand, sell the papers, keep a tally of the numbers and go back to the newsagent a couple of hours later with any unsold papers and my money-pouch full of the takings. Stand boys got 10 per cent of the money they collected plus any 'keep the change' tips. It was a lot cushier than walking around with the barrow, and I used to make a bit over a pound in an average week. (We were still a year off the switch to decimal currency.) That was pretty good, considering the average adult wage at the time was around twenty-two pounds a week.

In time my mate moved on and I got the stand outside the pub. I then picked up a lucrative sideline that meant I had plenty of money for the new jeans and other things I'd started to want. The key to it all was a bloke named Laurie.

I knew Laurie through the Sydenham United rugby league club, for which I'd been playing on Saturday mornings since age nine, not long after my dad died. Laurie seemed to have some role high up in the club, though I didn't know precisely what. He never seemed to go off to work like other men did, yet he clearly wasn't short of a quid: he was noticeably better dressed than the men around him, always in a classy shirt plus an expensive-looking pullover in cool weather, tailored pants, immaculate, good-quality shoes, and black hair slicked back like Elvis's. The padding around his middle was also testament to how well he was doing – he was on a good paddock, as we used to say.

I didn't realise it then, but Laurie was an SP bookie, and a highly successful one. SP, or Starting Price, bookmakers had first appeared in the 1930s when radio broadcasts delivered live horse- and greyhound-racing coverage to people in their homes. Lots of those people wanted to have a bet on the results, but at the time the only place where you could lay a bet was at the track itself. SP bookies sprang up to meet this need. Their activities were illegal, but the police usually turned a blind eye (in exchange for regular pay-offs) and ordinary people grew to accept them as part of the landscape. Throughout Australia, especially in working-class areas, men and women who would never have dreamed of breaking the law in any other way thought nothing of laying a bet with an SP bookie. It was as Australian as wearing thongs and drinking beer.

Seeing all that money passing through all those hands with none of it coming their way, the government decided to do something about it, and in December 1964 the NSW Totalizator Agency Board (TAB) was created to provide a legal outlet for off-course punting.

At the TAB everyone got the same odds, which could and did change right up to just before the race started. When you bet with SP bookies your odds stayed fixed as they were at the time you put your money on. The other big difference was that you could only bet at the TAB if you had the money in your hand, and if you did win you just went in and collected your winnings, no drama. There were plenty of SP bookies who would run up a tab for their punters, and if the punter didn't have what they owed when it was time to pay, some serious harm would come their way. There were also cowboy operators who would set themselves up as bookies without the cash on hand to pay out if the day's racing went against them. If that happened the punter might well turn up to claim their winnings, only to find the bookie had nicked off into the sunset. In time, the TAB would spread far and wide and kill off SP bookmaking completely. But when I had my first dealings with Laurie it was brand-new and had made almost no impact.

Laurie ran most of his business out of the pub; that was the closest thing he had to a workplace. I was right there on the spot every afternoon and one day he said to me, 'I need to collect a couple of things from a couple of blokes, just some envelopes, but I have to leave for a while. If I ask these blokes to give you the envelopes, do you mind just hanging on to them for me until I get back?'

A couple of hours later he returned and said, 'Have you got those envelopes, Stevie?' I handed them over and thought no more about it. Then he did it again, and a few more times over the next week or two.

I didn't realise he was testing me. The envelopes contained the details of bets these men wanted to put on with Laurie. More importantly, they contained the money to pay for those bets – Laurie was too smart to give credit to any of his punters. He was, I suppose, waiting to see if I would try to skim any of the money or if I'd go blabbing about it to anyone. I did neither, and he came to the conclusion that he could trust me. That was when he told me what was going on: 'Look, there are people around the place who are having a bit of a bet, and if you start collecting the details and the money from them for me, I'll make it worth your while.'

He was true to his word. It started with my collecting the money to be bet and the details of the bets – 'Melbourne, race seven, number six, 10 shillings each way' or whatever it might be – from the men in the pub. I'd carefully keep everything in my pouch, in a separate pocket from the news-stand money. Selling the papers would have been a great cover, except that I didn't need a cover because everyone knew what was going on, including the local coppers. On Saturday afternoons they'd pull up outside the pub in their police car. Laurie would already have given me a nice fat roll of money to hand on to them and I'd tuck it inside a copy of the *Mirror* and go over and hand the newspaper through the window: 'Here's your paper, Sarge,' I'd say.

'Thank you, Stevie.' The sergeant would take the paper and off they'd go. I have no idea whether the owner of the newsagency knew what I was up to, or knew the extent of it. He never said anything to me about it, but then again he used to place bets with Laurie along with everyone else.

The next job Laurie gave me was to ride on my hand-me-down pushbike around Sydenham and neighbouring St Peters to pick up the bets from people who didn't frequent the pub, including the old ladies. In the beginning he would give me a list of addresses, but I soon got to know them all by name – Mrs McLaren and old Tom and all the rest of the inveterate gamblers who were his customers. I would call at their homes, little weatherboard cottages and semi-detached houses that most of them had lived in their entire lives. I'd wait at the front door while they got out their money. No matter what time of day, there would be a thick fog of cigarette smoke rolling down the long gun-barrel hallway, and the races or some other sport were always coming from a radio in the background. If it was afternoon there would be a distinct smell of beer. Everyone drank, men and women, and the men would come to the door still holding the longneck bottle they were drinking from. They'd tell me what they wanted and I'd write it all down.

Mrs McLaren, who must have been eighty-five in the shade, was typical. She'd have a fag in the corner of her mouth, around which she'd say, 'Here y'are, Stevie. Two-and-six on number four in the first in Melbourne, all up, then the same again on number six in race two, then …' and on it would go, with any winnings from one race being wagered on the next. She'd say, 'I worked it out that if I get the eight winners I'll win ten thousand pounds.' Early on I would reply with something like 'Well, that's right, Mrs McLaren, but getting eight winners in a row is going to be pretty hard. Why don't you just have a bet on one, and–'

'No, no, no,' she'd interrupt, intent on her imagined fortune. In reality, of course, she would lose her money almost every time. But that never stopped her or any of the others and it was obvious nothing I said would make any difference. Sometimes they would invite me in or offer me a drink of beer, but even if I had ever wanted to I was too busy – there were too many people who just couldn't wait to give Laurie their money.

The punters didn't always lose. I guess they won just often enough to keep them interested. I didn't have to be listening to the races on the radio to know if Laurie was having a bad day, I only had to watch him. He'd be standing there in the front bar of the General Gordon, crankiness coming off him in waves. His hands would be deep in his pockets, unconsciously twitching away as if he were trying to stop his money from escaping. When he was listening to a close-run thing and it became clear the favourite was going to lose – the desired result if you were a bookmaker – his hands would fly out of his pockets and he'd clap them together, again without even realising he was doing it. If the hands stayed in the pockets it was best to steer clear.

But there weren't too many bad days for Laurie. One look at what the punters wore and the houses they lived in compared with Laurie's smart clothes and his spiffy lime-green Ford Fairlane 500 with its white canvas top was enough to show you which way the money flowed. Right from the start he paid me generously. For a few hours' work he'd hand me at least as much as I made in a week from the news stand, often considerably more.

I was too young to understand how the whole thing fitted together, but Laurie was part of some kind of syndicate of numbers men, bookies and runners. They were shady characters, but they'd never hurt a 'civilian' and there was room for them all. There were no territorial wars: such and such an area was Laurie's, and where his ended another bookie's started. They were honourable in their own way.

They were collegial, too. At the end of the day you'd see them all getting together for a drink. They kept a vacant house that they all used, and Laurie invited me there after a while. There were a couple of rooms up the front where blokes might crash out if they were too drunk, but the real action happened down the back, in the kitchen. Radios would be on, broadcasting races from various cities, and at the table there would be money in stacks piled high, and a couple of guys with the accounting books in front of them keeping tabs on everything. Before I went to work for Laurie, if I saw more than two five-pound notes together I thought it was impressive, but I never saw that table with anything less than thousands on it.

The funny thing was, even though they made their living from punters' losses, they all loved a gamble themselves. They played cards together and they couldn't resist a bet on anything, including the proverbial two flies crawling up a wall. By the time I'd been working for Laurie for a year or so they all knew me and accepted me, and they'd often have a bit of good-natured sport with me when it came time for me to get my money.

They'd have a big bag full of cash, the classic bookmaker's leather bag, with clasps on the top and hinges that could open almost flat. They'd give me a choice: I could take my two or three pounds and walk away, or I could risk a lucky dip –

without looking, put one hand in and pull it out, and keep whatever I'd grabbed.

'Okay, Stevie, what's it going to be?' they'd say while showing me the contents of the bag. Ten shillings was the lowest denomination of notes, then it went up to one pound, five pounds then ten pounds. They'd make sure I saw the ten-pound notes they'd placed strategically on top.

About half the time I'd take the gamble and say yes to the lucky dip. At this, they would close the bag and shake up the contents. A lot of times they conned me: the only pounds were the few that had been on the top and all the rest were ten-shilling notes, so I'd walk away with four or five of those. But sometimes I'd get a ten-pound note, and on a couple of thrilling occasions more than one. When that happened they would all give me a cheer and tease me by immediately asking for a loan.

Everyone knew I held money for Laurie, but because all the crooks were honest in the way they ran their crooked businesses it never occurred to me to fear for my own safety. One day when I was fourteen, I was packing up my news-stand stool and getting ready to go when someone came at me from the side and cracked me on the head. I just got a glimpse of the bloke who hit me before I crashed down onto the footpath. I woke up in Marrickville Hospital with a broken nose and a bunch of broken and missing teeth. I'd been rolled for the SP money; it was all gone.

My mother came to see me and I gave her the official story: I'd fallen over. As unconvincing as it was, she didn't probe further and I wouldn't have told her anything if she had. I was very good at keeping things close to my chest, which was why Laurie and his 'boys' trusted me.

Laurie came in as soon as he heard I'd been hurt and I told him the truth. He came back to see me every day I was in there, and when my face had healed enough for me to go to a dentist he paid for the caps and false teeth needed to repair the damage. Someone else looked after the stand until I was well enough, but I never considered giving up that job, or the one on the side for Laurie.

A little while later I was back on my stool outside the pub when Laurie's car pulled up. He was driving and the back seat was occupied by two huge blokes I'd never seen before, tough as nails, with another guy squeezed between them. Laurie gestured towards the guy in the middle. 'Do you know that bloke, Stevie?'

I took a proper look at him. 'That's the prick that hit me!'

Laurie said 'Thanks', and they drove off down the road. I don't know what happened after that but it wouldn't have been anything good. Those bookies certainly weren't murderers, but they were extremely effective at persuading anybody who wronged them to mend their ways. I never got robbed again.

2

SOOTY: THE HAPPY-HOUR DOG

You get out of life what you put into it. It's the same principle with animals: the more you give to them the more enjoyment you get back.

In my second year of high school I finally got a dog of my own. It happened purely by chance but it had a big effect on my life. We were doing a class in the music room at Enmore Boys'. Music was better than maths, but there was still too much 'Sit down and be quiet' for it to be really interesting. Any distraction was milked for all it was worth, and this particular day delivered up a beauty. The teacher was trying to get us engrossed in tonics and scales or some equally uninteresting topic when through the classroom door walked a little black ball of fluff.

It was a tiny eight- or nine-week-old puppy – a labrador cross, as it turned out. The best guess we could make as to what had happened was that there had been a litter and the owner hadn't wanted this particular little mouth to feed, so they'd thought, 'I'll dump him in the school yard. Someone will take care of him.' He'd meandered around, managed to climb the stairs into the building we were in and just happened to choose the music room to explore.

When the uproar had died down a bit the teacher called up a boy to go over to the school office and ask them to ring the dogcatcher. I said, 'Oh no, don't do that. I'll take him home.' I knew my mother would blow up about it but so what? I was used to that. My news-stand job had given me the confidence to stand up to her, and the work I did for Laurie even more so. I knew I wouldn't win her over, but I didn't care. I'd just weather the storm. As expected, she went off, but I stood my ground and said, 'I'll feed him, I'll look after him, you won't have to do anything.'

I named him Sooty. He was a good little dog and I loved him. Dog ownership was different back then. It was rare to see a dog on a lead and they often just wandered the streets alone quite happily. You'd know they belonged to someone because they'd be wearing a collar, but they'd be allowed to come and go as they pleased. When he was old enough, that was how it was with Sooty. He would disappear for a couple of hours in the morning, do the rounds of the neighbourhood, then trot back home.

As I'd found with my terrapin, my rabbit, my fish and the pigeons, there was a real joy in being close to Sooty. I bonded with them all to varying degrees, but I grew particularly close to my new pup and he was the one who really developed my interest in animal training. I'd had a tiny inkling of how it could work with the goldfish, and I'd seen it in action in Ray

Halright's loft, but my first real taste of success came from Sooty. It happened through a chance reading of a Little Golden Book called *The Lone Ranger and the Talking Pony*.

The book starts out with an Indian boy who has taught his pony to do tricks. This attracts the attention of a villain who comes along and steals the pony so he can be used in the villain's carnival. The Lone Ranger and Tonto cleverly defeat him and order is restored.

It was far from a literary masterpiece but the effect it had on me was electric. Not the supposedly suspenseful plot, but the early pages where the boy was getting his pony to do the tricks – stamping its feet and 'talking' by nodding its head on cue – to the delight of all his friends. The particular page that riveted me showed the boy standing next to the pony, holding a carrot out of sight of his friends. It was a true lightbulb moment: 'So *that's* how you do it,' I thought. The pony wasn't stamping and nodding to please the boy's audience, he was doing it for the reward he knew he would get. *Of course*, training was a reward-based process. It made perfect sense.

I thought a great deal about this reward system, and what it meant and how it could be applied. I understood it instinctively: after all, I hadn't been riding my bike around for miles calling on Mrs McLaren and the other old dears just for the fun of it; I did it because I knew I'd get paid. That was how the world worked. That principle – finding a reward that was substantial enough to repay the amount of work required – could easily be applied to teaching animals to do all kinds of things.

I started out training Sooty in the basics of obedience – Sit, Stay, Roll Over, Heel – and rewarding him with little dog-biscuit treats. He quickly got the hang of those things, so just for fun I moved on to teaching him to balance a biscuit on his muzzle. Gradually I increased the weight using extra biscuits, and then at some point I decided to see if he could balance an empty glass on his head, then one with a little water in it, and a little more water and so on. He seemed to enjoy it. Dogs will let you know pretty quickly if they don't like the game, but he was keen, so I kept going over about two months until he could easily balance a full glass on his head.

I showed my friends and they were duly impressed, showering Sooty with praise. Word got around, and one evening, when I was walking with him past a pub where people were sitting out on the step having a drink, as they used to do then, a bloke who recognised us made a comment about how Sooty was a clever dog. On the spur of the moment I said, 'I'll show you how clever he is. Give us your drink.' He handed me his half-full schooner glass and I balanced it on Sooty's head, just as we'd practised. The next thing I knew, all the other blokes outside the pub were calling out for their mates inside to come and have a look, and suddenly there were maybe forty people standing in a circle around us, cheering. Then they started throwing twenty-cent coins, saying, 'Here you go, mate, get the dog something to eat.' I walked away with my pockets heavy, thinking, 'I'm onto something here.'

Taking Sooty up to the pub became a weekly event. I soon learned that Thursday evening was the go. Thursday was payday and men would arrive at the pub with a full pay-packet, all cash of course. Timing was crucial. I had to get there when they'd had just enough to drink so they were loosened up and generous but not so much that things were turning ugly. Around a quarter to seven was perfect; that was happy hour for me and my dog.

There were always men sitting on the step or standing around on the footpath outside the pub drinking. They'd call to their mates inside and a crowd would gather. We'd start with a few simple tricks like rolling over and begging, and build up to everyone's favourite, where Sooty balanced a schooner of beer on his head. It was pretty much the same crowd that drank there all the time, but they didn't seem to tire of it. In fact, people used to be outside waiting for us. And they rewarded us generously – it was definitely worth continuing to show up.

Because nothing was ever said between my mother and me about the money I got from Laurie, I just kept it and used it to buy what I needed, as I would have if my only source of income had been the news-stand job. But sometimes when I came home from the pub with what seemed like a small fortune, I would give her some of it as a contribution to the household. The first time she said, 'Where does all this money come from?' I replied, 'Oh, I take the dog up the pub and do a few tricks.' That was all that was ever said, even though, as time passed and I became a regular attraction, blokes would offer me beer and sometimes I would accept. Did she smell it on my breath? If she did, she didn't make any comment, just continued to take money whenever I offered it to her.

By this point I knew with certainty I would never have the kind of relationship with my mother that I used to wish for. Something had happened that had ended those hopes once and for all.

I'd reached my mid-teenage years, fourteen and fifteen, just as the world was hitting the 'Summer of Love' and the full flowering of hippie culture. My generation had watched throughout the 1960s as music stars led the way with new fashions, including 'long hair' for men. It's easy to forget how much panic there was about this among the older generation. In 1964 Normie Rowe was just another employee of the Postmaster-General's Department when he was told that if he wanted to keep his job he'd have to cut his collar-length hair. He kept the hair, quit the job and became a huge pop star. Three years later The Beatles, the cheeky 'mop-tops' who were supposedly a threat to respectable society, had hair that only just reached their collars. The 'dangerous' Rolling Stones weren't much different.

So in 1967 and '68, when my generation started to grow our hair and let it get shaggy, we did it quite mildly. It was common – about a third of the boys in my year at school had hair below their collar – but it was too much for my mother. She let me know in a way that cut me to the quick. It was so scarring I can still remember every detail.

We didn't have a car, so when my mother did the grocery shopping she caught the bus and bought just as much as she could carry. If I wasn't working I would generally meet her at the bus shelter in Foreman Street, Tempe, the closest stop to our house, in order to carry the bags home for her. This particular afternoon started out just like all the others. I was there waiting at 3.45 pm when she got off the bus. I took the bags and we started to walk home. Then she said, 'I don't want you to meet me no more because I don't want no-one to know you're my son.' It was purely because of my 'long' shaggy hair – that was all it took for her to disown me in public.

I was devastated, but no matter what it cost me I wasn't going to show her that. We walked on and got home, I put the bags down in the kitchen and that was that. It was such a horrendous thing for her to say that it snapped something inside me. I had tried so hard to be a good kid, self-reliant, no bother to her, staying away from serious trouble. But none of that counted with her. I understood then that nothing I could do would ever change things. It wouldn't matter what I tried, none of it was ever going to work. I'd never be good enough for her and she would never love me the way I wanted her to.

Some part of me got that it wasn't my fault. As I grew older I was able to understand that my mother was an ignorant woman in the sense that she never experienced much of life. She got married at nineteen and had those seven pregnancies and five surviving children. She saw nothing of the wider world and she was widowed early. I suppose she did the best she could, although I know that there were plenty of others who had similar or worse circumstances in their lives, yet were wonderful people.

Even at the time, though, there was that part of me that was strong enough to think, 'I'll put this away in the vault and deal with it later when I'm better able to.' But I was just a teenager and there was another part of me that thought, 'What's the point even trying? No-one cares, I might as well do as I please.'

So I did. For a while I went right off the rails.

We moved to Rockdale and I had to give up working for Laurie and the newsagent. I started spending all my time with surfer friends, some who were mates from school and some I just met along the way. Cronulla was our beach and people came from all over Sydney to surf there. Decades later Cronulla would become infamous as the site of racist violence, but back then everyone got along. I became part of a tight-knit group that took the place of my family. We'd set out at 5 am, catching the train down there nice and early so we could enjoy some waves before school, or get a good go at the beach on weekends before it became crowded. I loved being out there, doing something physical surrounded by the beauty of nature.

Being on the board felt healthy and pure, but back on land we partied hard. We were particularly fond of speed and we could always get our hands on 'wide-awake pills', aka the amphetamine methedrine. We used to gobble down these bitter pills like lollies. It was fun while it lasted; we were young and bulletproof. Except that we weren't, of course. One night I took too many and was taken to hospital.

Despite my fitness from the surfing, I had pushed my system way too far and the overdose was just the beginning. It turned out that I had encephalitis, a very dangerous swelling of the brain tissue. I woke up thinking it was the morning after the night before, only to learn I had been in a coma for two weeks and was lucky to have survived. Even after I was discharged I was frail and thin, too crook to go surfing for quite a while. It gave me a hell of a shock and I knew I didn't ever want to be in that position again. There were too many things I wanted to experience. It just wasn't worth the risk.

Throughout this difficult period I still had Sooty, my main source of companionship and affection at home. But back then I didn't know how to look after a dog properly, nor did anyone else in the family, so he'd never been given any vaccinations or other vet care. He was still a young dog, only six, when he started acting strangely. His mind just wasn't right. He became aggressive – never to me, but increasingly to other people – and in the end he bit my mother pretty badly. My best guess was that he had been struck with a virus whose symptoms we hadn't spotted, and he had survived it physically but it had caused some kind of permanent neurological damage.

I wondered often in the years afterwards if there was a simple preventative measure I could have taken to protect him. Whether or not that was the case, something had happened to him and it was obvious we couldn't let him go on as he was. I was forced to make the hard decision to have him put down.

I had learned so much from Sooty and with him that it was extremely difficult to say goodbye. But that, too, was a lesson in the responsibilities that come with pet ownership. If you love animals you have a duty to do the best for them no matter what. You can't let them suffer or live half a life, even though you might grieve deeply as a result. It was a good few years before I was ready to own another dog.

As for my relationship with my mother, the more time passed, the more I was able to deal with the change in my feelings. But the raw pain caused by what she'd said to me has never gone away. In fact, although five decades had passed before I started writing this book, I'd only told a handful of people what she said to me that day.

One of the people I'd confided in was a friend who also had a childhood lacking in love and approval. When my friend was just five, his father pointed to a homeless person in the street and said to the boy, 'See that tramp over there? You are going to end up exactly the same as that.' My friend grew up determined to do things differently – and he did: he's a fine man and loving father who has raised two exceptional children. I grew up with the same goal.

There wasn't anyone else in my family I wanted to use as a role model either. Being so much older, Ray might have been someone I could look up to in that way, but I'm sad to say he had no ambition or drive. My late brother never owned a house, just rented his whole life; he never got his driver's licence; he never even ventured beyond New South Wales, and hardly even beyond Sydney. I couldn't understand it; I just knew I wasn't going to be like that.

So I made opportunities where I could and grabbed every chance going – even those that weren't necessarily respectable – as long as they fell within my own code of ethics. I'd learned to play poker very well from Laurie and his mates, and by sixteen or seventeen I'd found out about regular games that were held around the place at rented houses that smelled of stale bread and beer. These weren't games for novices; I was playing with adult men, and hard men at that, crooks many of them. At the start there would be a bit of good-natured chaffing about my age: 'Don't lose your lunch money, son' and that kind of thing. But once they saw I could really play, that all dropped away, and when I started winning we were all just equals.

I lost plenty, too, but even on the nights when I won and walked away with $150, a good deal of money at the time, I didn't feel threatened. Heroin hadn't really entered the scene yet. When it reared its ugly head some years later things went downhill quickly. The crooks selling drugs didn't follow a code, they were just out for whatever they could get. But the blokes I was playing against were honourable in their own way, just as Laurie had been.

That was also true of the women who worked in the illegal brothel that just happened to be next to my school. The 'girls' (as they were universally known, although some of them wouldn't see forty again) knew many of my friends in the

SP underworld. They used to ask me to run little errands for them – get their smokes or chocolates or whatever they wanted. But if anyone knew the value of labour they did, so they didn't expect me to do it for free: they'd give me a bit of money for the job. They were just as worthy of respect as anyone else, as far as I was concerned; after all, everyone had to make a dollar.

But my real money came from the operation I was running at school. Over my years in high school I was able to count on one hand the really good, talented, enthusiastic teachers. I did well in their classes because I wanted to please them. But on the whole I was a mediocre performer in class, and I couldn't wait until the bell rang for the end of maths or English or whatever it was so I could get out onto the oval with my friends and kick a ball around. I felt just as uninterested in science – but there was a time there when I got great marks in that subject, thanks to my teacher's fondness for a punt.

When I was in fifth form I set up my own SP bookie operation at school. At first I only took bets from kids I knew well, but the word spread. Other students began seeking me out and asking to lay bets, and it became a really lucrative business. I'd take bets of up to five dollars, which doesn't sound like much now but it was then. In a good week I'd make $100 or so; in a bad week I'd lose that much.

I tried to be discreet, but clearly the news got out because my science teacher (whose name I'd better not reveal) asked me to stay back one day after class. When the coast was clear he asked if it was true that I had an SP bookie operation going. I was quite wary, as you can imagine, but he was quick to reassure me that he wasn't about to turn me in – instead he wanted to lay some bets 'for a friend'.

I didn't extend credit to other kids, but after he'd become a regular customer he asked me to take some bets for which he'd fix me up later. Well, he obviously had a regular pay cheque, so I said sure. But the money somehow never quite materialised, and when he did win it was nowhere near enough to cover what he owed me. In the end he was so far in debt I said to him, 'We've got a problem.'

He said, 'Yes, we do. How can we fix it?'

I was very sure of myself for a kid that age; after all, I'd been largely independent for a long time. 'Well, we've got that big exam coming up,' I said. 'Let's make sure my mark's in the nineties, eh?' He agreed, and lo and behold, that was what happened. If only all my other teachers had been mad punters my school record would have looked a lot better!

Plenty of kids left school in fourth form, as it was called then (Year 10 now). They'd go into apprenticeships – the boys as mechanics or tradies, the girls as hairdressers. I stayed on for the final two years, though, not because I needed the qualification – however I made my living I clearly wasn't going to rely on my school results – but because I didn't know what I wanted to do. The idea of an apprenticeship didn't grab me. Apart from anything else, it would mean a drop in income! First-year apprenticeships were a lot more work for less money than running an SP book.

I passed my final exams – just. The result reflected the effort I put into it. The day I took my English exam the kids around me were writing furiously. I was staring blankly out the window when I noticed the leaves start to move differently. The wind had shifted offshore. I thought, 'Bugger this, I'm going surfing', and I got up, walked out, went home and got my board and headed for the beach without a care in the world.

If I could have repeated and stayed at school for another year I would have, just to maintain my income. But I was about to turn eighteen and the real world awaited.

3

SWEET SALLY AND BIG AMBITION

Dare to dream bigger than the people around you, but seek out the expert help you'll need to reach those impressive goals.

When school ended, I took off for New Zealand and spent a few adventurous weeks hitchhiking and surfing. When I got back to Sydney, I stayed in the Rockdale house with my mother and my sisters Elaine and Aileen until I could get a job, accumulate some money and get a place of my own. I still had no clue about what kind of work I might do in the long term, but I didn't need to worry about that for the moment. It was the beginning of the 1970s and the national unemployment rate was just two per cent. You could literally walk into a job pretty much anywhere you liked, especially if you weren't picky. You turned up at a factory or some other likely place and said you were looking for work, and half the time they would start you right then and there. When you got sick of it you could just leave knowing there was another job waiting around the corner.

I began a series of unskilled, unexciting labouring jobs, including working on building sites and in an iron foundry. I didn't mind hard work or early starts as long as I could still fit a surf in sometime before dark. But I really disliked monotony and I really, really disliked being indoors. The worst job I had during this period was working in a factory where I stacked boxes hour after hour, day after day. I couldn't wait to get out of there.

I was ready to have another dog in my life. I didn't have any particular views about breed. But all-black Sooty was still strongly on my mind and I wanted a dog who looked distinctly different, so my one requirement was that my new dog have white markings.

The selling of pets was completely unregulated in those days – it was terrible, looking back – and you could buy animals in all sorts of places. One of the easiest was the free-for-all that was the original Paddy's Market, right in the heart of town.

I went down there one Saturday and, as usual, you could pick and choose between all the puppies in the cages. You just pointed one out, paid your money and off you went. There were no vaccinations, no registration, nothing like that. I chose a little border collie cross (crossed with kelpie is my best guess). She was a lovely dog with the typical border collie black-and-white colouring. I named her Sally. I'd learned a lot from Sooty's death, and so at the first opportunity I took her to the vet and had her desexed and started her on a proper program of being vaccinated and wormed and generally taken care of.

I hadn't discussed getting a dog with my mother, I just brought Sally home. And strangely enough, after all the friction over

SWEET SALLY AND BIG AMBITION

animals in my childhood, my mother took to the dog almost immediately. Now that I was working I was paying board, and at first my mother allowed Sally to stay on the understanding that I would take care of her and all her needs. But then my mother fell in love with her. The whole family did. Perhaps those years with Sooty had got them used to having a dog around the place. But Sally was also a different kind of dog. She was a female, with a gentle personality, less boisterous and independent than Sooty had been: a soft dog.

It was good to have a dog again. I taught her basic obedience and other little tricks using what I'd learned with Sooty, and when the job permitted it, I took her to work with me. She also spent time around my friends. We were a loose group of twenty or so guys who all loved to surf, enjoyed a beer and appreciated girls our age. I started to get serious with a very nice girl (who just happened to be a real head-turner), and increasingly when I wasn't with the boys or at work I was with her. Fortunately, my family were so fond of Sally that they were perfectly happy to care for her in my absence.

I'd seen very clearly through working with Sally, and my other pets, that you get out of life what you put into it. The more I gave to my animals, the more enjoyment I got back. It's an approach that never fails, and it applies equally in the wild. There's no welfare in nature. In any group of animals, be they zebras, kangaroos or anything else, any individual who can't work for their own survival will die. Effort is rewarded, and I wanted to be a winner in life.

By twenty-one I'd figured out that whatever my 'real job' was going to be, I wanted to work outdoors. I looked at the various options and settled on horticulture. That meant doing a three-year course at a Technical and Further Education (TAFE) college, after which I would have the qualifications needed to work in landscape gardening. I successfully applied for a paid apprenticeship that would be done through my local council, Rockdale. I would work for the council and learn on the job, but also get time off to attend TAFE classes.

I took to it straightaway and enjoyed the physical work. To my surprise I found I also enjoyed the TAFE classes. Partly it was because, unlike at school, everything we learned had a practical application. But mostly it was because the style of teaching was completely different. We students were only a couple of years past high school, but we were treated as adults, not naughty kids as we'd been seen then. While we had to pass tests and do well in assignments, it was up to us to be organised and independent in the way we did our work. I had a huge amount to learn, not knowing much about plants at all when I started, and it was a revelation to me how effectively I could learn through this style of teaching. (When I eventually started to teach people myself, I drew on that sharp contrast between the way I'd been taught at school and the way it had been done at TAFE.)

Things were pretty good in the rest of my life, too. My earlier relationship had come to an end but I'd met a lovely girl called Diane. She was a friend of a friend, and when I first met her I knew that not only was she was attractive and very good at her floristry job, but she was also already in a long-term relationship. A while later I heard that they'd split up, so I tracked down her number and called to ask her out. She wasn't ready to start dating again, so I left it for a bit, then asked a couple more times, without success. I couldn't quite tell whether things weren't fully over with her former boyfriend or she just wasn't interested, but I'd given it my best shot; it was time to withdraw from the field. This was the best move I could have made: Diane then called me up and asked me out. I was happy to accept.

We got on well, but it wasn't intended to be anything serious, because in a few months Diane would be leaving for England; she already had her ticket. She was going there to travel and work and generally have fun. I could understand that. I'd been thinking how nice it would be to do some more travelling myself. I had less than a year of my apprenticeship to go, and if I could afford to, maybe I'd be able to take a decent break and see some of the world before I got down to work. But things quickly got surprisingly serious between Diane and me, and we started talking about meeting up in London. By the time Diane left, the plan was that I would save as much money as I could and meet her in London the following year, 1977. In the meantime, we were two red-blooded young people free to have whatever romantic adventures came our way.

In the end I didn't make it to London. Instead, I spent several months in Greece then Spain, and ended up in Bali, where the surfing was just as great as I'd heard.

On my return to Sydney I moved back in with my mother, sisters and Sally. Even before I left, Sally had firmly become the family dog rather than mine so when, in time, I moved out into a share-house with some mates, there was no question that she would remain settled at Rockdale.

I got a new job at Kogarah Council looking after the council's small parks. I also went back to TAFE to do a two-year greenkeeping certificate.

There was another significant change in my life around this point, although, as is often the way, I didn't realise at the time how important it would be. I had a steady job, no more travel plans and I was missing canine companionship: I was ready for a puppy. I told John, my flatmate, and he had no objections.

Having got to know border collies through my experience with Sally, I'd fallen in love with them and this time I wanted a purebred. That would involve a very different process from just rocking up at the markets and coming home with a pup, as I'd done with her. I knew I'd need to get the dog from a breeder, but I wasn't entirely sure how it would work.

There were a few people working for the council who I knew had a strong interest in dogs, including one bloke whose animals competed in shows. One day towards the end of 1978 I asked him about breeders. He offered to bring me in the latest issue of the journal put out by the organisation that oversaw purebred dogs in New South Wales. (At that point it was called the Royal Agricultural Society Kennel Control; the name was later changed to the NSW Canine Council and these days it's known as Dogs NSW.)

This journal contained a list of all the officially recognised breeders in the state and the types of dogs they specialised in, but it also had a calendar of dog-related events, including Dog Shows, in which dogs would be judged based on their appearance and demeanour; Agility Competitions, in which they had to complete an obstacle course against the clock; and something called Obedience Trials. It was the last of these that caught my eye. There was one coming up not too far away from me in a couple of weekends' time and I decided to go and see what it was all about.

When the day came I got in my red MG convertible and headed over to Centennial Park in the city's east. As I found out later, these Obedience Trials were put on by the dog-training clubs that operated throughout the city. Each Trial day would be organised by a specific club, in this case the Eastern Suburbs one, but as long as you belonged to one club or another you could compete in any of them, and spectators were welcome.

That first day it was hard to understand exactly what was happening, but by piecing together information from the event announcer and the printed program I started to get the picture. There were three levels of competition, catering for skills from beginner to elite. Back then I would have said the dog owners were the ones competing but, as I learned, the dogs are unequivocally regarded as the competitors and all awards are made in their name, although they do refer to the owner, for instance: 'Rover, owned and handled by Jane Smith'.

People and dogs were split into groups and the easiest category was up first. This was Novice. The dogs had to complete a series of off-leash tasks in a demarcated area ('the ring') and they were judged on each, with points adding up to a possible maximum of 200. A dog had to get at least 170 points in three separate competitions (with at least two different judges) to earn the title of Companion Dog (CD). Some of the dogs competing there that day were attempting their first win; others were trying for their second or third.

Once the judge gave the command, the dog had to come to heel for the handler; it had to stand perfectly still while the judge examined it; it had to change position in response to a verbal command; then it had to Sit Stay (just as the name suggests, sit on command and remain in that position) for one minute; and finally lie on the ground for a Down Stay for three minutes. Being slow to respond to commands would mean points off, while failing to remain at heel or getting up during a Stay task would be an automatic disqualification.

Dogs who had been awarded their CD title could then compete for the CDX award: Companion Dog Excellent. The points worked in the same way: again, there had to be successes in three separate competitions. In addition to the Novice basics, the dog had to Drop on Recall (stop instantly when commanded during its return to the handler); retrieve a light wooden dumbbell first on flat ground and then by going over a dog-sized jump; then do a three-minute Sit Stay and a five-minute Down Stay with – here was the bit that really got me – the handler out of sight.

The final competition step was Utility Dog (UD), where the skills really jumped to another level, taking in scent tracking and scent discrimination; silent commands (made by gesture alone); and a ten-minute Down Stay with the handler out of sight.

I had already been intrigued by what was going on and by the relationships between people and dogs, but when they got to the Stay tasks where the handlers were out of sight, I became completely riveted. With the dogs all lined up in a row in a Stay position, the handlers had to walk away until they were hidden, in this case behind a screen that had been brought in for that purpose. The majority of the dogs didn't take their eyes off the spot where their handler had last been seen. But neither did they get up to follow; they obeyed the command they'd been given. It was an intense display of loyalty and connection, and I was hooked. The discoveries I'd made with Sooty had already set me thinking that I wanted to do some kind of training with this new dog I planned to get. Now I knew exactly what form that training would take: competition obedience work.

As soon as the competition part of proceedings was over, I approached the judges and other club officials, all of whom were volunteers. I had a million questions about how everything worked and what you had to do to compete. There were all kinds of dogs, but particularly German shepherds, labradors and border collies. As I discovered, only purebreds were allowed to compete (though that rule has changed since then). I gravitated to the border collie owners. They could see I was genuinely interested, and they spent a lot of time answering my questions about how the different parts of the competition worked, how long it generally took dogs to pass through the stages and all the rest of it.

They told me that the Holy Grail was the title of Australian Obedience Champion (AOC). To compete for this, your dog had to have passed through all the stages, collecting every award up to UD, plus it had to have achieved a separate Tracking Dog Excellent (TDX) award. The reverence with which these dog owners spoke about AOC status made it clear it was an extremely rare achievement. As soon as I heard that I naively thought to myself, 'It can't really be *that* hard. That's what I'll go after with my new dog.'

4

SUNNY: A BORN CHAMPION

Make sure praise is earned or it loses all effect. The less you talk to a dog during training, the more you'll get out of it.

Armed with information from the Kennel Club journal, I made contact with a breeder called Peidje Vidler, who had been breeding border collies for decades and was quite elderly when I met her.

I knew so little about purebred dogs that I barely understood they are either working-line (sometimes called field-line) or show-line dogs. Show-line dogs are bred to compete at Dog Shows and working-line dogs are bred to do a job, which makes them much better suited for Obedience Trials. Now I can tell with just one look at a purebred border collie or springer spaniel or many other breeds which line they're from. The build is different, the colouration is different, even the temperament is different between the two lines.

Take the springer spaniel, for instance. This is a breed I've come to know and love over the decades, and it's the one with probably the greatest divergence between the two lines. The ears on a show-line springer are far longer than on a working-line springer and sit a bit lower on the head. The coat is also much longer and the body is generally taller and longer: characteristics that would seriously slow the dog down in the field, but ones that show judges reward.

But the most telltale difference between the two dogs is in attitude, particularly their hunt drive. Working-line springers are genetically driven to hunt and find. It's an absolute imperative for them. Show springers aren't. They're bred to be, well, nice, I suppose you could say. They need to be passive and sedate while show-ring judges handle them thoroughly, testing them against the ideal physical measurements. (The 'perfect' shoulder height, for instance, is 51 centimetres in a male dog and 48 centimetres in a bitch.)

Of course there are individual variations — show-line dogs who have a keen hunting instinct, or working-line dogs who would be quite happy to be on show. But in general, the vast majority of dogs from each line have the characteristics of that line. It doesn't mean that show dogs can't be trained, but if you do so you're starting behind the eight ball compared with someone with a working-line dog. You can succeed, but you have to get lucky. And I did — in a big way.

Breeders specialise in one line or the other. I didn't know it when I made contact, but Peidje specialised in show-line dogs. I called her up to find out when she might have some dogs for sale. My timing was perfect. She told me she had a litter of eight pups who were three weeks old. I went to see them and there were two who seemed particularly lively and inquisitive. I watched for a while and one of the pair really stood out to me. He was very outgoing, keen to play with me and already fetching things. We bonded there and then, and I said, 'I'll take this little fellow.' Five weeks later, when he was old enough to leave his mother, I went back to pick him up and he lay happily on the floor of my red MG as I drove him to his new home.

You can get a reasonable idea of a dog's breeding from the way it looks. Does it conform with the classic German shepherd characteristics? If so, the majority of its forebears have been German shepherds ... probably. It's far from certain. I've known a dog whom 100 people out of 100 would have confidently described as a German shepherd, because that's exactly what he looked like. But he was actually a crossbreed. His father was indeed a shepherd, but his mother was a black labrador. Looks are no guarantee.

That's where pedigrees come into things. A pedigree is basically a genealogy chart for the animal, going back five generations and naming all the individuals who form the dog's bloodline – the sources of its DNA. Of course, this all comes at a price and a dog with a pedigree is relatively expensive. My new pup came with such a pedigree and he cost $400, as opposed to the twenty bucks I had paid for Sally.

All pedigree animals have what's technically called a Breeder's Prefix but is better known as a Kennel Name. This is their formal name for competition, but it's too unwieldy for everyday use, so they have a pet name by which they're addressed. (It's the same with thoroughbred racehorses: the Melbourne Cup winner famed as Phar Lap was known to his strapper as Bobby.) My new pup's Kennel Name was the rather posh Borcat McAllister, but I decided my pet name for him would be Sunny. I think the name you give a dog is really important and should encapsulate the character and qualities you want the dog to have. I wanted a bright, happy dog, and 'Sunny' captured that.

I told Peidje I wanted to train Sunny for Obedience Trials. She explained to me that he was a show-line dog, but in my naivety I was still sure I could train him. I had it all planned out in my head. I thought I knew what I was doing and I was blind to all the mistakes I was about to make. But that was where my luck came in: Sunny turned out to be an extraordinary dog, a born champion, in fact.

When they reach four months old, pups are allowed to attend dog clubs. I went down to my local, Sutherland Shire Dog Training Club, which met on Sunday mornings, and signed up. Everyone was very friendly and welcoming. That first day was just about doing the admin needed to join – presenting Sunny's vaccination certificates, paying the membership fee and filling out the forms, which seemed to be missing a box for handsomest pup in the world, though that's what I had.

Like every other suburban dog club, this was a place for people to train their animals for everyday pet obedience. Such classes are terrific for regular pets, but doing competitive work requires a whole different approach. In obedience classes, for instance, having your dog sit when you tell it to do so is an ideal result. However, in competition the dog must sit automatically when you stop moving – it must understand what is required without being given the command. (To use an equine analogy again, it's the difference between teaching a horse to walk sedately along a trail and teaching it to do dressage, with all the precise and specific movements that requires.)

But I didn't understand any of that as Sunny and I were being put in the first of the five levels of classes, the Novice. All the instructors, like the club officials, were volunteers. Classes ran for an hour and you only moved up to the next level when the instructor was satisfied your dog had gained the skills needed to do so. There was a test for each level at the end of every month and you could attempt it whenever you thought your dog was ready. The dogs who attempted the test weren't just given a pass or fail, they were also graded, and the top three passes in each group were awarded ribbons.

I spotted a smaller, more intensely focused group who were clearly training for obedience competition: they had jumps set up and their dogs were fetching dumbbells and doing scent-recognition work. This was very much a specialised pursuit. Most of the people who joined the club just stayed long enough either to train up a new puppy so it became a well-behaved, well-socialised dog or to belatedly tackle behaviour problems in an older, disobedient dog. For 95 out of 100 people there, that was enough. I wanted to become one of the others, those working on highest-level skills. But first I had to pay my dues by moving up through the ranks.

The Novice-class requirements were suitably basic; it was designed as the 'kindergarten' level. The dogs just needed to obey Heel, Sit and Stay commands. I was so enthusiastic I worked with Sunny at every possible opportunity, and it only took three weeks before he was ready to be tested, alongside other dogs who had all been in the class longer. I have lost count of the number of times I've competed with my dogs in different ways over the years, but I remember every detail of that day. A collie rough who was a month older took the first-place blue ribbon and Sunny got the second-place red ribbon.

I was ecstatic and told everyone I knew. This was back in the days when cameras used real film. I had a thirty-six shot roll and I took every single one of them of Sunny with his ribbon – draped over his back, next to him on the ground and in any other position I could think of. I'd taken out a place on my first attempt at competition. Yes, it was in the Novice class at a local dog club, but to me it was nothing less than amazing. I was already ambitious but now it really stepped up a notch. Even so, I didn't dare attempt to talk to the people training for Obedience Trials just yet. I was full of questions but, red ribbon or not, they were the elite, way out of my league.

I was still working for Kogarah Council, where my job involved tending to the parks and gardens around the municipality. I began taking Sunny with me. We'd drive to whatever park was on that morning's schedule, I'd tie him to the fence while I mowed the lawn or worked on the garden, and in between the various jobs I'd spend a couple of minutes practising with him. Then we'd work through lunch. Heel, heel, heel. Sit, sit, sit. Stay, stay, stay. Over and over and over again. If you'd told me that an optimum training session, like the ones I do now, should run for less than two minutes, I'd have thought you were stark, staring mad. In my ignorance I thought the more you trained a dog the better. The truth is you can ruin a dog by over-training and I trained Sunny until he must have been bored rigid. How he put up with me I'll never know.

I did do one major thing right: I used food rewards. Believe it or not, that was almost unheard of in the dog world at the time. The view was that it was bribing the dog and that anyone who used food rewards was weak. More than once I'd heard it put in these sexist terms: 'You're a bit of a girl if you food-reward them.' What you were supposed to do instead was correct the dog if it did something wrong and do nothing if it did what it was supposed to.

That was exactly what had been done to me by my teachers at school. It hadn't worked on me and I instinctively felt it wouldn't work on Sunny. In fact, it had had such a negative effect on me that there was no way I was ever going to do that to a dog of mine, no matter what anyone said. Instead, when Sunny did whatever we were practising the way I wanted him to, he got a reward of food, praise or both. If he got something wrong nothing bad happened to him, he just didn't get a reward. We simply tried again, and when he did get it right, however many tries that took, good things followed.

It worked, just as I had believed it would. Despite my overtraining, the combination of positive reinforcement and Sunny's innate abilities meant he progressed remarkably quickly. We moved up through the classes month after month, and after Novice it was blue ribbons all the way. The old hands at the club took notice. They were generally very encouraging, although when I revealed that I intended to take Sunny to Australian Obedience Championship level, they all said that was too high an ambition.

I can understand how it must have looked. Some of them had been training dogs and competing at the highest level with various dogs for decades, and in that time they might have had just one dog achieve AOC status, or perhaps none at all. Here was I, my dog was from a show line, I'd never even been in a local dog club before let alone competed in trials, and yet I was saying I was going to land this major title. I might as well have been a first-time suburban parent saying they had a four-year-old they were going to turn into an Olympic champion. These old hands told me how hard it was and urged me to set my sights a bit lower. But I was too young and too determined to be discouraged. I listened politely and secretly thought, 'Just watch me.'

Sunny was barely twelve months old and he'd already made it through all the dog-club levels as winner. I'd been along to watch a few more Obedience Trials, soaking up as much information as I could. I'd seen that in the trials you weren't allowed to praise your dog during the exercise that was being tested; you could only do it after the judge formally said the exercise was finished. That was another big difference from what I'd been instructed to do in the dog club, where we were told to use praise as encouragement while the dog was performing.

It's worth making a point here about praise that many people still don't realise. Praise is a fantastic tool in dog training, but there is a really important distinction to be made between using it as encouragement and using it as reward. If you have a strong relationship with your dog, that animal will do anything to please you, so lavishing praise on it when it does what it's supposed to makes it feel great. But using praise as encouragement is a really dumb thing to do because it gives the wrong message.

Let's say your dog is lagging behind rather than walking at heel as it should be doing. Back then in the dog club we were taught that you were supposed to turn back and say, 'Good dog, good dog, good dog' to get the animal to come up beside you. But how is the dog going to know that the praise is for the thing it hasn't yet done? Instead, it naturally thinks it's being praised for what it's already doing – in this case, lagging – and so it continues doing it. If you want to bring about change you should ignore the undesirable behaviour and praise only when the dog gets it right, in this case when it comes up next to you.

I was still only at the beginning of the process of working all this out for myself. I just knew that since I couldn't use praise during the Obedience Trial exercises, I should not use it that way when Sunny and I were training, so I adjusted my technique accordingly.

I was itching to have a go at an Obedience Trial. I was so sure Sunny was ready that I ignored the accepted protocol of asking the Chief Instructor's permission first. I simply went ahead and entered the Novice event in the next available trial.

As luck would have it, the host organisation was the Eastern Suburbs club, the one that had put on the trial a year earlier kick-starting the whole thing for me. I spent three hours the day before washing, brushing and combing Sunny, then groomed him again on the Saturday of the trial before we left. I dressed neatly – no jeans and surfer t-shirt that day, the whole thing was very formal – and got there in good time. As with the previous trials I'd seen, there were competitors from dog clubs all over the city, maybe 200 of them, and even in the Novice category, almost all of them were more experienced than I was.

I was fired up and ready to go, then as soon as we walked into the Novice ring the nerves hit me. There were twenty other dogs in there. But I just kept my focus on Sunny and tried to stay calm, knowing he would pick up on my feelings.

The judge confirmed the handlers' names and our dogs' names, and then asked if we knew the rules and regulations of the NSW Canine Council. Yes, I said, though I wouldn't have had a clue beyond the basics. C'mon, the rule book was inches thick!

Each competitor would do all of the required tasks one after the other, then it would be the next dog and handler's go. The score for each competitor was displayed on a blackboard for everyone to see, with each cumulative total updated after every exercise.

Heel on Lead was the first task, with the handler making a left turn, right turn and back turn while the judge walked behind with his pen and notebook marking the performance. This was followed by Stand for Examination on Lead, during which the judge touched the dog all over its face, chest, back and legs while the animal had to remain perfectly still and calm. Then came Heel off Lead followed by Stand Free for Examination, in which the handler had to be 15 metres away while the judge handled the dog. Then came Recall, in which the dog had to stay while you walked away until the judge said 'Halt', at which point you turned back. Then he said 'Call your dog', and when you did the dog had to go straight to you and sit in front of you. Then the judge said 'Finish' and the dog had to go around behind you then move into position next to you, sit and stay. You could use verbal commands but you could only give each command once.

Sunny and I were to go third. The two competitors ahead of us didn't make it all the way through the sequence of exercises, getting automatically eliminated for moving during a Stay. But I took no pleasure in their failures. From that first competition to now I've never looked at a dog and thought, 'I've got to beat that one.' For me it's always been about performing at my best and getting the best out of my dog.

There were no worries on that score. Sunny went through every task beautifully, doing exactly what we'd practised after I'd studied the requirements. When he got through the first exercise I started to relax a little, and I breathed even more easily after the second. The further we got into things the more confident I became, and the more confident I became the better Sunny performed. The remaining competitors went through the tasks, some doing well and others getting eliminated.

When I entered the competition my goal had been just to pass, which meant getting 170 points out of the possible 200. As ambitious as I was, I'd have been very, very happy with that for my first competition. It would mean Sunny was one-third of the way to his Companion Dog title: a great result by any reckoning. But something completely unexpected was happening: he was leading the field.

Two final tasks remained in the category but you could only compete in them if you had accumulated enough points, which meant having scored above 70 per cent in each of the preceding tasks. The dogs who had done so lined up, including Sunny, and suddenly I was nervous all over again. Having never dreamed of winning, that goal was now almost within our reach. But it could slip away with just one wrong move.

First up was the Long Sit. You had to move 20 metres away from the dog, gesture to it to Sit, and it had to stay there nice and still for one minute on the stopwatch. Then came the Long Down. Again the handler was 20 metres away. You had to send your dog into the Down position and it had to remain there for three minutes.

As mentioned, in the categories above Novice you went out of the dog's sight for this exercise. We remained in the ring but it was still nerve-racking. All a dog had to do was scratch itself or get distracted and start to rise and it would be eliminated. It was made all the more difficult by the fact that all the dogs were lined up just a metre apart from one another.

You can train and train a dog, but it's almost impossible to duplicate the conditions of a trial arena, simply because there is so much nervous energy coming from both other dogs and other people, and your dog picks up on that. So you can never know how he or she is going to perform until they experience the real thing for the first time. Many, many trials have been won and lost in these final events.

But Sunny wasn't fazed by any of it. He did exactly what he was supposed to do, and he won! His score was 170 out of 200 – by coincidence the cut-off score that needed to be achieved to build up to the CD qualification – and he had got there on his first try. In fact, he had done even better. As his judging card revealed, the judge had inadvertently scored him out of ten in a task that was supposed to be out of twenty: his real score would have been closer to 180. What an incredible result.

There was a ceremony at the end of the day during which they gave out the awards to the winners and place-getters in each category, and awarded the dogs who had qualified for their CDs and CDXs. The Novice-category winner was announced: 'Borcat McAllister, handled by Steve Austin.' I went up with him and was presented with a trophy and ribbon.

Well, guess what: dogs aren't the only ones who respond to praise and positive feedback. I'd already been keen on competing because my ideas about what worked and what didn't in animal training were firming up into a technique I thought had huge potential. Now I was absolutely determined to keep going. Having set a goal, having reached that goal (actually, far exceeded the original goal) and having been rewarded for it in this way made me feel great. After all those years as a kid of not being recognised for anything good I did, this kind of recognition meant a huge amount to me. It wasn't the ribbon or the trophy, it was what they represented: the sense of achievement that came with working hard to achieve something and having the world say, 'You're a success.'

The next morning I went to my usual weekly dog-club meeting. A couple of the other club members had been at the trial, apparently, and had seen Sunny and me in action. They'd come along to dog club and said, 'That young bloke with the border collie was competing yesterday …' So when I arrived some of the more senior people asked how I'd gone. I told them I won. I wasn't cocky at all. My inexperience protected me, really, because I still didn't quite get how unusual this achievement was. They were clearly surprised: 'What do you mean you won?' Once they saw that I wasn't kidding they were really pleased for me, and for the club too, since each competitor's club is always identified on the program of events and any successes reflect back on the club. I'm sure there were some mixed feelings as the word spread; after all, there were people at the club who'd been competing for a long time without ever landing a win. But if there was envy I was oblivious to it.

I entered the next two available Obedience Trials, which were held over the following two weekends. I'd thought going into it that having a bit of experience might help me feel less nervous, but as soon as the competition started it was just the opposite. Now that I'd had a taste of the thrill of winning, I wanted more. But it wasn't quite to be: we came second in the next trial, which was still a great result and put Sunny just one more pass away from his CD title. We got that third remaining pass at the following trial, in which Sunny was again placed second.

In a little over a year I'd gone from not even knowing what an Obedience Trial was to training a CD title-holder. I was well and truly addicted to competitions now.

The Sutherland dog club officials were thrilled with my results. They asked me if I would become an instructor. I understood what an honour this was and happily agreed. People at work were interested in how Sunny was going, and they'd ask for updates every Monday if they knew we had competed over the weekend. The local newspaper got to hear about it and something about the story tickled them. With the council's permission they came out to photograph Sunny and me at work and ran a front-page shot of him 'pushing' a lawnmower alongside me. I felt like I was really onto something.

Fired up by Sunny's Companion Dog title win, I started training him straightaway for the next level up, Companion Dog Excellent (CDX). As I've said, this meant competing in the Open (not Novice) category and demonstrating all the CD abilities plus others that were on a whole new skill level.

Several of the new exercises involved retrieving dumbbells. While they had the classic hand-weight shape, these were made of wood so they weren't heavy and were very easy for dogs to pick up in their mouths. For the simplest of these exercises you had the dog sitting by your side while you threw the dumbbell away from you on flat ground. When the judge told you to, you signalled the dog to fetch. It then had to bring the dumbbell back and sit in front of you, offering it up. You could only take it when the judge indicated you should do so. The judge would then say 'Finish', at which point the dog had to go behind you and emerge to sit by your side again.

Some exercises required the dog to clear jumps. In one, the dumbbell was retrieved from the far side of a vertical dog jump. Another used a broad jump. This involved having the dog leap at your command over what looked like three palings from a white picket fence lying side by side on the ground. Drop on Recall required you to send the dog away, have it wait for your command to return and then, as it was racing back to you at full speed, the judge would say 'Now.' The dog would instantly have to respond to your non-verbal command to stop and drop and then would have to remain there until the judge said, 'Call your dog.'

There was a Sit Stay and Down Stay as there had been in the Novice category, but these were the kind that had drawn me to obedience trialling in the first place – the ones where the handler went out of the dog's sight. They also ran for longer: Sit Stay was for three minutes rather than one, Down Stay for five rather than three.

Sunny lapped up all these new skills and we were soon ready to compete. As with CD status, to be awarded the CDX title the dog needed to get at least 170 out of the possible 200 points at three trials under at least two different judges. Having won our first ever trial and accumulated the three scores needed for CD in consecutive trials, I was pretty cocky. But as good as Sunny was, he wasn't infallible and we did fail some trials, though we passed a lot more than we failed.

Okay, well it hadn't been quite as simple as I'd imagined, but we did get there without *too* much difficulty and I became the proud owner and trainer of a CDX dog. There were a few other people at my dog club who had achieved this, but they were all much older than I was and had trained many dogs and been doing it for many years. They were impressed with what I'd achieved, but not as impressed as I was.

I was self-taught and Sunny had been my first attempt at getting a dog to trial standard. Clearly I was a genius at this stuff. Next would come the Utility Dog title and then the coveted Australian Obedience Championships. Obviously the reason why all these older and supposedly wiser heads had tried to warn me off such lofty ambitions was because they just didn't have my innate ability. I didn't say any of this out loud, but I firmly believed it.

Fortunately, my ego hadn't swollen quite enough to blind me to the fact that there were one or two people from whom I might still learn. Chief among these was a lady called Terri Safner. She had trained several dogs right up to UD and I had huge respect for her. Like me, she built her training around positive reinforcement.

It wasn't only in the Obedience Trial ring where things were going well. My job was steady, and I had met up again with Diane, the girl I'd been supposed to meet in London. Our relationship once more became serious quickly and we moved into a place of our own. She didn't share my interest in the dog world, but she loved Sunny and was supportive of me, even though training and trialling and instructing at the club chewed through a lot of my leisure time. She understood when I got stuck into the training needed for Sunny to compete for the UD title.

The exercises for the UD title were a quantum leap from everything Sunny and I had done so far. It wasn't just that he was required to stay down for a stint of seven minutes then a stint of ten minutes with me out of sight, or even that he was required to move in whatever direction I indicated by gesture, in response to the judge's random choice. It was the introduction of scent work that was a whole new level of challenge. And though I didn't know it yet, it would change my life.

There were two different scent exercises to be completed. The first was Seek Back Lost Article. For this, handlers would be supplied with a thin piece of leather about 15 centimetres long – picture a section cut from a belt. As handler, you would rub it to get your scent on it, then the judge would take hold of it using a pair of tongs so as not to confuse the scent. With your dog at heel you would walk in front of the judge, following their directions: 'Forward. Left turn. Forward. About turn. Right turn. Forward', or whatever it might be. Somewhere along the way the judge would drop the leather piece. When you had made a sufficiently complicated track the judge would say, 'About turn. Halt. Send your dog.' You'd give the dog the scent of your hand and the command, 'Find!'

The objective was for the dog to follow the scent back along the track you had created, find the piece of leather and bring it back to you following the usual protocol of sitting and presenting. Dogs who hadn't quite got the idea would stick their noses up and scent it on the air then make a beeline for it. As long as they brought it back they'd get some points, but they would lose marks for not scenting their way along the track.

Training for Seek Back was tricky and required an extremely high level of communication between dog and handler. But here's something a lot of people don't understand: intense communication does *not* mean incessant yammering. In fact, the less you talk to a dog during training, the more you'll get out of it. I encounter people all the time who simply refuse to believe this. We'll be doing some kind of basic obedience task – Sit, for instance. Instead of giving the dog the command once in a calm, firm tone, they'll repeat it over and over, assuming that more is better: 'Sit, sit, sit, sit, sit.' It's just babble raining down on the dog, and the way I get people to understand this is by asking them, 'What was the last song that played on your most recent visit to the shopping centre?' Of course they have no idea. None of us does. Muzak is a background constant that becomes white noise and we simply tune out. And that's exactly what dogs do when owners flood them with commands. I'm sure if they could reply they'd say, 'For pity's sake, shut up! I'm working here!' If you want to communicate with your animal, no yammering please. Give the command once clearly, then pipe down and give the dog the space to work it out for themselves.

It's not just dogs who get rubbed up the wrong way by that kind of relentless babble. I once spent a couple of weeks working closely with a ranger, doing conservation work. He was a great bloke – capable, dedicated and good company, someone who spoke only when he had something to say. We were taking a lunch break one day, enjoying the sights and sounds of nature and making the occasional remark. I commented on how pleasant it was to be with someone who didn't feel a need to fill every silence. He told me about a pig hunter he'd once been assigned to work with, clearing feral animals from a forest. This hunter had two pig-dogs with him. He started talking at them as soon as they got out of the truck and didn't let up for nine hours straight: 'Where's the pig, where's the pig, where's the pig? C'mon, where's that pig, where's the pig, where's the pig? Where's the pig, where's the pig, where's the pig? Get the pig, get the pig. Get the pig, where's the pig, get the pig.' The dogs just ignored him.

My ranger mate is the nicest bloke you'd ever want to meet but he told me, 'After a couple of hours of this I was thinking, "We're in the forest and I have a loaded gun in my hands. I could shoot him out here and no-one would know."' That bit of desperate black humour was the only thing that kept him sane during that long, long day. This motor-mouth pig hunter comes to mind every time I hear someone bombarding a dog with verbal commands.

The second of Sunny's two scent exercises, Scent Discrimination, was even harder than Seek Back. Here there were three groups each containing five identical objects, all of them again about 15 centimetres long: one set of five made of metal, one of wood and one of leather. They were all numbered. At the start of the exercise you handed over the three sets to the judge then you and the dog waited at least five metres away from the test area, with your backs turned. The judge randomly chose one item from each set. He or she then scattered the rest at random on the ground and brought the designated items to you and your dog, using tongs. You rubbed each one to get your scent on it. The judge then took them and placed them among the others on the ground.

When the judge directed you to do so, you turned around and sent your dog to retrieve the three marked objects, in the order you had just specified to the judge. Again, all communication with the dog was by gesture only. You lost points if the dog picked up the wrong object or the right object in the wrong order. You even lost points if you fumbled and dropped the object after you'd taken it from the dog. Getting the task right required complete concentration from dog and handler, working in sync.

Scent Discrimination training took about three months to get right, and the only reason why it took that long was because I over-trained Sunny. These days, using the peak training methods I developed in the mid-1990s, I could achieve the same result in three days.

Finally we were ready to compete. Even though we had taken part in quite a lot of trials by this point, going into my first UD ring was a nerve-racking experience, and I didn't walk out of it feeling much better. We failed at that first trial. In fact, it wasn't until number four that we got a pass, although things went pretty smoothly after that. We continued to compete, and once Sunny had gained the UD title and that pressure was off me, my confidence lifted and so did Sunny's. We started to win consistently.

Then an exciting thing happened. As a result of my success with Sunny in the Obedience Trials, I had been asked to put my name forward as Sutherland dog club's Chief Instructor and I'd been very happy to accept the role.

The excellent results I was getting with Sunny were important; they served as my credentials to take on the role. But it was my absolute enthralment with all aspects of dog training and my desire to see just what could be achieved with it that gave the club's committee members such confidence in me. It was an honour to take on the role.

* * *

By now Diane and I were keen to have a family. In 1980 we got married and by mid-1981 we were expecting our first child. I knew I'd eventually have to curtail my dog training, which was, after all, still a hobby that I fitted around my full-time work as a gardener and greenkeeper.

Our first daughter, Lauren, arrived on schedule on 9 April 1982. I was present for the birth and it was without doubt the most breathtaking and scary thing I had ever seen. The nurse handed me this tiny delicate creature wrapped up in a foil space blanket, and as I took her in my arms for the first time the blanket crackled loudly and I thought I'd broken every bone in her body.

While nothing can top the excitement of the birth of your child, particularly your first-born, something came close in the form of an Obedience Trial. But not just any old trial. This trial was being held as part of Sydney's annual Royal Easter Show, the biggest show of its kind in Australia. Only twenty dogs took part and you had to be invited to compete. I was absolutely thrilled when Sunny got one of the coveted spots.

These days the Show is held at Sydney Olympic Park in Homebush, but back then the showgrounds were in Moore Park. Tens of thousands of people came to watch the dog events in the main ring. The stands were packed, and as we stood with our dogs waiting to go out into the ring the atmosphere was electric.

As was usual in a trial, the position in which the dogs competed was decided by random draw. Sunny got a number a fair way down the list, but rather than giving me time to settle down this only made me more and more nervous, because dog after dog ahead of us was failing to get through the very first exercise, the Seek Back.

It's a challenging task at the best of times, but these dogs were the best of the best, so you'd have expected them to get through it easily. However, none of them had competed under these circumstances before. In the days before the Obedience Trial, the Dog Show events had been held right on this spot. The rules don't permit bitches on heat to take part in trials but they are allowed to compete in Dog Shows. So as well as all the unaccustomed noise and excitement and the food smells coming from the crowd, the ground still held the scents of all the dogs who left their mark, including the siren call of those on heat.

One after another these excellent, brilliantly trained dogs failed to find the scent they needed in order to track back to the piece of leather that held their handler's scent.

Finally it was Sunny's turn. My chest felt like it had iron bands around it. But on command that wonderful dog of mine got his nose down and followed the scent like a train on rails. Nothing distracted or confused him; he went straight to the leather, picked it up and brought it back faultlessly. I was so relieved that he'd done the one thing I'd hoped for that for a second I turned to walk out of the ring – before I realised what I was doing and stopped myself.

After that we went through exercise after exercise in textbook style. As I got more confident, so did he. By the time we got to the task of Send Away, I thought, 'We're actually going to win this.' This exercise involved sending the dog between two jumps, one a bar, one solid. The judge told you which one the dog had to jump each time and you had to indicate it by gesture to the dog. Sunny seemed even more confident than I was – he was already a champion, but he was performing better than he ever had before.

He streaked along towards the solid jump just as I had directed him to, left the ground about two metres away from it and sailed over it effortlessly. He was athletic canine perfection; you could hear the crowd gasp. He went round once again and this time came over the bar jump, if possible looking even more like a four-legged Superman. It was mesmerising.

Now there was only one more exercise, the ten-minute Down Stay. There were only four dogs left in the competition, and one of them, a German shepherd, was a mere one point behind Sunny. The dogs were lined up in the middle of the ring, and we had to give them the Down command then walk away, in this case right inside the officials' rooms under the stands.

As well as having to contend with the crowds and sounds and smells, the dogs had to ignore something else. A chairlift ran overhead, taking people from one side of the showgrounds to the other. People who were on it looked down and, seeing the dogs lying there, thought it was great entertainment to chuck popcorn and bits of Pluto Pup at them.

If a dog fidgeted it might lose a point, but if it started to get up or even slightly shifted position twice, it was disqualified. Sitting inside that room not having any clue as to what was going on out in the ring felt like the longest ten minutes of my life.

I heard over the loudspeaker: 'Exercise finished.' But what had happened? Who had won?

Then I heard the voice of a trial judge I knew who was there observing. He sang out from outside the room, 'Good on ya, Steve', and I knew we had it. I couldn't quite believe it, though, until the judge himself appeared, shook my hand and said, 'Congratulations, full marks.' The shepherd hadn't moved, but neither had Sunny, so we won with a score of 186 out of 200: a terrific achievement.

They made the presentation; I left with a huge silver trophy and three-year-old Borcat McAllister left as Sydney Royal Easter Show Utility Dog Obedience Champion. Even now, more than three decades later, it remains one of the absolute high points of my entire dog-training career.

An excellent opportunity came my way that brought yet another change for the better. I was appointed to a new job that was jointly funded by Kogarah Council, for whom I was already working, and the Kogarah-based St George Rugby League Club. The job was as greenkeeper–caretaker of Jubilee Oval, home ground for the much-loved club, and it came complete with a house right next door to the oval. In the mornings I could throw on a t-shirt and a pair of board shorts, take ten steps and I'd be at work. It couldn't have been more perfect.

I started work at 6 am, which meant I was all done by 3 pm, and I made good use of the remaining hours of daylight in training Sunny for the final elements necessary to gain Australian Obedience Champion status: his Tracking titles. He would need five separate passes in Tracking tests that started out hard and grew even more difficult and demanding as he progressed.

As difficult as the scent-detection task had been in the middle of the Royal Easter Show ring, it was an absolute doddle compared with this kind of Tracking. For a start, the Tracking took place in bushland, not on a mown field. In each of the levels the judge laid out the track and then (at least six hours later, so the judge's smell had dispersed) a 'tracklayer' walked the track. They put an item marked with their scent (typically a sock or some other small piece of clothing) at the beginning of the track and took others with them to drop along the way, then they waited at the end to be found. It got harder and harder as you moved up through the levels; the final test was a 1500-metre track with three-hour-old scent, two strangers' 'crossover' scents, and three dropped items to find.

Dogs couldn't deviate from the track by more than 10 metres and they and their handlers had to deal with whatever else found its way onto the track and whatever muddling effect that had on the scent. We'd get kangaroos jumping up in front of us. Cows would wander through and leave cowpats to be dodged.

Logistically, it was incredibly challenging to train for: not only did you have to locate a bit of bushland somewhere, but you also had to find a helper who was prepared to lay the track and would wait 'still and silent' and 'as inconspicuous as possible' (as the official rules put it) until the dog found them. For the most advanced level you needed your two track-crossers and then someone who would wait for up to three hours to be found. That was a very big ask.

Sunny passed all his Tracking tests on the first attempt, giving him his Tracking Dog (TD) and Tracking Dog Excellent (TDX) titles in addition to his UD. That meant he qualified as an Australian Obedience Champion, the ultimate obedience accolade. It was just four years since I had taken him home as a tiny puppy, and now we'd reached the pinnacle together. There was only one other person in the whole Sutherland dog club who had taken a dog to AOC. It was a huge achievement, and in due course the club recognised it as such.

SUNNY: A BORN CHAMPION

They went to a lot of trouble, having a special 14-carat-gold medallion made up with the words 'Sunny, AOC, 1983' and a picture of a border collie engraved on it. That would have been special enough, but it wasn't just a picture of any old border collie, it was Sunny himself.

I was very touched.

5

TV STARS AND COOL HOT DOG

It's impossible to get a dog to do what you want if you're inconsistent. And don't yell in anger at it. All yelling at dogs or kids achieves is to make them fear you and stop trusting you.

Sunny's competition success opened up a whole new world for us: television. Many of the locally made adverts and TV shows in which an animal appeared back then would try to get away with using the producer's kids' pet or the director's neighbour's dog; that way the animal didn't cost anything. But smarter, more experienced people used properly trained dogs, and they relied on casting agents to find them.

These agents kept an eye on the upper levels of obedience competition, looking for dogs that might come in handy, and Sunny's many successes had brought him to their attention. One day in early 1983 I got a call asking if I'd be interested in trying him out for a new four-part children's miniseries being made by the ABC. They were after a border collie and they'd heard Sunny looked great and was very well-trained, so would I like to bring him along for a screen test?

I knew nothing about that world but it sounded like a good opportunity. Sunny and I arrived on the appointed day and learned that the miniseries, *Hedgerow House*, was a mystery–adventure about some children who find their way into an abandoned house concealed behind a huge hedge. The kids' dog had a crucial role at the beginning of the story because it had to run down a lane and go through a gap in the hedge; when the children followed the dog they discovered the house and the action kicked off. Later on, when they were exploring the house, the dog would end up falling down into a cellar and one of the kids, a young boy, would have to pick it up in his arms.

We were being auditioned to check that Sunny lived up to his reputation, that he would behave well around the child actors and that the boy (who was about twelve or thirteen but had been cast because he was small and looked younger) could pick him up. We went through some basic commands – Sit, Stay, Come – then the boy joined us. Sunny was gentle and calm while the boy played with him, and the boy picked him up with no problems. We got the job and were given the address where filming would take place the following weekend.

I was really looking forward to showing off my dog and I pictured arriving and getting straight into things. But turning up and seeing the trucks and vans and cables and lights and generators, and all the rest of what I now know is the usual organised chaos of a film set, was daunting. There were people milling around everywhere, most of whom seemed to be doing nothing much (though as soon as the cameras rolled it was a different story).

Before any filming started, the director wanted to see Sunny run down the lane and then, in what would be a separate shot, go through the hedge. Coming down the lane couldn't have been simpler: I just had to get Sunny to stay back out of sight and then, when I was positioned behind the camera, give him the command to come to me. They seemed surprised that he got it exactly right first go, which I thought was a bit odd given how basic a task it was.

Then he had to go through the hedge. They seemed to be expecting Sunny to take hours to nail this, but I just mimicked Seek Back, setting up a track that led along to the hedge then throwing the article through the gap. I gave Sunny the command and he did it perfectly.

They asked if he could do it again. Sure, he'd do it all day if you asked him to. Now the director and other key crew were seriously impressed. When you're given a dog as a freebie favour you get what you (don't) pay for. Lots of these people had been on sets where time (and therefore money) had trickled away as the animal couldn't do what they wanted. On that scale, if a dog sat when it was told to it was doing well. No wonder they were blown away by Sunny.

When I'd arrived on set it was, 'The guy with the dog is here.' After a couple of days of seeing him in action it was 'Steve and Sunny'. They started asking me whether he'd be able to do this and that, and when I said yes they began writing new bits into the script for him. It was a great experience all round and I got paid $1100, which was the equivalent of three weeks of my greenkeeping wage.

TV STARS AND COOL HOT DOG

I wasn't going to be giving up my day job anytime soon, though. In America there were people who make a living solely out of training animals for TV and movies, but the Australian market wasn't big enough for that. Even Aussies who made it the main part of their business had to do some other kind of work, generally obedience training, to supplement their income. But it would certainly be a nice bit of icing on the cake, so I made it known that Sunny was available.

He was such a great performer and a handsome dog that we were soon getting interest. This came particularly from ad agencies, since dozens of TV commercials were made for every one drama or film, and plenty of them were for pet food or featured pets in some other way.

My job at Jubilee Oval was flexible enough for me to fit this extra work in. During footy season I worked the weekends and got Tuesdays and Wednesdays off, and otherwise I just built up enough extra hours to take time in lieu. My life was increasingly focused on dogs. As well as the on-camera work Sunny was doing, I was still competing with him. And I was volunteering my time down at the dog club every Sunday morning and on Wednesday nights as well for elite competition training.

Sunny did some fantastic commercials over the following few years. One of my favourites was a Good-O dog-food ad in which he was on a fishing boat tied up to a dock. He had to be eating out of one bowl with another full bowl next to it when a labrador came along the dock, looked hopefully towards the second bowl and barked. Sunny then needed to pad along to the bow and pull on the mooring rope, bringing the boat close enough for the labrador to jump on so they could munch away side by side.

The commercial was on high rotation and a lot of people I knew were amazed that he was able to do this seemingly sophisticated sequence. But break the task down to its basics and it was so easy to train him for it. Sitting, eating and moving into position on command were things he could practically do in his sleep. And as for the rope, well, that was just a version of tug-of-war, which he loved to play. All I had to do was give him the command to get the rope and pull, exactly as he would when we were playing at home, and the director got precisely what he needed. Being on a boat while he was doing it didn't faze Sunny at all.

In fact, it didn't matter what he was asked to do, he could do it perfectly first time, every time.

Well, almost every time. There was a PAL Meaty-Bites ad in which he had to eat food that an actor playing his owner poured into a bowl. But when he was a puppy I had taught him not to take food from anyone but me, so he refused to play along. In the end they dolled me up and put makeup on me and I made a blink-and-you'd-miss-it appearance in place of the actor.

Word spread and Sunny was soon in high demand. It got to the point where production companies would specify to their casting agents that it had to be him who did the job; they knew he would deliver for them.

Auditions weren't something we needed to do any more, but I did get persuaded to go along to one on the grounds that it was for a major film with a big budget and big-name stars to match. We arrived in good time but as soon as we got there I was tempted to leave. They were running way behind and there were a whole lot of dogs and handlers waiting ahead of us. But

I'd said I'd do it, so I waited. And waited, and waited. An hour and a half later, Sunny and I were finally ushered in. This was the eighties, the era of pretentious men with designer ponytails wearing sunglasses indoors, who had no time for people who weren't like them. There were half a dozen of them sitting there waiting for us and they were clearly bored beyond belief at having to watch yet another bloody dog go through its paces.

As I sat down in the chair provided, the bloke in the middle piped up and said in the most patronising manner possible, designed to get a laugh out of his pals, 'Oh, and I suppose you've got the best dog in the world, have you?' Now, I was already well and truly fed up by this point, but before I had a chance to react Sunny did something he had never, ever done. He walked up to the table behind which they were all sitting, turned his back to them and dropped a big poo right there. Then he calmly walked back to my side. I kept a straight face, stood up and said, 'Well, the dog's just given his opinion of your attitude. I agree with him!' And we walked out, leaving them spluttering in our wake. It was the one and only time Sunny ever relieved himself indoors – he always did have perfect timing.

In 1984 I was approached to take part in something called PAL Super Dogs, basically a crowd-spectacle version of an agility trial put on by the pet-food company. It would be half-time entertainment at major sporting matches and a headlining act at big regional events around Australia like the Ballarat Show. I got a call asking if we'd like to try out. Of course I said yes. They liked what they saw and invited us to join.

Dogs of various breeds including labradors, Old English sheepdogs, German shepherds and golden retrievers would go around a course that featured various obstacles and scaled-down versions of what you might see at a horse show-jumping competition. The obstacles included a row of brightly painted, cricket-stump-height poles that the dog had to weave between, and the jumps included ones painted to look like brick walls with a row of loose wooden brick-shaped blocks on the top. One by one the dogs had to complete the course, with the handlers running beside them. They were timed and there were penalties for things like knocking the loose bricks off the 'wall' jumps. Supposedly it was a competition, but it was really just fun for the spectators, so we tried to arrange for different dogs to win each time. Our 'pay' was unlimited dog food, but the real benefit was the exposure it brought and, for me, the chance to gain experience in presenting to the public.

Some of the events were huge: Sunny performed in front of 60,000 people at the tea break of one West Indies versus Australia day–night match at the Sydney Cricket Ground (SCG) and a similar number at the Melbourne Cricket Ground. It was demanding on the dogs physically – some of the jumps were very high, even for a border collie – and after three years I felt he'd had enough and withdrew him. But the marketing people who organised it asked me to stay on and manage it. That also meant commentating live.

Unless you counted talking to small groups of dog owners at obedience classes, I'd had no real experience of public speaking. It was definitely scary, but if you don't challenge yourself you don't learn, so I gave it a go and got better every time I did it. I'd introduce each dog and describe what was happening ... 'This is Billy and he's a four-year-old labrador. There he goes, clearing that first jump easily. He's going through the vertical obstacles beautifully but, oops, he's knocked the bar off that final jump. That gives him a time of thirty-three seconds, so next up to see if she can beat that score is ...' and so on. I got more and more confident and relaxed, and more and more able to keep the crowd involved and interested.

I didn't know it yet, but that PAL Super Dogs exposure would lead me to take on a massive challenge in the service of the whole nation. But I'd have to wait a couple of years for that ...

By 1987 Diane and I had three children. Rochelle was born in 1985 and Claire a year after her. The girls enjoyed coming along to see Sunny perform occasionally, but it was no big deal for them. He was the beloved pet they played with every day, the one who pulled them on a rope attached to their tricycles around the whole of Jubilee Oval and played hide-and-seek up in the grandstand with them. As kids do, they took it all for granted – doesn't everyone's dog perform at the SCG and do TV ads?

As well as my full-time job and whatever film and television work came Sunny's way, I was teaching occasional paid dog-training classes. These came about as a natural offshoot of my voluntary work running the group training classes at the dog club. People who wanted some more intense one-on-one work with their dogs would occasionally ask me if they could make a time to see me separately. There was a good grassy area near Jubilee Oval that I could use, so I would arrange for them to come along after I'd finished work for the afternoon. At first I didn't ask for money for these sessions, but eventually I was getting so many requests and it was taking up so much time that I reluctantly started charging a modest fee, from memory something like $10 an hour. People were happy to pay; in fact, they told me I should increase the price, and over time I did.

I was working long and hard but I was young and full of energy, and most important of all, I loved what I was doing. My home life was good. The girls were all very different from one another but a delight to be around. I'd been determined to be a better parent than my own parents had been and dog training had been a huge help. People sometimes think I'm kidding when I say that, but it's absolutely true. I'd learned things from working with dogs that I applied to my girls and it made for much calmer, happier kids.

The first thing was consistency. If you are straightforward and consistent with children you will get great results. Being consistent is hard at first, no question, but it pays off in a big way. What this means in practice is if you say 'Go to bed' you have to follow through. You can't change your mind because they don't like it or they make a fuss (although changing your mind is really tempting, and we've all done it at some point). Nor can you do your block if they don't do what you've told them. Don't argue with them and don't repeat yourself endlessly. Instead, gently and calmly take them by the hand or pick them up, take them into the bedroom and put them to bed. Every time they get back up, do the same thing again. If you can stick with this approach night after night, the child eventually realises you mean it when you say 'Go to bed.'

I learned all this the hard way, making mistakes with my dogs before I ever had kids. It didn't stop me from making mistakes with my kids too – just ask them, they'll tell you! – but I made a hell of a lot fewer than I would have otherwise.

Experience had taught me what worked and what didn't, and I had discovered it was impossible to get a dog to do what you want if you're inconsistent.

I'll give you a simple example. You train your dog to sit beside your gatepost before you come in or out, teaching it to wait until the gate is fully opened and you've given it the command to go. Then one day you're in a tearing hurry and you urge the dog through as soon as the gate starts to open. The dog can't understand that this is the exception to the rule, only happening on that one day because of unusual circumstances. Maybe rushing through the gate from now on will get it into trouble, but maybe it won't. In that moment the dog learns it doesn't have to follow the routine. As understandable as it is to hurry that one time, by doing so you've undone a whole lot of good work and you'll have to start over again to entrench the behaviour you want. It works just the same with kids.

Being inconsistent was just one of the mistakes I made with dogs early on. Another was losing my temper. I've never hit my dogs, but I've certainly been guilty of getting angry and yelling at them. I'm not proud of it, but I'd be pretty interested to meet any dog owner who can honestly say they've never done the same. It's a pointless thing to do, though, because the dog doesn't have any comprehension of what you're angry about. The same goes for young children. All yelling at dogs or kids achieves is to make them fear you and stop trusting you.

It can take every bit of self-discipline you've got when kids are behaving badly, but if you make yourself act calmly and just keep repeating the same boring, consistent message, you'll get the result you're after. And because they know you're consistent about sending them to bed from the time they're three, they know you'll be consistent when you tell them as teenagers they'll be grounded for the weekend if they don't change their behaviour. It's a long game, but in the end it's win–win for you and them.

My involvement with dogs had given me those insights, but it was also teaching me about managing behaviour more indirectly, thanks to my dealings with the owners at the dog-club classes. Here I saw the good, the bad and the ugly, and in time I learned how to enjoy the good and deal with the bad and the ugly. The majority of people were just fine, but I had to figure out how to manage the ones who simply did not want to be there and made no effort to hide it. They expected that they could turn up, put in absolutely no effort and magically their dog would end up fully trained. I had to find a way of communicating with them that was clear and polite but that would cut through. The ones who were too hard on their dogs, yelling and screaming at them, had to be shown another way without being made to feel humiliated. The ones who were too soft and let their dogs jump all over them and get away with anything had to be taught how to be firmer in a way they could handle.

I firmly believe that, with a few exceptions, there are no 'bad dogs'. Ninety-nine per cent of the time, when a dog behaves badly it's the owner's fault. In all the years I've been working with dogs I've come across a tiny number who weren't right mentally. I once worked with a border terrier for three weeks and could not teach him a single thing, not even Sit, the most basic of commands. Physically he was fine, but there was something missing, something … off. However, cases like that are very, very rare. Usually, if I can get the owner on-side, the dog will follow.

As an instructor, I very quickly figured out that when people rubbed me up the wrong way I had a stark choice. I could tell them what I thought of them — that they were stupid or rude or a bully or whatever. Doing so might have given me a few seconds of release, maybe, but the consequences for the dog could have been dire. That was because if the owner felt embarrassed or threatened they wouldn't come back to dog training and the dog would remain unmanageable. It wouldn't get walked because it was too hard to handle, so it would stay in the backyard barking all day long in frustration. Before long either the owner or the neighbours would have had enough, and the dog would have become a problem to be disposed of — it would probably be sent to the pound, where it might well be put down. But if, instead of driving those owners away, I could find a way to get through to them and encourage them to come back and learn how to manage their pet, I'd have given that dog a real chance at a good, happy life.

Understanding that gave me all the motivation I needed to hang in there and keep trying with even the most hostile owners. A good example is a guy I had once in puppy class, a big macho bloke, covered in tatts and wearing a death's-head t-shirt, radiating aggression. He had a labrador called Jack. We were working on the right technique for teaching the puppies to come when called. I showed the class what to do and this bloke did the steps in the wrong order. I said to him, 'That's good, what you did, but this time when you call him, say "Come" and *then* pull the lead.' He said, 'Nah, I've already done it.' I tried again. 'Yep, I know, that's good. But what happened was you pulled the lead and then said "Come". You'll find he learns it a lot better if you do it the other way round.' He said, more loudly this time, 'Nah, already done it.'

From the way he was glowering I knew that if I kept pushing him there was a good chance he might thump me. So I let it go, focused on other dogs and when I got back around to him I talked as if none of it had happened. I was pleased to see him come back the following week, but again I acted with complete neutrality. Without being obvious, I kept a close eye on him and his pup, and as soon as the dog did what he was supposed to I said, 'Geez, Jack, that is fantastic!' You could see the hostility melting away from the bloke and he said, 'He's a good dog, isn't he?' I said, 'He's a *great* dog.' From then on, because he felt proud of his dog and not afraid that he'd be shown up in front of other people, Jack's owner listened and worked on his skills and ended up with a good, well-trained animal.

By 1987, Sunny was only eight but he'd reached the pinnacle of obedience work, and there were no more mountains for him to climb. I wanted to continue competitive training but I didn't just want to do the same thing with another dog. I'd seen people on the circuit with that approach – take one golden retriever to UD or AOC level, then get another golden retriever and do the same thing all over again. There's nothing wrong with that, it just wasn't for me. I wanted a new challenge. I would have loved to have done true sheepdog work with Sunny, but where do you get sheep in Kogarah?

A stroke of luck brought me precisely the kind of challenge I was looking for. I was asked to represent the NSW Canine Council as an independent observer at an upcoming Field Trial. Along with Retrieving Championships and Utility

Championships, this is one of the main types of competitions held for what are known as gun dogs, a category that takes in setters, retrievers, spaniels, pointers and other breeds such as cocker spaniels, clumber spaniels, flat-coated retrievers, curly-coated retrievers and Irish setters (all working-line, of course).

I knew a little bit about Field Trials. They were designed to test the ability of dogs for hunting and shooting under real conditions. The dog handlers carried guns with live ammunition. The trials were held in areas that were habitats for game – rabbit, quail or hare. Under strict conditions, the dog had to find the game and flush it from its hiding place, i.e. send it running or flying. The handler then had to shoot the game and the dog had to run to where it fell and retrieve it, delivering it back to the handler. The events were held during the relevant hunting season, but if an animal or bird that wasn't in season was flushed out, the dog would still get marks, although the game wouldn't be shot.

To be honest, I went there thinking, 'What do these dogs do, really? They just run around and pick up a couple of dead animals, that's it.' As soon as I saw them go to work I realised my mistake. I arrived at the event feeling I was a pretty good dog trainer. In fact, I felt I was the ant's pants. Within minutes of the start of the trial, I thought to myself, 'You'd best shut up here and just look and listen', and that was the smartest thing I could have done. Man alive, did I learn something that weekend!

It was astonishing what those dogs could do. I watched them find a quail from 200 metres away, get to within a few centimetres of the bird's hiding place, hold point (stay motionless indicating the location of the target) until they were given the command to flush it out, and then, after they'd done so and the bird had been shot, run out on command, pick it up and bring it back as delicately as if they were handling it with kid gloves.

I knew I could learn a lot from people who could train dogs to that degree. It was a two-day event. We camped out that night and I took the opportunity to ask as many questions as I could. The trial competitors were a great bunch. They could see that my interest was genuine and were happy to give me lots of good answers. By the time we turned in for the night I was totally hooked on gun dogs.

There are separate trials for the various breeds: one for spaniels and retrievers, one for pointers and setters, and one for 'utility dogs' (a category that includes Weimaraners, Hungarian vizslas and others). The trial I attended was for spaniels and retrievers. When I got home the following evening, I looked up a big illustrated book I had of different dog breeds. In the section on gun dogs there was a photo of a black-and-white springer spaniel holding a duck it had retrieved and brought back to its nuggety-looking old owner. There was something about the picture that really spoke to me. I decided a springer spaniel was the breed I'd get.

The springer spaniel Field Trial group recommended a breeder called Lynley Fox-Cummings. I called her and was very impressed by her knowledge and approach. We arranged that I would get a puppy from her next litter, and in due course she called and said he was ready for me. His Kennel Name would begin with Rossmore but Lynley let me choose the last part of it and I decided on Steely Dan, to honour one of my favourite bands. Rossmore Steely Dan: that was a fine formal name. For his everyday name I chose something suitably purposeful: Hunter. But the girls weren't having any of it. They started calling him Hot Dog and pretty soon I just gave up trying to call him anything else, since the only names he would answer to were Hot Dog and Hottie.

It took more than a year to get ready to compete. I had to train him but I also had to train myself. In England, thanks to the good old class system, the handlers don't have to shoot, they let 'the guns', as they are known, take care of that part of it. In Australia, the handler does the lot. Well, I'd never done any shooting before. I got my shooting licence, bought a gun, joined a clay-target shooting club and practised week after week. I wasn't a natural shot by any means, but I kept on trying and I gradually improved.

The second big hurdle in preparing to compete was giving Hot Dog some field experience. You can train for Obedience Trials on any flat bit of grass: get your jumps and dumbbells and you're away. Tracking training is more demanding, but you can still find a bit of bush to use within the expanse of the city. Field Trial training is a whole different thing: you can't exactly head out with a gun and a hunting dog and start shooting rabbits in the bush at Lane Cove or Heathcote or any other part of suburban Sydney. That kind of thing tends to get a bloke arrested. Instead, you have to drive for five or six hours to reach a suitable spot, even though when you get there you might not see a rabbit all day.

Then there was the challenge of teaching a dog to go against its instincts. It has to hunt to the point of flushing the game, then stop. That's a mighty big ask for a dog whose innate response is to chase down the prey. I trained Hot Dog by doing dummy retrieves and giving him a big reward every time he stopped. After a while the 'Stop!' whistle command took on a positive association for him and when he heard it he would pull up straightaway and look at me, awaiting instruction.

Finally we were ready to put ourselves to the test in our first competition.

Sometimes ignorance is a blessing. It sure was the day Hot Dog and I competed in our first ever Field Trial, in a cold and windy field outside Cooma, in southern New South Wales. There were about twenty people there, mostly competitors, plus one or two hardy spectators. The way it works is that two dogs ('a brace') and their handlers go out at a time, head to head. The draw is done randomly, just numbers picked out of a hat. The name of the handler I was up against was Rod Watt. That didn't mean anything to me, but the competitors I'd got to know saw the draw and their eyebrows went up. I wondered about that, but there wasn't really time to talk about it; the judge was calling us.

What the old hands knew was that Rod's spaniel was one of the best Field Trial dogs in the world; they had won countless events together. Well, you can't be intimidated by what you don't know, so Hottie and I went out there and did our best. We didn't win, but we didn't lose either – the performances were so closely matched that the judge couldn't split us on points. Both dogs would go through to the second round.

One of the guys who'd been involved in the trials for a long time came up to me as soon as the announcement was made and said, 'Do you know what you've just done?' My mind raced through all the things I'd been trying to remember and I said, 'What? Did I make a mistake?'

The glory I felt after he explained didn't last too long. In the second round Hottie took off after a rabbit at the wrong moment and we were eliminated. Well, he was still a puppy, after all. But it had been a great start. It taught me that my dog had what it took to get ahead in Field Trials and that I wanted to keep on going until we got to the top. It wasn't going to be quick, that was obvious, but I'd wanted a challenge.

As I'd learned with Sunny, the relationship you form when you work with a dog, as opposed to a relationship with a dog who is purely a pet, is almost indescribably strong. That applies to dogs being trained to compete in Obedience or Field Trials, dogs rounding up stock for farmers, police dogs, army explosive detection dogs, you name it. The communication is so intense that a few words and a look can convey more to those animals than half an hour's wrestling with a pet on the lounge-room floor might. I could look at Hot Dog when he was performing brilliantly and say a heartfelt 'Good boy, mate' and it represented an explosion of love and attention to him.

He could also clearly communicate his feelings to me, and he wasn't shy about it when I was letting him down. My shooting continued to improve but it was a very slow process. As the months went by, we lost a lot more trials because I couldn't hit the target than because of his performance. Hottie would plunge into a blackberry bush as big as a room to go after a rabbit. He'd flush the rabbit out and I'd be waiting, I'd take aim, fire and … the rabbit would hop off across the field to live happily ever after. I got some filthy looks from my faithful companion when that happened, let me tell you. I swear there was an equal mix of disbelief and exasperation in his eyes. What could I say? I was trying, really I was. But for now, the only thing I could do to make it up to him was to apply antiseptic cream to the scratches on his testicles when it was all over.

Mind you, the disappointment wasn't all one-way traffic. Occasionally Hot Dog would be the one at fault, like the time I worked all day at the oval, then went on to my second job as a doorman at the St George leagues club, finished there at 1 am, popped home, picked him up and drove for seven hours down to Cooma. In retrospect that was pretty stupid, I know, but I just loved competing in Field Trials. I parked at the meeting point in town and managed to get all of thirty minutes' sleep before the other blokes who were competing came along, fresh as daisies after a cosy night in the local motel. Off we went out to the paddock where the trial was starting. In the draw to see what order people would compete in, my number had come up in the first pair.

The judge said, 'Are you ready, fellas?' We answered yes. He said, 'Load your guns.' We did so. He said, 'Okay, are you set? Send your dogs.' I sent Hottie, who went a grand total of four metres, put a rabbit up and then proceeded to chase the bloody thing off into the distance: instant disqualification. Time elapsed since the competition started? All of twenty-two seconds. Surely a world record for the shortest ever time in action. The other blokes waiting their turn collapsed with laughter. The judge looked at me sympathetically and said, 'That's just bad luck, mate.'

To say I was disappointed is an understatement. Mostly with myself for not having trained Hottie better, and for underestimating how wound up he would be after a night in the car with no run to burn off some energy before competing. Even so, he wasn't my favourite that morning. On the way down I'd chatted away to him, keeping myself awake: 'You're a good dog, you're going to do great' and so on. It was no talkies all the long drive back.

To be awarded the title of Field Trial Champion, a dog had to accumulate points, which were earned by coming either first or second in a trial. It took three years from when we started competing, but we got there and Hottie officially became 'Rossmore Steely Dan FT Ch'.

After he'd achieved that I decided to put him into some Obedience Trials, not with the same sense of ambition I'd had with Sunny but mostly because it would be good for his stud fees and for my growing reputation as a dog trainer. I didn't even aim for Australian Obedience Champion status this time; if we could get to Companion Dog Excellent (CDX) that would be fine, because while he had become an exceptional gun dog, obedience work required quite different skills. But his field experience did deliver him one brilliantly unexpected victory.

He was taking part in an Open competition as part of the attempt at his CDX title. The event took place at Castle Hill Showgrounds in horrible conditions, with rain on and off all day. By late afternoon, as we were getting to the last of the competition exercises, Hottie was coming dead last. I wasn't worried, because it looked like he'd just scrape over the 170-point mark needed for a pass and that was all I was aiming for. Nine dogs got to the Sit Stay exercise and they all passed and made it through to the five-minute Down Stay with the handlers out of sight. We each gave the Stay command to our dog and walked over to the toilet block.

Just as we went behind the building the heavens opened with torrential rain. Then the thunder started. The storm must have been passing almost directly over us because the noise was unbelievable. The tiny eaves over the back wall of the block offered almost no protection from the downpour and the second hand on my watch seemed to be moving in slow motion.

Finally, five minutes had passed and we went back out to where the dogs should have been.

Hottie was the only one left. The others had all freaked out at the thunder and taken off to their owners, but Hot Dog was sitting there as happy as Larry. The judge, Bob McGarvey, a man with years of experience, said to me, 'I can't believe your dog stayed. The louder the thunder got the happier he was!' I said, 'He's looking for the ducks to come over, Bob. He thinks that thunder is gunshot and he's wondering what's keeping those damn birds.'

Hottie took first place in the Open that day – lowly score or not, he was the only dog left at the final whistle! I would think back to this day more than a decade later, when speed-skater Steven Bradbury won gold at the 2002 Winter Olympics by being the only man left standing at the end of his race. Some people started referring to that as 'doing a Bradbury'; personally I thought Bradbury had 'done a Hottie'.

6

A TRICKY PIG AND ONE CLEVER CAT

Cats interact with people in a completely different way from dogs, but you can still train them if you can find the right stimulus.

I'd been involved in dog training for over a decade by now. It occupied a great deal of my leisure time and even more of my thoughts, but it was still just a hobby, albeit an all-consuming one. All that was about to change. The new decade that was unfolding, the 1990s, would bring me some remarkable opportunities and experiences.

But first there was a terribly sad incident: the death of Sunny, who had taught me so much and taken me so far in the canine world. I wouldn't be where I am today had it not been for that wonderful dog.

He was only twelve and in fine health; he should have had a number of years more to enjoy life. But a tick got him. Tick-control medication in those days wasn't as good as it is now, and while I checked him every day, the thickness of border collies' coats makes detecting ticks difficult. I wish I could replay that time and search and search him until I found that deadly parasite. I rushed him to the vet as soon as he showed symptoms, but by then it was already too late. (Having said that, while the vet took every step he thought reasonable and I agreed at the time, I am much more questioning now and much more forceful as an advocate for my animals' care.)

In hindsight, I made more mistakes training Sunny than with any other dog I've ever owned – I'd do it so differently if I had the chance. But it didn't matter how many things I got wrong, he rose above them all. He was a born champion who had excelled at every challenge he was given. It was a very big loss.

I still had Hot Dog, of course, and I might have waited a while longer to get another dog, but my girls were extremely keen to have a puppy. My bond with Sunny had been so strong that I didn't want to get another border collie. He was irreplaceable, so I thought it would be better to get a different breed of dog entirely. But a friend of mine had a dog called Caspar who had been sired by Sunny and inherited his abilities, becoming so highly successful in both obedience and agility competitions that he was the most titled border collie in the world at one point. Caspar, in turn, had fathered a litter, and when the girls found out about these puppies, that was it, they were desperate that we should get one. I resisted but they pestered and charmed – well, what chance does a father have? We got one of the puppies. His Kennel Name was Gotrah McAllister's Lad but he was Bobby to us.

He proved to be a brilliant dog, though quite different from Sunny. The best way to describe it is that Bobby was a real thinker, strange as that sounds. He was extremely clever and you could stand there and watch him seemingly reason things out, at least as far as dogs can be said to employ reason. He also had a sneaky streak: if you called him and he thought you couldn't see him he would often just ignore you, but if he knew you were within his sightline he'd come straight to you. But he was exceptionally lovable; in fact Diane, who tolerated most dogs rather than sharing my feelings for them, took strongly to him.

Over time I took Bobby to CDX level in obedience competition and, like his grandfather, he became a favourite of ad agencies and their clients. Perhaps his most famous commercial was the one the Meat and Livestock Corporation ran to change the way people thought about lamb, by selling it without fat and bone under the name 'Trim Lamb'. The ad was done like a modern take on a silent movie, with a corner-shop butcher trying to convince the sceptical women who tap on his shop window that his appealing display really is lamb. With the window between them, neither side can hear the other and the dialogue is shown in subtitles. My dog's big moment provided the smile at the end of the ad: the butcher finally succeeds in getting the message across to a woman who then happily enters his shop. Her place at the window is taken by Bobby, who goes from hopeful to downcast when the butcher kindly shakes his head and mouths, 'No bone.'

It wasn't too long after we got Bobby that I received a phone call from a gentleman called Bob Biggs who, with his wife,

Hannie, owned a pet-boarding kennel they'd named Hanrob, located in Heathcote on Sydney's southern edge. As well as caring for dogs while their owners were away, Bob and Hannie wanted to offer dog training as an optional extra. Bob had heard about me and was ringing to see if I was interested in going to Hanrob to work as a trainer.

As much as the idea tempted me, it was a big decision. For one thing, making the leap would mean giving up the employer-supplied house my family lived in. Moving house might well mean the girls would need to move schools. And while I could tell right from the start that Bob was a good man, at that stage his business was still quite small. So he and I agreed that rather than quitting my existing job and moving there full-time straightaway, I would work some hours training down at Hanrob around my existing commitments and we'd see where it led us.

On the days when I didn't have to work as a doorman at the leagues club I would finish my greenkeeping job mid-afternoon then tear down to Heathcote and start training dogs, often going until eleven at night, using a torch tied to a tree for light. Word spread and business increased, and as demand grew Bob built a shed especially for the training and we were able to take on more dogs. By 1993 there was so much demand for my services through Hanrob that it was time to take the plunge: I resigned from my Jubilee Oval job. I would be a consultant rather than an employee; Bob and Hannie would get the boarding fees while I would get the training fees and pay them a small amount to cover the cost of overheads, including advertising.

From here on in, my professional life would be centred around animals. It was a gamble, but I was ready to give it my all.

A TRICKY PIG AND ONE CLEVER CAT

It worked out beautifully – a real win-win situation. Bob and I had a great relationship. He taught me a huge amount about business and together we developed the training side of the venture from nothing to arguably the state's biggest and best.

Partway through 1993 I got a call from the producers of an upcoming movie called *Babe*. The movie went on to become a huge hit, of course, and even won an Academy Award. But at the start of that phone conversation I knew nothing about what kind of film it might be or whom it might be aimed at. The producers explained it was an adaptation of a children's story by British author Dick King-Smith. My daughters were just the right age for the story, but King-Smith wasn't a writer I'd come across and I'd never heard of the book.

They told me the basics: the setting was a sheep farm. In the book it was in England but the film would have a more general storybook-style setting and would be filmed in the lush highland country to Sydney's south. The hero, and title character, was a plucky piglet won at a fair by the sheep farmer and saved from the table when he developed the surprising ability to herd sheep. Humans definitely took a back seat in this story. As well as the pig there were significant roles for sheepdogs (border collies), sheep, horses, ducks, hens and a cat.

The animal characters would be voiced by humans, and part of the action would be done using animatronics and puppets, but there was still a huge requirement for trained animals. That was in large part why pre-production had started so early, more than a year before filming was due to begin. That sort of timeframe was unusual on local films, and so was the budget: $30 million, a moderate sum by Hollywood standards, but the most that had ever been spent on a film shot in Australia up to that point.

Initially, I thought the production people were calling to ask me to run the entire animal-training operation, but they explained they already had Karl Miller in place. He was a renowned American trainer who had done dozens of big movies, including *Beethoven*. That was fair enough: few animal trainers anywhere in the world could have competed with his work. They did ask if I wanted to train the dogs under Karl's direction, but while I would have been interested to see him in action, I didn't want to commit to perhaps two years of work – which was what it would have taken to get all the way through to the end of filming – in a situation where I would be applying things I already knew rather than taking on big new challenges.

I did, however, agree to do some experimenting with pigs for the producers, to assess the pigs' trainability and monitor their growth rates in order to help the movie-makers come up with a detailed plan that would provide them with the required number of pigs at the right stages of growth throughout the entire four-month filming schedule. I also agreed to give Karl whatever help I could in locating suitable dogs.

Karl came over to Australia and visited the Hanrob kennels. I'd gathered about twenty prospective border collies for him, and while some of them were what he was after, in the end he decided to buy dogs himself and train them from scratch. (A friend of mine called Luke Hura, a very good trainer from Melbourne, worked on the training with him and the dogs performed excellently.)

For the pig experiment the producers arranged for two eight-week-old piglets to be delivered to me. I named them Eggs and Bacon – my theory was that a pig would rather be *called* Bacon than become bacon.

A TRICKY PIG AND ONE CLEVER CAT

People often talk about pigs as very smart animals. I wouldn't get one to do my taxes, but some of them are certainly capable of quite intelligent behaviour. In fact, one of the most amazing pieces of wild-animal behaviour I've ever seen came from what must have been the Albert Einstein of porkers, in the Queensland bush. It was a number of years after the *Babe* experiment and I was there doing work for the state's Parks and Wildlife Services (PWS), clearing feral cats and foxes out of a national park near Bundaberg. There were also feral pigs in the park and the rangers had set some humane traps to catch them.

As we were moving from one target area to another, the ranger I was with suggested we make a brief detour to check on one of these pig traps and see if anything had been caught. The traps come in various designs, but this was one of the largest models, made of galvanised mesh panels with steel posts at the corners. The way it works is that the gate of the trap is left open for the pig to enter. The animal then moves right into the body of the trap, seeking food. The food is placed so that in the process of snuffling it all up, the pig touches a thin rope stretched a couple of centimetres above the peanut-strewn ground. This rope serves as a trip wire: when it's touched it sends the gate swinging down into place, trapping the pig. Pigs love peanuts, so they're the preferred enticement. The rangers set trails from a few hundred metres out, with little piles of nuts along the way leading to the trap, and more nuts in a lovely big pile inside. That was exactly what had been done in this case.

As we approached we saw that those little piles had all been eaten up, so we were expecting to see a pig in there when we finally reached the cage. Instead, the gate was still open and the trap was empty. That was a bit odd, and when we looked more closely we saw something so unexpected that for a minute I wondered if someone was playing a practical joke. Every scrap of peanut that was inside the trap on the 'safe' side of the rope and within snout's reach under the wire had been eaten. But all the rest of the peanuts – and there was a good treasure trove there for a hungry pig – were still in place behind the wire.

The rangers always put the peanuts in the traps in a heap any old how, just making sure there were some on the front side of the wire and the majority were on the other side. But now the demarcation line where the remaining nuts ended was so sharp it looked like it had been made using a set square. Somehow one very smart pig had come into that trap and had recognised the danger posed by the trip wire. It had freely helped itself to the safe food and then, ever so carefully, slipped its snout under the rope just as far as it could go without touching the rope and triggering the gate. Next it had hoovered up the nuts within reach along a perfectly neat line from one side of the wire to the other. And then it had turned away from all that other good, easy food that was left and had walked its clever self out of there.

If I hadn't seen it with my own eyes I wouldn't have believed it. How did this pig know to do that? The rope was separated from the gate by more than a metre. Had the pig seen another animal get caught in the trap previously? But even so, how could it have worked out the mechanism? How did it know there was a direct connection between touching the rope and the closing of the gate? It couldn't have been from personal experience, because every pig who was trapped was removed from the park. Also, where did it get the cunning and self-control to so carefully take only the nuts it could safely reach and leave all the rest? I'm still shaking my head about that one.

A TRICKY PIG AND ONE CLEVER CAT

Until the *Babe* team called, I hadn't attempted to train a pig. I began to work with my piglet pair, as well as keeping tabs on their growth. As time passed it became clear that while Eggs was a nice pig she wasn't picking up the training nearly as well as her brother. So she went off to live a happy life with a family on a farm and I focused my attention on Bacon. His training was based on exactly the same principles as I used with dogs: positive reinforcement with what the animal considers the right reward. Peanut butter was Bacon's chosen reward; he'd do anything for it.

I taught him to sit, stay and come when called with no problem. But I learned that it's remarkably difficult to retrain a pig. Once the behaviour has been entrenched, it is very hard to teach a pig to give a slightly different response or add to that behaviour. If, for instance, you have trained the pig to move to a certain spot and then wait for what amounts to four beats before returning, it's difficult if not impossible to retrain it to wait for *six* beats. Dogs will watch their trainer's face, keenly picking up signals, but pigs will just re-enact whatever behaviour has been entrenched. Once I understood that it became much easier.

The *Babe* production team only needed data from young pigs, so once Bacon reached maturity I asked them what they were planning to do with him. They said he would probably be sent off to meet the fate that most pigs meet, but I said I'd keep him instead. Bob was happy for him to continue to live at Hanrob. I continued to work with him and we moved on to more advanced tricks.

He became a really good performer, although he tested my ability to keep smiling no matter what one day when we appeared on *Midday with Ray Martin*. It's easy to forget just how huge this ninety-minute variety show, produced live in front of a studio audience, was back in the mid-1980s to early 1990s. Who has time to watch TV in the middle of the day? Well, back then millions of people did. But an hour and a half is an awful lot of airtime to fill every day, and there were frequent animal appearances of one kind or another. Ray would be looking alarmed as a snake-handler tried to get him to hold a big python, or the wildlife-rescue people would be on to talk about what to do if you found an orphaned wallaby by the side of the road, or there would be a segment in which animals simply came on to do entertaining tricks.

Bob Biggs and I had decided that a miniature horse might be an interesting and novel animal to train up for promotional demonstration, and TV and film work. Phantom, the horse, was easy to work with, using what's known as 'pressure and release'. I would put my foot next to his front hoof and he would instinctively move his hoof back a little. I would immediately reinforce that with a big 'Yes!' and his favourite food rewards of carrot and apple. After a short period of training I could simply move my foot a little within his eye line and that would be his command to stamp his foot or lift it up and down to 'count' the answer to a sum I gave him. It went over very well with audiences.

Before this, I'd been on the Ray Martin show numerous times with various dogs, demonstrating what they could do and talking about training. The show's producers kept in touch, calling me from time to time to ask what animals I was working with at the moment and what kind of segment they might be able to build around them. They were intrigued when I told them about Bacon and Phantom, and asked me to bring them and a couple of other animals in for an appearance.

It was all going well. Phantom showed off his counting, Bobby performed beautifully as always, then it was Bacon's turn. The audience had 'awwwed' and applauded the other animals in all the right places, but they'd all seen dogs and even horses respond in some way to commands before. They were a lot more surprised at the idea of a pig's doing so (remember, this was before *Babe* came out). Ray asked, 'And what does Bacon do?'

On the floor about three metres away I positioned the little jump he'd been trained on – a pig-sized version of a show jump, about 30 centimetres high – and said, 'I'll throw this plastic dumbbell over to the other side of the jump, he'll jump the bar, pick up the dumbbell in his mouth, jump back over the bar, sit and hold the dumbbell up for me.'

Ray said, 'No way!' and so did people in the audience.

I was completely confident; this was something Bacon had reliably done many times before. But the moment the dumbbell left my hand I realised I had failed to take account of something very important: television studio sets are carpeted. Bacon had been trained in a shed with a concrete floor, so every time he'd done this previously he'd been able to clearly hear a clunk when the dumbbell landed. This time, there was nothing.

Pigs don't have super-sharp vision and Bacon certainly hadn't followed the toy's arc through the air. He just stood there. *I* just stood there. Ray looked at us expectantly. With every moment that passed I felt the mood of the audience changing. Expectant smiles turned into scowls and people started to mutter the way they do when they've been tricked. Finally Bacon caught a whiff of the plastic, or maybe something just clicked into place inside that little piggy mind. Anyway, off he trotted. He did the whole thing perfectly, including returning to me, sitting, and presenting the dumbbell for me to take from his mouth. The response was huge. The tension that had developed when it seemed as though the trick might be a dud converted into a heightened sense of appreciation and enjoyment when the trick worked. I filed that observation away for later. I also made a mental note to bring a sheet of Masonite with me the next time Bacon performed on TV.

Bacon wasn't my only challenge around this time. I'd also decided to train a cat. I hadn't spent much time around cats and hadn't given them a lot of thought. But I never really bought the whole supposed 'dog person or cat person' divide. They occupied a similar place in my mind to, say, alpacas: I didn't have an opinion on them one way or the other. But then a dog trainer I knew said, casually, 'Dogs are easy if you know what you're doing. But cats? Now, there's an animal who can't be trained.' He was just making conversation, not issuing a challenge. But if ever you want to get me to achieve something there's no surer way than by telling me it can't be done.

The more I thought about it, the more I became convinced he was wrong. Yes, the way cats interact with people is completely different from the way dogs do, everyone knows that. But that doesn't mean cats won't respond to the right stimulus. I thought about all the lions and tigers who had been trained in circuses over the years. Those kinds of acts have largely died out now because most people have come to the view that it's cruel to treat them in that way. But for a lot of years 'lion tamers' had their animals responding to commands – jumping left or right, lying down or walking around, doing whatever their trainers wanted them to do.

The trainers certainly had whips, but most of them didn't seem to use those whips much, other than to indicate where they wanted the animal to go. So it must have been something else like the reward of food that was driving the behaviour of these big cats. 'After all,' I thought, 'that is exactly what lions and tigers are: simply much larger versions of the domestic moggy. Big or small, they are both predators. They both work by stealth. They like to chase things, and they like to eat things. I could build a training regime around that.' The challenge was on to prove to myself that I could do it.

I went to the local animal shelter to choose a cat. There was a range, of various ages, but the one that caught my eye was a little kitten, just eight weeks old. Physically he was a typical tabby, grey-and-white, but there was definitely something special about his personality. I watched them all for a while and he was the most mischievous, playful and curious. Some people would say the most obnoxious: he wanted all the food whether it was supposed to be his or not, and he wanted to get into areas he wasn't supposed to. I thought, 'That's the cat for me.'

I took him home and named him Batman. I introduced him to Hot Dog and Bobby in a careful, measured way. It was crucial that he not become afraid of dogs because he was going to be out doing demonstrations in public. The dogs themselves were so well trained I could get them to Sit Stay or Drop Stay while I brought the kitten out and played with him. Every single time I did this both dogs got rewarded and so did Batman. I used high-value rewards – cooked chicken for the dogs, fresh raw meat for the cat — so that they quickly developed a positive association. It was a lot of work, but it was effective, and after about a month they were completely at ease around each other. It's worth noting that despite the dogs' high level of discipline I was careful not to place any of my animals in a situation where they might get hurt.

As soon as Batman had settled in I started his training. I was using the scientific principles properly known as 'operant conditioning' based around the positive reinforcement I'd used so often before — rewarding him for getting things right and ignoring it if he got things wrong, so as to not deter him from having a go. In the end I taught that cat a lot but he taught me much, much more. I would never have guessed it when I started, but I learned so much that I was able to apply to dogs later on. In fact, in hindsight it was an absolute gift to me as a dog trainer.

One of the first things I learned was that you cannot correct a cat the way you can a dog and you have to have endless reserves of patience. If you start to get frustrated or the cat senses even the beginning of anger you're done for the day. He'll just go, 'See you later, Jack.' Unlike a dog, a cat works for itself, it doesn't work for you. A dog will, in effect, think, 'Even if I'm not getting the reward I expected, I'll do it anyway, just for some approval.' The cat is much more indifferent to all that.

Batman was a really wonderful cat but, like all felines, it was about what was in it for him. He loved his food — he remained a greedy thing all his life — so that was always a strong motivation, but he also loved getting a good scratch on his back, just at the base of his tail, and that worked well as a reward too. I was patient, and by giving him time he far surpassed my initial expectations.

Over a period of months he learned to sit, stay, drop and lift his paw to wave. I also got him accustomed to being in all sorts of different environments and around people and other animals. I did this by getting him used to wearing a collar and being on a lead, then taking him with me almost everywhere I went. If I walked to the shops I would take him with me. If I went for a drive in the car, he would come. When I took Bobby and Hot Dog for a walk, he would walk along with us. He lived with me, but I also quite deliberately had him spend time at the Hanrob kennels, again as part of accustoming him to a variety of environments. By the time he was twenty weeks old he was completely at ease no matter where he was or who was around.

With encouragement from Bob I'd started giving talks at local service clubs like Rotary and Lions. We'd take dogs along and make appearances at school fetes and other community events. It gave me great experience in learning how to keep an audience interested and how to present your material in a way that really works. I started taking Batman with me when I did these public appearances and people were absolutely fascinated by him. They couldn't believe that it was possible to train a cat to that degree. The word spread and I started getting inquiries about featuring him in TV commercials. He appeared in *Home and Away*, and did magazine photo shoots and all sorts of TV commercials.

One of the commercials called for Batman, Bacon and Bobby to all appear. The setting was a pub and the ad would feature Bacon 'playing pool', Batman sitting up on a bar stool 'ordering a drink' and Bobby as another 'customer'. The pub chosen for the filming was in the Sydney beachside suburb of Manly. I got all the animals there as scheduled, checked in with the director and confirmed what he needed them each to do. Then, while the crew was setting up the lights and all the rest, I took the opportunity to give the animals some exercise and a toilet break.

I was minding my own business, walking along the beachside promenade quite happily with the pig, dog and cat, all on their leads. We were a pretty odd sight, I'll admit, and there were plenty of double-takes from people in passing cars. But it was all too much for one man, who pulled over next to us and, pointing at Bacon, said with his eyes almost popping out of his head, 'What's that?!'

I said, 'It's a pig.'

He said, 'You can't walk a pig on a lead! Not with a cat!'

I thought the poor bloke might pass out, he was in such a state trying to get his brain to accept what his eyes were seeing.

I said, 'Well, you can … here we are.' There wasn't much else to say, so the animals and I walked on, leaving him sitting there open-mouthed in disbelief.

7

'CAN I HAVE A VOLUNTEER FROM THE AUDIENCE?'

What you do in the public eye gets noticed, whether you realise it or not. If your work is good, someone will remember, which can lead to unexpected opportunities far in the future.

During this period I got invited over to America to do a talk for the American Boarding Kennel Association, having met some of the key people when they came to Australia to do a presentation organised by the Pet Industry Association of Australia (PIAA), in which I was active. The talk, about how kennels could incorporate training into their services, was in Charleston, South Carolina. I took a few extra days before I flew home in order to go down to Florida and visit the island of Key West. This place has a very famous cat association thanks to Ernest Hemingway and his liking for six-toed cats ('polydactyl' is the proper name). The writer, who lived on the island throughout the 1930s and regularly visited the house he kept there right up until his death in 1961, was originally given one of these odd-looking animals by a ship's captain. That cat, Snow White, passed the gene abnormality on to more than forty feline descendants who live at the house, which is now a museum to Hemingway and his work.

But I went there for a different cat-related reason. I'd heard about a remarkable feline trainer who worked down there and I wanted to see him in action. His name was Dominique LeFort and he was a true eccentric – he still is. Born in France, he worked as a mime in Paris before travelling to Canada with his young daughter in the 1980s. He'd never owned a cat until someone in Montreal gave one to the little girl as a pet. By this stage LeFort had developed a clown act and he slowly incorporated the cat into it. After a while, he got another cat and then another, and when he and his daughter moved to Florida a few years later he worked up a cat-busking act. By the time I saw him he was famous, having been featured on lots of travel, animal and human-interest TV shows, and also been a regular attraction at Florida's Walt Disney World. But he still lived in his mobile home with his cats, and performed every day at sunset down by the water near where the cruise ships came in. He was in his fifties at least, but he looked decades younger and had the energy of a 22-year-old.

He was brilliant. He really took cat training to another level. He had various pieces of equipment set up, including some stools at bar height and others at head height. The audience gathered in a circle around him while he kept up a stream of absurdist commentary. When he had built up a good number of spectators he started getting the cats to do some basic leaps from one stool to another, then called for volunteers. He lined up two or three of these people between a couple of stools, telling them to bend over, leap-frog style, at which point a cat did a series of jumps from one stool to the other using the people's backs as springboards. Then he lined up five or six people between the high stools, getting them to stand tall. They were expecting the waiting cat to pad across their heads, but instead it leaped clear over them.

LeFort also had a thick ship's rope strung up and he got two cats to drop and stay on it while another walked down the rope, jumped over them and crossed to the other side. At one point he ran in a tight circle while a rushing cat wove between his legs. For the finale he took out two hoops on the ends of poles, set them alight and held them steady about 15 centimetres apart. The cats jumped from one high stool to the other through the burning hoops.

He was a great performer and the show was sensational. I introduced myself to him afterwards and we met for lunch the next day. We talked about all the various cat shows he had done and his time before that as a circus clown. He was full of enthusiasm and vitality, which accounted for his much younger girlfriend. A real character.

When I got back home LeFort's show really inspired me to up the ante with Batman, and he was up for everything I asked him to do. I adapted the rope-walking I'd seen and that clever little cat learned to walk along a thick tightrope. Then I trained Bobby to rest his head on the rope and taught Batman to pad right over the top of him. I also tried him on leaping through hoops and he did that beautifully too.

I was asked to appear at a series of events with the celebrity vet Dr Harry Cooper. At the time he was hosting his first TV show, *Talk to the Animals*. It was the beginning of what would become a strong friendship with Harry, as he moved on over the years to *Harry's Practice* and *Better Homes and Gardens*, becoming one of Australia's most popular TV personalities. Bobby and Batman and I travelled the country with Harry, doing vet-clinic openings and pet-store appearances. After Batman had become well used to the hoop training at home, I had acquired a hoop designed to be set on fire, and I'd tried him on that. It was just an experiment to see how he would react, but he took to it easily; it didn't seem to worry him at all. Where the space was appropriate I planned to incorporate it into my shows with Dr Harry. But we only did it once before the promoters asked me to drop it because, even though Batman was perfectly safe, they were concerned about how children in the audience might react. Fair enough – and there was plenty of other great entertainment in the segment anyway.

People went crazy for Batman and he cruised through it all. We'd fly to Darwin or Hobart or Perth, do the show and come back, often on the same day, and he was as happy and healthy an animal as you could ever imagine. He really was a terrific cat.

The only problem I ever had with him during these shows was that he was so unafraid of dogs. His previous experiences with them had been so positive that he assumed they were all friendly – he would walk right up to strange dogs to exchange greetings. People were encouraged to bring their pets along to these events, and some of the dogs who turned up made it clear when they saw him that they wouldn't mind having a chew of him, so I had to keep an eye out when we were in a crowd.

'CAN I HAVE A VOLUNTEER FROM THE AUDIENCE?'

As well as the personal appearances, I was being asked to make appearance with Batman on TV shows – Harry's, Ray Martin's and others – and he got better and better known. One day in 1994 I had a call from the Animal Welfare League of Queensland. They'd seen one of the TV segments and asked if I was interested in taking Batman up there for an event they had planned. They were promoting responsible cat ownership, including the need to get your animals desexed. That's a stance I wholeheartedly support and I was happy to help. The event was being held at Movie World on the Gold Coast, which was still quite new, having opened less than three years earlier. Batman and I headed up and did the presentation and it went down a treat.

Unbeknownst to me, some of the theme park's executives had been in the audience. As well as offering rides, theme parks like Movie World put on family shows at regular intervals throughout the day. These give visitors a chance to have a rest and be entertained for half an hour or so before they head back out to the fray. Animals were already being used in a small way in some of the Movie World shows, but the executives wanted to make them a real focus.

Sue Thompson was a highly experienced, very talented animal trainer based in Queensland and she'd been appointed head trainer for the park. The executives had liked what they'd seen from Batman and me at the cat-awareness day and they wanted to know if I might like to work up some kind of show in collaboration with Sue, starting in the lead-up to Christmas and running throughout the summer holidays. It sounded great to me, and I was fortunate that there was a good trainer called Sam Torrisi working with me at Hanrob who would be able to take over my work while I was away.

My family was excited about the job too. Movie World were not only paying me handsomely, but they would also supply a fabulous large apartment for the eight weeks of the show's run. While I worked, Diane and the girls, who were then ten, six and five respectively, could kick back and have a fantastic Queensland summer.

Soon after I flew back up to the Gold Coast and met Sue. We clicked immediately and sat down together to discuss how we might construct the show. The park executives had said right up front that they wanted it to feature domestic animals; that way they could avoid the tricky business of getting the necessary licences for 'exotics', as animals such as chimpanzees are known in the business. That was fine with us. There were all sorts of possibilities using animals one or both of us had already trained – dogs, cats, horses, birds, pigs and ferrets (which weren't usually allowed in Queensland, but we could get special dispensation). The park management was keen for us to include a positive message if we could, and we could immediately see how themes of responsible pet ownership and correct training habits could be built into the entertainment in a good and subtle way.

We came up with a structure that we thought would work well. By that point we had just six weeks before the show opened: three weeks to get everything ready, then three weeks in rehearsal. We set about acquiring and training all the animals, and the Movie World technical crew started building the sets and creating props so the whole thing would look top-notch. To allow for the possibility that the pig might continue to work with Sue after I left, I didn't use Bacon but instead acquired a new young pig, Puddles, while Sue located kittens in Queensland pounds.

'CAN I HAVE A VOLUNTEER FROM THE AUDIENCE?'

In late October I put Puddles, Batman, Hot Dog, Bobby and the two ferrets in their transport crates in the trailer I was towing behind my car – packed full with me, Diane, the three girls and all their gear – and headed up to the Gold Coast. We looked like something out of the TV show *The Beverly Hillbillies*, and whenever I stopped to refuel, Diane and the girls would flee into the service station in an effort to disown me and my travelling menagerie.

Sue and I ironed out the bugs during the rehearsal period, and when the show opened it was a huge hit. The props and costume people had done a great job and the animals performed exactly as they'd been trained to do – well, almost exactly. Puddles was the opening act. When the music started she would run out from backstage and pull on a rope that released a sign saying 'Welcome to the Movie World Animal Show'. She was a smash every day except the one when she took it upon herself to jump in the lap of a Japanese lady in the front row.

Sue's horse, Flash, did a 'counting' act, responding to her discreet hand signals. The kittens featured in a scene where they were 'trapped in a burning building' – though in reality they were safe in a basket, they were visible through the 'window' of a flat piece of scenery painted to look like an apartment, with artificial smoke and a fire-engine siren giving the right urgent feel. Sue's snow-white Samoyed, Ben, would run up a ramp and jump into the 'building' then emerge carrying the basket full of kittens and bring them back down the ramp to the 'ooh's and 'aah's of the crowd. The fantastic backstage crew made sure everything happened seamlessly and the audience absolutely loved it.

Initially I acted as the show's host, as well as doing the animal work alongside Sue. It was another huge learning curve that took me to a new level of professionalism in public speaking. But the show was going over so well that we decided to ramp it up a bit, which meant bringing in one of the theme park's presenters, an impressive young lady called Melanie, so that Sue and I could focus on the animals.

Diane and the girls saw the show when it opened and would come along now and then as the weeks passed. The costumed performers – dressed as Daffy Duck and Tweety Bird and Bugs Bunny – got to know the girls and would play with them and make a lovely fuss of them and their mum. Sue and I worked incredibly hard, doing four shows a day, seven days a week for eight weeks, with only Christmas Day off in that whole period, but it was a great time all round.

There were some wonderfully memorable moments. One section of the show was about how we trained animals to perform for TV. Bobby, for instance, sometimes had to act aggressively on camera. I trained him for this by doing what's known as bite work, where you put on protective padding and teach the dog to respond to very specific commands so you can precisely control what appears to all intents and purposes to be a genuine attack. Once the dog is starting and stopping on command you need to find a way to make sure it 'attacks' the stunt person in precisely the spot it's supposed to, since that's where the padding is, and if it misses the mark the stunt person could get badly hurt. The best way to ensure this precision is using flexible plastic targets. You train the dog to go right for the middle of the target, starting with quite a large target then getting smaller and smaller and smaller, so that by the time you've finished the target is so small it won't be seen by the camera shooting the scene but the dog will still know where to bite.

'CAN I HAVE A VOLUNTEER FROM THE AUDIENCE?'

That was exactly how I'd trained Bobby. I'd explain this in the show, demonstrating the different-sized targets as I went along. Next I'd show the crowd some of the other tricks Bobby could do on command – jumping over objects, and so on. Then I'd call for someone from the audience to come and help: 'Who wants to be my assistant?'

Now, the thing was, we always had a stooge planted and ready. They were actors employed by the park, generally aged around eighteen or nineteen and dressed in a t-shirt and board shorts so they looked just like the rest of the visitors. They were all good, but one in particular, a young bloke called Rodney, was brilliant at keeping the audience on the edge of their seats until the very last minute. You wanted people to believe that what was happening was real for as long as possible, because that focused their attention and kept them completely involved, but right at the end you wanted them to realise the stooge had been in on the whole thing. That way everyone had a huge laugh and the tension that had built up was defused.

The way the skit ran was that I'd call for volunteers and a whole lot of kids would put their hands up, as would our stooge. I'd pick an enthusiastic kid and ask them to come on down to the stage, and the uniformed ushers would let them through into the performance area. While all this was happening, our stooge would stand up and start loudly complaining.

One show stands out for me as especially unforgettable. On this particular day our stooge was Rodney, in top form.

'Hey, what about me?' he called out.

Following the plan I said, 'Thanks, sir, but we're trying to keep this for the children.'

Everyone then expected him to sit down rather sheepishly, but he was having none of it. 'No, I paid my money to come into the park and I want to come up and try it too.'

People throughout the audience were starting to mutter uncomfortably and a few of them were calling out, 'C'mon, mate, just sit down.'

Rodney continued, acting the part perfectly: 'I put my hand up first, I was before her. Why can't I come up?'

At this point a bloke across the aisle stood up and called out angrily, 'Just bloody siddown, will ya?'

He looked like he'd had a couple of beers and Rodney just couldn't resist the opportunity to give the bear a poke. He turned to the bloke and yelled out, 'Just mind your own business, all right?'

The bloke's wife, dying of embarrassment, was tugging at his arm and hissing at him, 'Sit down, sit down!'

Well, this was the perfect opening. 'What's wrong, mate?' yelled Rodney. 'Can't you look after yourself? D'you need your wife to fight your battles for you?'

All of this had only taken a minute or two, but by now the whole crowd was unsettled. What had seemed like a nice entertaining show had suddenly gone pear-shaped. They were booing Rodney and yelling at him to sit down, and the bloke who had stood up was torn between sinking back into obscurity and going over there to sort out this mongrel heckler. The young girl I'd chosen from the audience was standing next to me, wondering, like everyone else, where this was going to go.

Timing is absolutely crucial in this kind of situation, and at this point I stepped in and said to the crowd, 'Hang on, hang on.' Then, turning to Rodney, 'Right, come down here nice and fast, then. I'm going to give you a quick go then this girl gets *her* turn.'

Down he came, and by now even the nicest people in the stands despised him as a loud-mouth who went around pushing in front of kids and ruining things for everyone. I told Rodney and the crowd that we were going to get Bobby to jump over him. All he had to do was bend over and touch his toes and stay in that position. When he was set I pulled the bite target out of my pocket and, making sure the audience saw me doing it, I used the pretext of giving Rodney a matey slap on the butt to stick on the target. The people in the audience were whispering and nudging each other. I gave Bobby his Go command and on he latched! Rodney was nicely padded, but the crowd didn't know that, of course. They were laughing and cheering and egging Bobby on. Rodney was rolling around on the stage, with Bobby firmly attached to his butt, and he was screaming, 'Get that dog off me! I'm gonna sue you!' Again, he was perfect, doing it in such an over-the-top manner that people soon cottoned onto the fact that the whole thing was an act, so that by the time he ran off stage holding his backside everyone was grinning.

We also had a fun little bit of business with the ferrets that also relied on audience interaction. Earlier in the show I'd have brought out the ferrets and talked about how sharp their teeth were. Again I'd call for a volunteer: 'Who wants to learn to be an animal trainer?' I'd always pick out a boy between about twelve and fifteen. He'd come down, I'd ask his name and where he was from, then I'd say, 'If you want to be an animal trainer you've got to completely trust your animals. Do you think you can do that?'

'Oh, yes,' the boy would inevitably say.

'Okay,' I'd respond. 'Well, I'm going to show you what trust is.' And I'd take a ferret and put it down my waistband. It would run down my leg and reappear out of the bottom of my pant-leg. 'There we are, now it's your turn.' The looks on the boys' faces were priceless. Sometimes they were too horrified to speak, but occasionally the mic I was wearing would pick up a fervent 'No freaking way!' and the crowd would roar.

My favourite sketch was called 'Hot Dog the Mind Reader'. This was another one for which we needed a boy, for reasons that will become apparent. Age thirteen or fourteen was perfect. We'd pick out our volunteer, get his name – 'This is Mark, let's give him a big hand' – and put a blindfold on Hottie. I'd say, 'He can't see anything, he is completely focused on your thoughts. I want you to put your hands on his head and think about the thing that most interests you. It might be cricket or football or reading books, or a particular subject at school. Maybe it's cars, maybe it's your friends. Whatever it is, he'll read your thoughts then we'll take off his blindfold and he'll prove his amazing powers by going backstage and picking out from a box something that represents what was on your mind. For example, if you were thinking about football he'll pick up a soccer ball; if it's cricket, he'll bring back a cricket bat; if it's school he'll bring back a textbook, and so on.'

The kid would put his hand on Hot Dog's head. I'd say, 'Now, make sure you're really focusing, really concentrating.' He'd be nodding away. Then I'd take the mask off Hottie, and say, 'Are you ready, mate? Go.' He'd run off stage and return with something in his mouth. It would be scrunched up so the audience couldn't make it out. I'd say, 'Great, here he is. So, Mark, this is what you spend your time thinking about. Is that right?'

'CAN I HAVE A VOLUNTEER FROM THE AUDIENCE?'

Eager to see it, he'd say, 'Yep.' He'd take it from Hottie's mouth, at which point it would unfurl and be revealed as a bikini top.

The kid would be too open-mouthed with shock to notice the attractive young woman coming out from backstage with a beach towel wrapped around her upper half. She'd come over to him and grab the bikini top with a big 'Hmmpf!' and storm off. It reliably brought the house down, especially the time the kid turned with a guilty look on his face to where his parents were sitting in the audience and said, 'Honest, Mum, I was thinking about soccer, I promise!'

In fact, the show was such a hit that partway through the planned run management told us they'd like to keep it on. I had a life to get back to in New South Wales, of course, so Sue and I trained up some new animals to work with her in place of Bobby, Hot Dog and Batman, who would all return with me. In the end, that animal show ran for three years instead of the scheduled eight weeks.

There's an interesting postscript to the story of Hot Dog the Mind Reader. A decade or so later I was in Los Angeles doing a series of talks for the California Narcotic Canine Association, which also covers explosive-detection dogs and for which I'm a certifying official. There was a spare day in the middle of my visit and the organisers asked what I'd like to do. I was interested in seeing the animal show at the Universal Studios theme park, so off we went. It was well done, with lots of audience interaction and plenty of variety in the sketches. At one point the host said, 'We have a dog here who can read minds ...' Well, that caught my attention. It all unfolded exactly as I'd expected, and when the dog went backstage I said to the American colleague sitting next to me, 'It'll be a bikini top, you watch.'

Puzzled, he said, 'I thought you hadn't been here before!'

There was a nice twist, though, in that instead of having a young lady run out to get the top back in mock outrage they had an orangutan who came out wearing a bikini bottom, arms covering her chest.

My time at Movie World marked another big step up for me. The money I got for that job was great, but in retrospect I learned so much from that project I'd happily have paid *them* for the experience. Back at Hanrob I was also continuing to learn, particularly about how to handle customers. I had reluctantly stepped down from the Sutherland Shire Dog Training Club – the demands of my schedule were such that something had to give – and as much as I'd learned about dog owners there, I still had more to find out. People had very different expectations of a volunteer dog-club trainer from those they had of someone who charged for the service. Early on in my time at Hanrob I made the mistake of wanting to be friends with the people whose dogs I was training, rather than taking a more neutral, professional approach. It meant I would sometimes let it slide when they didn't quite do what I'd asked, but I later realised that wasn't good for them and their dogs or for me. I thought my way through it and came up with an approach that worked. One of the smartest moves I made came out of my understanding that every dog I trained was an advertisement – good or bad – to anyone else who might be looking for a trainer, and that it was extremely important that the clients who were paying your bills were satisfied.

'CAN I HAVE A VOLUNTEER FROM THE AUDIENCE?'

I decided that once a dog's paid training sessions were over, I would have a standing offer of unlimited free 'refresher' lessons for the rest of the animal's life. This may sound like a great way to lose money, but it was actually just the opposite. People loved knowing they could take up this opportunity if they wanted to – and they really could, the offer was genuine – but the open-endedness of the offer actually meant they used it much less. If you give people a limited number, say four lessons, they will tend to use them up. If you give people a timeframe, say thirty days, for free lessons, they'll squeeze those lessons in so as not to feel like they're missing out. But I found that if it was an unrestricted, unlimited offer people would rarely return. Funny thing, human nature.

In 1995 my next huge career challenge began. It came to me almost by chance. A bloke who had worked for PAL when I was doing the Super Dogs events with Sunny a decade earlier had made a career change and moved to Canberra to join the public service. He was waiting for a coffee one day when he overheard two staffers from the Australian Quarantine and Inspection Service (AQIS) saying they needed an experienced dog trainer but didn't know where to start. He didn't know them and he didn't actually know me either, but he had seen me in action and he remembered my name. He introduced himself to the AQIS staff and suggested I would be worth a phone call. From that overheard conversation came ten years of service protecting Australia's wildlife and agriculture by training quarantine-detection dogs.

An AQIS staffer got in touch with me and explained that Australia was going to follow the lead of the United States and a few other countries that used dogs to sniff out items not permitted to be imported for quarantine reasons – either because they might bring new diseases into Australia or because they were contraband, such as smuggled live animals. AQIS had had an American trainer out here for a little while to get the program underway and now they wanted to hire a local to oversee the development of a national program. They followed up the call by coming to interview me, checking on my credentials and experience and seeing me in action at the kennels. Then they asked me to sketch out a proposed approach. Satisfied with all this, AQIS appointed me National Trainer for its detection-dogs program. I was thrilled and set to work immediately.

The US trainer had prepared three dog-and-handler teams; I would have to rapidly provide enough teams to service all of Australia's international airports. The type of dogs had already been chosen, I was told: they had to be beagles. People sometimes ask if beagles were selected because they have an extra-good sense of smell. Not at all. In fact, the ability to smell is the last thing you'd look for in a detection dog, as strange as that sounds. That's because all dogs have an incredible ability to smell. If you compare one dog with another some have a better sense of smell than others, no doubt about it, but those are fine distinctions within the context of general excellence. All dogs have such an extraordinary sense of smell that even the ones right at the lower end are more than good enough for the job.

No, in choosing a detection dog you're actually looking for factors much more variable from one individual to another: personality characteristics. What you need are dogs who have a strong drive. They must be highly reward-focused, happy, outgoing, and not afraid of noises or crowds or indeed anything

'CAN I HAVE A VOLUNTEER FROM THE AUDIENCE?'

much. Given my choice I would have selected purely on these characteristics and not on breed. Labradors, who were already being used in Australian airports as drug-detection dogs for the Customs service, would have been fine. So would border collies, German shepherds, spaniels and lots of others. But someone had decided that beagles had an acceptable, non-threatening look and so I was going to have to find suitable dogs within the available pool for that breed. I would also be training quarantine-detection dogs for mail-sorting centres, and there, out of the public eye, they were allowed to be any breed — crossbred or purebred, it didn't matter.

The only beagles I'd had any real contact with before this had been pet dogs I'd encountered as a trainer; I'd never trained one as a working dog. I'd certainly seen them in action over the years at obedience competitions and admired the handlers who trained them to a high level.

Beagles are hounds, part of the group that includes Afghans, whippets, Rhodesian ridgebacks, bassets and so on. Working dogs, such as border collies Sunny and Bobby, are genetically wired to round up the herd and keep it under control. Gun dogs such as Hot Dog are genetically wired to find a quail or a duck. Both working dogs and gun dogs work closely with their human handlers.

Hounds operate differently. Their attitude is more: 'I'm going to get the rabbit and if you're there, good, but if you're not I'm still going to get it.' I always admire the trainer of a brilliant border collie, but I have even more admiration for someone who trains a hound to a high level, because it's an exponentially harder task — and one I was about to take on.

8

AIRPORT DETECTIVES: DOGS KEEPING AUSTRALIA SAFE

In dog training 'bridging' means giving the animal a signal that it has done the right thing, using a noise to help it link the task to the outcome. Some trainers use clickers but I prefer verbal cues. You can choose any word as long as it is emphatic, short and clear.

I had to train the quarantine-detection dogs to find any plant material, including all fruits; any meat product, cooked, raw or dry; live eggs; and live birds, bees and reptiles. That was a very large skill set for each dog to develop, but even though I had never trained a full-time detection dog before, I knew I could do it: it was simply an extension of the scent training I had done with my own dogs for Utility Dog competitions, Tracking events and Field Trials.

The first AQIS group I trained consisted of four dogs: two beagles, who would go to Brisbane and Adelaide Airports as quarantine-detection dogs, and a labrador and a cattle dog, who would be designated 'active-response dogs' and go to work in mail centres. It took at least a month to find suitable animals – clearly we would have to speed up this part of the process – but finally I was ready to begin.

The training was to run for thirteen weeks. First there would be five weeks of working solely with the dogs, just me and them. Then the handler who had been assigned to each dog would come and we would all work together for eight weeks. The dogs would be scrupulously tested in situ before they could be approved for work.

All I had to do was apply the same principles I had previously used. First, introduce the dog to an odour. When the dog next detects and recognises the odour, get it to sit. When it sits, 'bridge' it, in other words give it a signal that it has done the right thing. Bridging means you are helping the dog link the task to the outcome: in this case I wanted the dog to understand that if a certain odour was somewhere in the environment it was to home in on that odour and then sit to indicate it had detected it; when it performed this sequence a reward would follow. You 'bridge' by using a noise to let the dog know it has indeed done what you wanted it to. Some trainers use clickers but I prefer to use verbal cues. You can choose any word you want as long as it is emphatic and clear. Even the word 'Yes!' will do as long as you use it consistently and with focused attention on the dog.

When it came to rewarding my own dogs I'd used a combination of play and food. For the airport dogs it had to be food – play was considered impractical in such a crowded environment – but for the active-response mail-centre dogs it could be either food, or play using something like a tug-toy.

Exactly as I had done with my own dogs I used 'negative punishment' – and boy, is that a great concept in need of a more appealing name. I gave them no punishment for making a mistake, only reacting with a reward when the task was successfully achieved. I was now in my forties, but the memory of the terrible, discouraging way I had been taught still lingered strongly and I stuck firmly to the vow I had made to myself to do things differently. I wasn't about to make these dogs afraid to try in case they did something wrong, as I had been when I was young. Instead I let them make decisions, rewarding them when they made the right one and ignoring them when they got it wrong. If a dog sat in front of a non-target indicating a 'find' where there was nothing, I would say only, 'Leave it. Find', and move the dog on.

Unsurprisingly, given the newness of the program and the high expectations surrounding it, I was under close scrutiny as training got underway. My approach earned me scathing criticism from observers who had been taught to handle dogs the old-fashioned way, 'correcting' them when they got anything wrong. Where my focus was on developing the dog's drive and attitude so that it *wanted* to do the job, they believed results could only be achieved by 'checking' the dog – pulling it up and letting it know it was wrong, *forcing* it to perform. This was more than just a mild difference of opinion. Their approach was the polar opposite of mine and my methods were absolutely vilified by some of these so-called experts.

People come through airports carrying and smelling of all sorts of things, so it was very important to expose the dogs to lots of potentially confusing odours during the training. Chocolate biscuits were a good thing to use, given their strong scent. One day one of these 'experts' was watching as a dog I was training stopped at a non-target, a bag that didn't contain any quarantine no-nos but did contain chocolate biscuits. He saw me ignore this mistake and move the dog on and said, 'Don't do that! If he sits at the chocolate biscuits, give him a good whack.'

Of course I wasn't about to do this, but he wouldn't let it go. So I asked him, 'What happens one day when the dog's at the airport and there's a real odour in there along with the chocolate biscuits?'

His answer was, 'Well, a strong dog will know the difference.'

That was complete nonsense. Far too many dogs have been ruined by the kind of training he was advocating. What they learn from it is that if they make a mistake they will suffer for it. In the case of a detection dog, it means if they come to a bag that contains narcotics, explosives or quarantined items along with, say, chocolate biscuits, the dog will pass the bag, in effect thinking, 'Well, there's a target odour but there's also chocolate-biscuit odour and that leads to punishment, so it's not worth it.'

In time I got to see this particular handler in action with his own dog. He was keen to show off, saying, 'My dog's got 100 per cent proficiency; every single time the dog sits at a bag, it's got something in it. Every time.' There were a range of target and non-target bags set up and yep, he was right, every time that dog sat at a bag there was something in it. But to me there was a glaring problem: there was no other scent in the target bags competing with the fruit or plant the dog had been trained to detect. There were no biscuits or chips or noodles, or any of the other things people carry in real life.

I said, 'Could I try something with your dog?' and arranged some boxes in a line, just like the bags. Some were non-targets and others contained apple targets, but I also prepared some with apples (a target) and crisps (a non-target) in together. The handler took his dog along the line and, just as he had done before, the dog got every one of the targets when that was the only thing in there. But he didn't indicate any of the three boxes that contained both apples and crisps.

I said to the handler, 'You missed three targets.' At first he refused to believe it, then when he saw the apples he made various excuses. But it was clear to me that, having been whacked for mistakes, the dog had learned the hard way not to take the risk.

I would rather a quarantine-detection dog I trained make a hundred 'false positive' mistakes, indicating something where there turned out to be nothing, than miss a single real target, because the stakes are so high. It was endlessly surprising during the training to see how many people just didn't get this – the amount of ignorance about the program was astonishing.

There had been initial opposition to it from some of the handlers of the Customs drug-detection dogs, who felt that the quarantine dogs would get in their way and interfere with their work. (AQIS and the Customs service, a.k.a. Border Control, now work closely together on their detection-dog programs: a very welcome improvement from those early days.) Underlying this was the view, shared by many outside Customs, that what *they* were doing was important, while AQIS's work was just a dinky operation on the side. Even intelligent, otherwise well-informed people would sometimes say things to me like, 'Oh, well, you're only finding apples, it's not really a big deal.'

That attitude used to bug the hell out of me. They simply didn't understand the possible consequences of bringing infected material into the country. Take foot-and-mouth disease, for instance. Thanks in large part to our being an island, Australia is blessedly free of this highly contagious, damaging livestock disease. Lots of other parts of the world are not so lucky. It's taken a huge economic toll in a number of European and Asian countries. The 2001 outbreak in the United Kingdom and mainland Europe had a devastating effect, causing losses of more than $19 billion in Britain alone.

Foot-and-mouth is spread by infected animals but also by things such as straw and hair that have been in contact with those animals. Because legal livestock and agriculture imports are so carefully controlled, by far the most likely way the disease would enter Australia is via contaminated animal products illegally brought in.

Rabies is another disease that would be catastrophic if it made its way into Australia. (Johnny Depp learned a thing or two about this danger after he was busted in May 2015 for bringing in his pet dogs on a private jet and not declaring them.) And those are just two examples. Yes, a kilogram of smuggled heroin could have a very bad effect if it got through, but nothing like the potential effect of a kilo of animal products infected with foot-and-mouth disease or a live animal infected with rabies. And that's not even to mention the plant diseases: one such disease carried in on a single infected piece of fruit such as an apple could potentially wipe out the whole of Australia's apple-growing industry.

So it was a huge responsibility, and one I took very seriously. Understanding the risks involved if something infected slipped through only confirmed my commitment to the 'negative punishment' approach.

The breadth of what we were training the dogs to detect didn't pose quite as big a problem as it might initially appear. In theory, they had to be able to detect every plant in the world, tens of thousands of which they had never encountered and might only do so for the first time when it was in a traveller's bag. But rather than training them in scent discrimination for the specific odour of each and every one of those plants, it was much more practical to train the dogs in scent association or scent generalisation. The common denominator in plants is chlorophyll, so I acquired many different kinds of plants and trained them to detect that. It was the same idea with fruits: they generally have a high concentration of sugar, so by introducing lots of different kinds of fruit the dog begins to understand what might be called the odour 'theme'.

The AQIS training took place at Hanrob and soon became my full-time focus, leaving no more time for training boarded pets. With help from Hanrob staff, I set up the training shed so it was as close to an airport environment as possible. True, I couldn't simulate thousands of people moving about, but I could get lots of other elements in place to replicate the experience. I had music playing in the background, and we set up a PA system to broadcast alerts and announcements and had radios going all day too, mimicking walkie-talkie noise. We set up all kinds of different bags and backpacks and cases on the floor filled with clothes and gear and cosmetic bottles in various combinations for the dogs and handlers to move past and check, just as they'd be doing for real at the airport. I asked everyone I worked with to save their empty cosmetic and personal-care-product bottles – shampoo, shaving cream, perfume etc – which were useful because they retained their strong smell and added layers of complexity to the task as the dogs got better and better.

My experience in training Batman proved to be priceless when it came to working with beagles. There are exceptions, of course, but generally speaking they are very aloof dogs, quite catlike in the sense of only being interested in what's in it for them. That's a perfectly fine attitude for a working dog because as long as you can find the right reward the dog will do its bit.

After I'd worked with those initial four dogs for five weeks and their handlers for two weeks, we were ready to make our first visit to Sydney International Airport to start getting them accustomed to the real thing, and so I could check the handlers' techniques. The handlers were already AQIS employees, but in order to be allowed into the airport in an official capacity I had to be formally made a federal quarantine officer. We all wore uniforms and displayed our security passes and had strict protocols to follow.

After the concentrated work in the training shed it felt strange to be on display at the airport, particularly on that first run, when a great many people who either wanted the program to succeed or were sure it wouldn't were there to see us in action. It was like being in a fishbowl, but there was nothing I could do about that so I just encouraged the handlers to focus on the task in front of us.

Fortunately the dogs performed well. One of the beagles, Charlie, was particularly good, as was Rowdy, the cattle dog.

Even the most sceptical observer could see that the dogs were going to be a great asset. In fact, on his second airport outing Charlie not only detected the targets we had planted, but also found secreted fruit and plants and stopped them from being brought in. And he hadn't even finished his training yet.

The official validation at the end of the training was a two-part process. First came an intensive day-long test. There were thirty boxes containing a combination of targets and non-targets, including fresh bread and chocolate, all mixed in together. Each dog had to run up and down the line seven times, with the contents changed each time. It lost points for not getting a target and for responding to a non-target, and the pass mark was 80 per cent. If the dog passed the box test, the next day it went to the airport, where it was observed and marked as it moved past people, checking bags on the ground and climbing up onto loaded trolleys to check there. The handlers were also marked on how well they followed the protocols I'd trained them in – approaching people and asking them a very specific set of questions: 'Is this your bag? Did you pack it? Can I see your travel statements? Can I see your passport?'

All four dogs and handlers in that first group passed. Gus went off to work at Brisbane Airport and Charlie to Adelaide, while the other two went to mail centres in Brisbane and Melbourne respectively.

Hanrob was only paid for a dog if it passed. In the ten years I was in the position of National Trainer we had a validation rate of over 98 per cent.

Having proved that the program would work, we turned our attention to sourcing beagles in much greater numbers, since there simply weren't enough available through animal pounds. The answer was a national media campaign involving friendly spots on TV shows like *A Current Affair,* and TV and radio ads whose message was: 'If you have a beagle you want to rehome who loves his food and does naughty things like pulling washing off the line, we want to hear from you.'

AQIS would pay up to $800 for a suitable dog. The old saying that you can't teach an old dog new tricks is flat out wrong. If a dog is fit and healthy it doesn't matter if he's eighteen months or eight years old, you can teach him equally well. But because these would be working dogs, we were seeking beagles between eighteen months and three years old, on the basis that we expected a working life of between seven and ten years. After that, just like for us humans, the physical demands of the job started to become a bit much (at which point the dog would go to live its remaining years in a loving home).

It was surprising how many beagle owners there were who no longer wanted their dogs. Some were getting divorces or moving interstate, but in other cases it was the all-too-common story of people who had brought home an extremely cute puppy and been surprised when twelve months later it was a boisterous animal who needed exercise and training.

Calls flooded in from people who thought their dogs were suitable. They all came through to me for an initial phone assessment. First I got the basics about the dog's age, sex and whether it was purebred or crossbred (the latter didn't rule the dog out, as long as it still looked like a beagle). I also checked on the dog's medical history, then there were questions about its behaviour that were designed to weed out all but the dogs with the highest drive. For instance, the owner might be asked, 'If your dog's walking along the street and there is a hamburger on the ground would the dog eat it?' They'd say, 'Oh no, she's too well trained for that!' I'd have to say, 'Sorry, then, but she's not what we're after.'

I lost count of the number of times I was told, 'This is the best dog in the world.' Early on I got a call from an owner describing a dog in such glowing terms that I drove nearly three hours to Newcastle to see it. It took me more than an hour to get the dog to come out from under the house. I only kept trying with it because I'd already spent all that time making the trip. When he eventually came out, one look confirmed how unsuitable he was.

Perhaps only one in a hundred dogs merited an in-depth assessment at the training shed over a couple of days, and people did not like to hear that theirs wasn't one of the chosen few: 'But the advert said ...' So I quickly got better at weeding out as many unsuitable candidates as possible over the phone, before having to pay them a visit. I would make it clear to the owners that our assessment was very tough. In fact, I would exaggerate, saying, 'If I come and see your dog I'm going to bring a cat or a rabbit in a cage, and your dog is not allowed to harass that animal.' I never had any intention of putting a cat or rabbit through that, but it was a useful way of eliminating people who would otherwise insist their dog was perfect. The same thing happened when I said, 'I'm going to make a lot of noise, including firing a cap gun, and the dog has to stay calm.' The vast majority ruled out their dogs during the course of the conversation, saving us a lot of wasted time.

It didn't matter how many people I dealt with, there was always someone who could surprise me. I had a call one day from a woman who had a female beagle called Alice. She sounded like a fantastic dog: eighteen months old, loved her food, very outgoing, great with kids and everyone else, well exercised, fit and healthy and had done puppy-class training. I listened to all this and said to the owner, 'That's fantastic. I'll definitely come and have a look at Alice, but even if only half of what you are saying is true you should pack up her bags.'

The lady said, 'Oh that's great. Now, as far as the pick-up and drop-off go …'

I said, 'Er, I beg your pardon?'

She said, 'Well, can you come and get her each day about seven in the morning and drop her home after I'm back from picking up the kids from school?'

She'd thought being a working dog meant one who went out to work and came home each day like a human would. When I gently set her straight she said in a shocked tone, 'Do you expect me to give my dog up for ever and ever? Oh, I couldn't do that!'

You just never knew your luck. You might go two weeks without finding a single suitable dog and then you'd get a call from a pound saying they had a beagle put aside for you to look at, and you'd walk in and see a little dog jumping out of his skin with curiosity and drive and you'd know instantly he was worth taking. But making it to the training shed for assessment still didn't mean the dog would actually be accepted into the program. Of those who didn't make it through the first step, if they had come from private homes, we would ask the former owners if they would take back their dogs. Most said no, in which case a good new home was found, as it was for any pound dogs who didn't make it through. Those who did make it through went straight into the program and soon proved their worth.

People who've seen the dogs in action when they've been passing through an airport ask me if the dogs are really, truly checking every bag, given how fast they move past them. They certainly are, and if you want to understand this a bit better do your own little experiment. Get a piece no bigger than a twenty-cent coin of something that smells quite clearly to you – such as a fresh cake, some coffee or a slice of pineapple – or put a few drops of an antiseptic like Dettol on a cotton ball. Put your chosen scent in the bottom of a glass. Then get some other glasses and fill them with either water or unused cotton balls. Put on a blindfold and have someone quickly move each glass past your face at nose level, asking you to say when it's the glass with the scent. Assuming your nose works fine, you'll get it every time. It will be obvious. Now think about how much more precise a dog's sense of smell is than yours.

Even the most expert scientists in the field don't know exactly how good that sense of smell is. The closest they've been able to pin it down to is between 10,000 and 100,000 times more effective than ours. James Walker is the former Director of the Institute for Sensory Research at Florida State University and he did some of the leading research in this area. He's explained it this way: 'Let's suppose they're just 10,000 times better. If you make the analogy to vision, what you and I can see at a third of a mile, a dog could see more than 3000 miles away and still see as well.'

So if you're ever among a plane-load of arriving passengers and a quarantine officer says to you, 'Ladies and gentlemen, this is a quarantine-detection dog, can you please put your bags and backpacks on the ground so we can run the dog through and check them', and you see that dog check all 700 bags in a little over ten minutes, rest assured that in the few seconds it has spent with each bag the dog has gathered all the information it needs.

I've never needed any convincing of this, having been astonished by what dogs can detect time and time again. But even I was absolutely floored the time I witnessed an FBI blood-detection dog working in the United States. This springer spaniel found one single drop of blood in the drawer of a desk inside a shipping container – and alerted his handler to it *outside* the container, in a warehouse full of them.

I saw this dog in action while at the California Narcotic Canine Association's annual conference. I'm always happy to speak at these conferences because they bring in experts from many law-enforcement agencies to give fascinating demonstrations. One time a young FBI agent spoke to us about explosives detection. She was standing next to a table that held an array of perfectly ordinary things available at any hardware store. She ran a video showing a street of parked cars and told us to watch the red car in the middle of the screen. It went up in a huge explosion, blown into tiny pieces. There were 300 hardened police and Customs officers in the room but every person there was dumbstruck by the force of the explosion we'd witnessed. The agent told us it had been made using the ingredients on the table.

This device had no battery and no metal components – even the timer fuse had been made using organic materials (for obvious reasons I'm not going to go into details). That meant that it could not be picked up by metal detectors or x-ray scanners. If a trained person knew *precisely* where to look they would find it, but otherwise the only way such an explosive device would ever be detected was by a trained detection dog.

I have subsequently trained explosive-detection dogs for various security purposes, such as working at mass public events that might become targets for terrorists. As with training quarantine dogs to find unknown plants by using chlorophyll, you train explosive-detection dogs by focusing on what are called the precursors – the things that set off the explosive. The vast majority of the work these dogs do is out of the public eye, but when I'm travelling or out and about at big gatherings I get enormous reassurance from knowing that explosive-detection dogs are on the job.

Throughout the program I had to train the handlers every bit as much as the dogs. They needed to be at the top of their game every hour of every working day, and that meant I had to be tough on them in the training stage. At a certain point in the course we would prepare to do a bag check in the shed and I would say to the handler in question, 'The red bag's got a target in it.' They would prepare their dogs then give them the Find command and go along the line and, sure enough, when they got to the red bag the dog would sit to indicate a target. The handler would confidently open up the bag and become confused when they couldn't see a target. They'd turn to me and say, 'I can't find it.' I'd say, 'That's because there's no target in there.' Inevitably the response was, 'But you said …' I would then tell them why I had lied: to prove to them the subconscious influence they were exerting over the dogs with their body language and tone of voice. They'd fully expected to find something in that bag and they'd unconsciously communicated that to the dog. Understanding that effect was the first step in learning to stay neutral.

The next, related lesson was TYD: Trust Your Dog. For this one I would tell them it was a blank run with no targets, but I'd secretly have put a target in one of the bags. As before, they thought it was the dog being tested when actually it was them. They'd give the dog the Find command and it would stop in front of the relevant bag. Believing it was a 'false positive', they'd start to move it on without even checking the bag. Asked why, they'd say, 'You said it was a blank run.'

'I lied,' I'd tell them.

'But that's not fair.'

'But,' I'd say, 'it's the best way to show you the importance of the number one rule: TYD. Forget your expectations about what's in the bags. Keep yourself neutral and Trust Your Dog.'

Keeping the dogs safe was an everyday challenge at the airport. Right throughout the terminal, people would push trolleys and heft suitcases without always looking where they were going, but around the baggage carousels things got particularly rough. At some point someone must have told a whole lot of these people that if you don't get your bag off the carousel before it disappears through those rubber flaps, it will be chopped up and burned – why else would they push and shove so frantically? If the handlers weren't continually on their guard, ensuring their dogs stayed next to the carousel as they moved along checking bags, the dogs could get badly hurt here – slammed in the stomach by a swinging suitcase, or worse. I was only partly joking when I said to the handlers in every course: 'Protect your dog, always. Better you should get injured than put your dog at risk. Handlers are easy to replace, good dogs are bloody hard to find.'

Then there were the dangers you didn't see coming. Sometimes people carrying an illicit substance would see us approaching and just drop it, as discreetly as possible, where they stood. That was what we figured must have happened one day when we were out there training with a dog called Jessie. She'd been working just fine, everything normal, when all of a sudden she started acting very strangely. She stood in front of a garbage bin and wouldn't be moved, just stayed there staring at it for five minutes, then started making a peculiar howling noise. Our best guess was that someone had panicked and dropped a tab laced with LSD or ecstasy on the ground and she'd picked it up and swallowed it. We had her checked immediately, but there was nothing to be done other than stay with her and keep her calm until the drug passed out of her system. The poor little thing was in doggy Disneyland for two days, but fortunately she was perfectly fine after that.

There were people who were uncomfortable around the dogs for cultural or religious reasons. There are cultures that regard dogs as unclean or even, in some cases, vermin, and people from those cultures will not let the animals near them. When this happened you had to direct them to put their bags down and step away so that the dogs could check the bags: it still had to be done.

Some people just didn't like dogs. One Thai air hostess completely freaked out at the sight of a beagle and nearly broke her neck running away from it; high heels or not, she could have taken on Cathy Freeman. One of the dogs was seriously wounded by a South African passenger who lashed out with a kick for seemingly no reason. He was arrested and it turned out that his son had committed suicide just days before; he was so beside himself with grief he barely knew what country he was in, let alone what he was doing.

Others had friendlier intentions and just wanted to pat the dogs. But well-meaning as that was, it's a no-no with working dogs. So we used to carry cards featuring a picture of the dogs that we would give out as souvenirs, particularly to children. Some people really didn't want to take no for an answer and weren't mollified by the offer of a card, but these weren't pets, they were doing a job, so we had to be firm.

Overall, though, considering the numbers of passengers and bags, the problems with the new program were few and far between. The naysayers had been proved wrong: dogs were a brilliant quarantine-detection tool.

At the airport one day we found two live bees – a queen and a worker – being smuggled in inside a pen. That might not sound like much, and indeed, it's not the bees themselves who are the problem, it's the parasitic mites living on their wings who can wipe out Australian bees by the tens of millions.

One mail-centre dog found live pigeon eggs that had been elaborately hidden and mailed from Europe. They were inside a box all done up as a child's gift. On first glance the box seemed to contain six perfectly normal Kinder Surprise eggs. But the dog had alerted staff to the package, so the foil covering on one of the eggs was unwrapped. So far so normal: inside was the expected chocolate egg. But inside *that*, where there should have been a plastic egg containing a toy, there were the live eggs.

We sometimes found drugs that had made it past the Customs-detection dogs, and other contraband items such as two huge suitcases jam-packed with Levi jeans being smuggled in in an attempt to avoid paying Customs excise. The dog had reacted to the unusual smell of the new clothing; I could see that it wasn't a response to a target, but clearly there was something in there that needed to be checked out.

The government was very, very pleased with the program's success and we got lots of positive media attention. Federal ministers would often greet arriving overseas dignitaries and then have us go through our paces for them, or arrange PR events at which our work was featured.

A government minister said to me at one of these events, 'Steve, I have a really good idea.'

'Yes, Minister?'

'The dogs are doing such a great job – why don't we kill two birds with one stone by training them to find explosives as well?'

I said, 'Well, that's a really interesting thought, Minister. But are you available to open the bag?'

He looked puzzled. 'What do you mean?'

I said, 'Well, if a dog who's been trained for both explosives and quarantine items sits at a bag, I won't be the one checking it.'

Still puzzled, he said, 'Why not?'

'Because I don't know if it's an apple or a bomb in there.'

'Ah yes,' he said, 'very good point.'

Fortunately that was the last we heard of that.

Unless I was actually standing next to a VIP at one of these media events, I was almost guaranteed to miss seeing them, because when I took the handlers out with the dogs to train in situ we'd take a spare dog, whom I would use for the demonstration. Like the rest of the handlers, my focus was firmly down at bag-on-ground level. I missed countless big names, only finding out afterwards they'd been in the line I checked, including then captain Allan Border and the entire Australian cricket team. I even failed to register supermodel Elle Macpherson – though how I missed those legs I don't know.

During my time working at the airport I was often amazed by what people tried to bring into the country. One dog who'd only been in training for four weeks or so went up to an arriving passenger and put his nose in the guy's crotch. Not 'in the vicinity of', right up in there. Well, this was a novice dog who was really just supposed to be getting used to the place and, as we all know, plane trips can be very long and sweaty, so I gave the traveller the benefit of the doubt and started to lead the dog away, but he wouldn't go, he was absolutely focused on this bloke, a Swede who had flown from Europe via Singapore.

So I said in a fairly casual way, not yet moving into official mode, 'Have you got anything in your pocket there, sir? Any fruit or meat or anything?'

He said, 'No, no, no', but just at that moment his two pants pockets started moving. The problem was, his hands were by his sides.

I said to him, 'Mate, either you're awfully glad to see me or you've got something in there.' As protocol required, I radioed for the appropriate AQIS officers and when the passenger was searched he turned out to have ten baby cobras strapped to his thighs. The snakes had been kept cold so they would remain sleepy and inactive while they were hidden on him and now they were waking up. Given the strength of the venom even in baby cobras' bites, he was lucky we caught him when we did.

Even before incoming passengers disembarked they were given information in a variety of languages and in diagram form about what they weren't allowed to bring in. They had to sign travel statements to say they didn't have any of these prohibited items, or to declare them if they had. Then all along the way through Customs and out to the baggage carousels there were reminder signs and bins in which they could dispose of the orange they'd only just realised they still had in their bag, or whatever it might be. Even at the point of collecting their baggage, if they saw us checking and then suddenly remembered, they could still come up and say, 'Hang on, I do have something after all', then we'd show them the special bin to put it in and off they could go with no problem. It really was staggering what some people brought in, either because, despite all the information and warnings, they genuinely did not understand they were breaking the law, or because they thought they could get away with it.

I was out with a group of trainee handlers and dogs one day doing one of these familiarisation visits when one of the beagles responded to a bag being carried by an elderly lady. We always wore gloves while searching bags and looked carefully at what we were doing: no-one was ever to put their hand in and feel around blindly, because you never knew what might be in there, from a dirty hypodermic needle to a deadly creature. The handler who had to delve into that particular bag was particularly glad of the gloves that day: what he found in there was a shrunken head. The only ones I'd ever seen before this were props in cheesy 1950s jungle movies or joke-shop novelties, but you could tell instantly this was no fake. The dog was trained to respond to all meat products and this fit the description. It was a genuine dried and shrivelled human head which had had the skull removed then been ceremonially boiled up just long enough to make sure the hair didn't fall out. It turned out to have been the uncle of the lady who was carrying it.

On a number of occasions we found placentas being brought in by women who had given birth overseas but were bringing the afterbirth back in a plastic container so it could be buried where they lived. I'll leave the smell and sight of a placenta that has been left unrefrigerated for twenty-four or more hours to your imagination. Equally unpleasant was 'mice wine': a supposed health tonic made in China and Korea in which a litter of newborn mice is put into the bottom of a bottle of rice wine then left to ferment.

Lots of people don't like aeroplane food, but some came up with their own extreme solutions. I thought eight cooked rats on a skewer brought in as a snack was bad until the day we encountered a very elderly Vietnamese lady who'd planned even further ahead. She had one of those large red-white-and-blue striped zip-up bags you get at two-dollar shops. One of the dogs responded to the bag, then backed away, went back in and backed away again. The woman was screaming at the dog to get away and attempting to hit it. We calmed her down and I unzipped the bag. My heart stopped for a moment when I saw a baby-sized newspaper package oozing blood. What I found when I unwrapped the paper was unpleasant but it was a relief compared with what had first flashed through my mind. It turned out to be two chickens whose heads she had pulled off just before boarding so they would be as fresh as possible when she landed.

The live animals we found in people's hand luggage included monkeys, birds and puppies, often brought in from Bali where rabies was uncontrolled, so they all had to be sent to be destroyed. Even when they had been caught out, many people continued to lie bare-faced. One man had two large pieces of hand luggage that turned out to contain two cedar-tree saplings, each more than half a metre tall. 'Oh,' he said, having carried the bags halfway across the world, lifting them onto and off the plane. 'I don't know how those got there.'

As well as the hair-raising moments, there were some very funny moments when it was a challenge to keep the straight face the role demanded. A whole lot of work with fruit-flavoured hair products had made the dogs good at distinguishing peach or apple shampoo from the real fruit, but some fake scents could still confuse them. I had to check the bag of a young Japanese couple who were on their honeymoon as it had generated a positive response from a dog. The couple didn't speak English, so the first step was to show them a picture displaying all the things we'd be looking for and asking, by gesture, whether they had any with them. They both shook their heads, and then the young bride looked again at the pictured fruit, burst into giggles and said something to her husband. He dug around and pulled out a packet of banana-flavoured condoms. Even though you thought you'd found the thing that had caused the dog to indicate a find, you had to be sure, so you had to show it at snout level and make sure the dog indicated that yes, this was what it had responded to. With that confirmed, the couple were able to take back their honeymoon supplies and head off laughing and blushing.

On another occasion a novice dog rightly identified a meat product in a woman's bag but got a bit too excited and stuck his head into the bag's opening: something he was meant never to do. He obviously nudged something, because suddenly a strange, ominous noise started coming from in there. Could it possibly be a bomb? I asked the woman what was causing the sound, but she just looked at me and shook her head, she wouldn't speak. I followed protocol and radioed it in, asking for assistance, at which point she hurriedly owned up: it was a vibrator that had been somehow set off by the dog's movement. I reassured her that was fine, it was none of my business. We used to see intimate, adult things on almost a daily basis inside people's bags – and on one memorable occasion going round and round and round unclaimed on the baggage carousel.

One of my very favourite moments came courtesy of Sam Torrisi, who had taken care of the training at Hanrob when I was doing the Movie World show. Sam came from an Italian background and spoke the language fluently. He worked with me in training the AQIS dogs and, like all the other handlers, had to undergo regular revalidation to make sure none of his skills had slipped. I was observing from a slight distance as Sam checked a line of passengers arriving on an Alitalia flight, having first explained (in English, as always) what he was doing and what the dog was checking for. Partway along the line was an elderly couple, and as the dog approached Sam heard the lady saying urgently to her husband in Italian, 'Papa, Papa, tell them you've got the tomato plants!' The husband's reply was, 'Shut up, woman. These are from Sicily, my grandfather's plants. They won't find them.'

Now, of course I knew none of this and Sam's expression didn't flicker. The dog didn't hesitate when it reached the couple's bag; it alerted Sam confidently. Sam then did exactly what he was meant to, saying to them (again in English, as always), 'Good morning, is this your bag? Did you pack it?' Then he asked, 'Is there anything in your bag – any plants, fruit, meat, anything else?'

The old man said, 'No, no.'

To which Sam said, 'Thank you', and started to walk away.

I knew he was a really good handler, but he seemed to have forgotten everything he had ever learned. His dog had indicated a target but he hadn't even asked to see the couple's travel statements (the cards they had signed saying they had nothing to declare), let alone checked the bag.

There was just enough time for all this to go through my head before Sam stopped and, looking towards the beagle, said, 'Excuse me?'

Was he having some kind of strange episode? What a shame it would be to have to fail someone who had previously been so good.

Sam bent down to the beagle as if he were listening to what the dog had to tell him, said, 'Oh', then straightened up and stepped back to the couple. 'Sir?' he said to the man.

The man was looking a bit wary and confused by now. 'Yeah?'

'My dog tells me you have plants in your bag,' said Sam. He bent back down to the dog again, saying, 'Excuse me, what?' then straightened up and turned back to the couple. 'Oh, it's tomato plants from Sicily.' Bending down again, he asked, 'Sorry, what?' Then, straightening up once more, announced, 'The beagle says they were your grandfather's.'

The woman gave her old man a mighty elbow in the ribs and said, in Italian, 'I told you, you fool.'

The man just stood there with his mouth open and finally managed to blurt out, 'I didn't know the dogs were *that* good!'

There were flurries along the rest of the line as other passengers suddenly ducked over to the quarantine bins, and Sam passed his revalidation with flying colours.

9

HUNTING THE WORLD'S UGLIEST TREASURE: TRUFFLE HOUNDS

Dogs live for today and that makes them eternal optimists.

I'm always up for a professional challenge and I love being taken by surprise, as I was when a Tasmanian farmer called Peter Cooper called me up out of the blue in February 1996, the year after I had begun work on the AQIS contract. He wanted to talk to me about something I had almost no knowledge of: truffles. What he said intrigued me, but even so I never could have guessed the hold that these strange, ugly, incredibly expensive delicacies would have on the next three years of my life.

Peter explained that he and agronomist Duncan Garvey had been exploring the possibility of growing truffles in Australia. I found out later that the idea had come to Duncan in a Hobart café in 1991. He'd overheard someone at a nearby table talking about the amazing experience they'd had eating truffles in a Paris restaurant.

Duncan was a sixth-generation Tasmanian who'd studied at universities on the mainland and come home full of fresh ideas. He wanted to do things differently, and that conversation had been enough to spark his interest.

The following year he and Peter had set up a company called Perigord Truffles of Tasmania. They thought truffles might represent a new opportunity for local farmers, and the national Rural Industries Research and Development Corporation agreed, giving them a grant to look into it further. Peter was also awarded a Nuffield Scholarship, designed to let young farmers with exceptional promise explore the best practices in use around the world.

Peter and Duncan made the first of a series of intensive research trips to France. There they found out just how specific the conditions have to be for truffles to appear in the first place, how hard they can be to find, and how carefully they have to be handled once you've got them out of the ground. They also learned that there had been a lot of money spent in France trying to propagate truffles (as opposed to harvesting wild ones), in an attempt to revisit the glory days before two world wars and the rest of the twentieth century wreaked havoc on the industry, and that these efforts had shown only limited success. But none of this put them off. They came back more convinced than ever that Tassie's soil, landscape and weather could work for truffle growth, and that they might be the ones to successfully start such a business.

It's a slow-burn process, growing truffles. Three years before Peter called me, he and Duncan had created Tasmania's first truffle-growing areas, truffières, as they are called. They knew it would take at least four or five years before any truffles were found at all, and another one to three years after that before they could expect significant harvests. But they were on a mission: they wanted to prove that it could be done. Where I came into the picture was to help them find their crop using dogs.

People who are familiar with French truffle hunting often associate it with pigs. That's certainly how it used to be done, and still is occasionally. Do a web search for images of truffle hunting and you'll still get lots of pig shots coming up. But there are some pretty good reasons why pigs aren't the best animals to use, and looking closely at the historic photos of the old-style trufflers will show you one: they often have a knuckle or two or even whole fingers missing.

As I had learned training Puddles and Bacon, pigs aren't exactly flexible thinkers. And the pigs these old farmers used weren't even trained as such. They were pretty much just farm pigs who got to go out into the forests during the season and follow their noses. Pigs love to eat truffles, so they weren't hunting a target in the hope of getting a 'well done' and a pat on the head. They were sniffing out a feast. If you've ever tried getting between a pig and its tucker, you'll know what a bad idea that is. Once these French pigs had nailed the scent, the race was on between human and animal to get to the truffle first. If a hand was in the road the pig would just chomp down anyway.

Peter and Duncan didn't fancy having to do battle every time they found a truffle, so, like sensible modern European truffle hunters, they would be using dogs. They had looked into the work being done by scent-detection dogs in Australia and heard about the training I was doing for AQIS; that was why they called me.

Once he'd given me the background, Peter asked me if I thought I could train a truffle-detection dog. I knew I could, as long as they could supply the odour. Truffle hunting was a different task from those I had trained dogs for previously but I was sure similar methods would work.

I was intrigued by what Peter had told me, but more importantly I liked him from the get-go. I responded to his energy and genuine enthusiasm for trying something new. We arranged that I would make a recce visit down to Tasmania. He and Duncan would show me the set-up and we would talk through the possibilities.

A couple of weeks later I was stepping off the plane at Hobart. Peter picked me up and we drove for thirty minutes to his farm near New Norfolk, where he lived with his lovely wife, Jill, and where he and Duncan had created a truffière.

Truffles are the 'fruit' of a fungus. The kind Peter and Duncan were hoping to produce was the prized French black version – *Tuber melanosporum* for the science buffs – often called the Périgord truffle after the region of France with which they are associated. Black truffles are among the rarest, and therefore priciest, ingredients you can buy. (White truffles from Italy are even more sought-after but haven't been successfully cultivated.)

Black truffles are often called 'black diamonds' or 'black pearls'. Foodies struggle to describe their aroma, but *The Truffle Book* author Gareth Renowden says it combines 'old socks and sex'. Paris-based *New York Times* writer Elaine Sciolino goes further, saying they smell of 'lust: soil, mold, garlic, sweat, ripe mushrooms, hazelnuts, sweet onions, an animal in heat'. That doesn't set my mouth watering, but whatever floats your boat.

The way they grow is that the fungus forms a symbiotic relationship with the roots of hazel and oak trees – in other words, the fungus and tree benefit one another. The resulting truffles can vary from about two centimetres in diameter to grapefruit-sized or even bigger. They are black, warty and ugly. Some people think the texture resembles a dog's nose. Personally I think it looks a lot more like something that comes out the other end. These days France only produces about 36 tonnes in an average year (it used to be three times that). Demand around the world far outstrips supply, so people pay a lot. The price goes up and down depending on the size of the harvest, from around $1800 a kilogram to more than $3300.

In France the majority of truffles are harvested from native forests; in Tasmania everything had purposely been created from scratch. The truffières Peter and Duncan had set up looked like commercial orchards or plantation forests, with row after row of evenly spaced trees, all of which had been 'inoculated' with fungal spores. But unlike an orchard, the trees here were small, no more than two-and-a-half metres high. They were kept that way because the idea wasn't to grow hazelnuts or acorns, it was the roots that mattered. The resulting truffles would mature in the winter – June, July and August in our part of the world.

This wasn't a wild forest, these blokes knew where the trees all were, so the obvious question was why did they need dogs to find the truffles? Couldn't they just dig for them X number of days after the inoculation? If only things were so simple. As Duncan told me, it wasn't like sowing a crop in a ploughed field where you could predict the outcome. Not every tree would produce a truffle. And those that did would not do it to a precise timetable. Then he and Peter told me something that made me wonder if they were crazy for even trying: once the truffle matured you had a maximum window of seventy-two hours to find it before it started rotting and became worthless.

You could check a tree on a Saturday morning and there'd be nothing to find – chefs weren't interested in immature truffles because they lacked that distinctive aroma. By Sunday afternoon a truffle worth thousands of dollars might be maturing, but if it wasn't harvested, by Wednesday morning it would be a valueless rotting lump. If that happened, the best you could hope for was that spores left behind in the soil (what fungi have instead of seeds) would get swallowed by a passing animal. Travel through a digestive tract activates spores, so if they were then to get pooed out near another suitable tree you might, just might, be lucky enough to get truffles in that spot five or more years later.

That really wasn't much of a back-up plan. Clearly it was vital to dig up each truffle during its brief window of maturity. Inspecting the truffière, I looked around me. The rows of young trees stretched off into the distance. And this was just *one* of Peter and Duncan's truffières; there were more than thirty scattered throughout the state's centre and north-west, containing many thousands of trees in all.

But as daunting as the task was, I was fired up by the challenge of it. My positive impressions of Peter from our phone call had been reinforced in person, and I liked Duncan just as much. We were all getting on famously. This was clearly going to involve a lot of hard work, but it looked like it might be fun too. (I turned out to be right on both counts.)

Still, it was a decision I would have to talk over with Diane and the girls, because, as Peter and Duncan explained over lunch, this was very much a start-up venture and the returns were uncertain. They had formed joint-venture arrangements with landowners, who had paid them for the inoculated trees and for their expertise and agreed to split the profits from any truffles harvested on their land and sold. (I was fascinated when Duncan and Peter told me that many of these investors were like me in never having tasted or even seen a truffle up to that point.)

The proposition Peter and Duncan had for me was a similar profit-sharing one. They would provide the materials needed to train Bobby and Hot Dog as truffle-hunters and they would pay all the expenses involved in my bringing the dogs down on weekends throughout the upcoming winter season. If it turned out to be as lucrative as they hoped, I would be handsomely rewarded. If not, well, that was the risk I had to decide whether I was willing to take.

I flew back to Sydney, keen to give it a go. At that point I thought my commitment would be for ten to twelve weekends over a single winter. But even that was a big enough ask for my family. They would see me for a few hours after I got home from work at Hanrob between Monday and Thursday, and that would be about it for three months. On Friday evenings the dogs and I would fly to Tassie to be ready for work bright and early on Saturday morning, and I'd arrive home late and exhausted on Sunday nights. The girls were in high school, with Lauren close to her final exams and the other two navigating their teens. But I'd worked long hours for so many years that Diane had become used to keeping everything running smoothly in my absence. She and the three girls were a tight unit, and I knew they would be fine.

Loading the dogs onto the ship headed for Macquarie Island in 2009. On one journey, the ship hit some very bad weather – it was so bad that I wasn't able to get to the dogs in the hold for quite a while.

Me, Gus and Ash.

I was completely unprepared for the wild and remote beauty of Macquarie Island – it's certainly one of the most spectacular places I've ever been.

Some of the island's king penguins. Sceptics were concerned the dogs might harm the native wildlife, but we were able to prove that the dogs could be trained to move through groups of birds or seals off-leash without harming or even disturbing them in any way.

An elephant seal checks us out. The seals themselves didn't cause us too many problems, but I very nearly lost Gus in a seal wallow, a disgusting mixture of seal faeces, shed fur, mud and the occasional dead seal that Mawson once described as 'quick-mud'. It was a pretty hairy moment!

Eventually the dogs were able to completely eliminate all rabbits and rodents, and restore the island to its former pristine glory. In September 2015, their hard work was recognised with this set of commemorative stamps.

(© Australian Postal Corporation 2015. This material has been reproduced with permission of Australia Post.)

Training fox detection dogs for the Tasmanian government in 2012.

Training dingoes (or trying to anyway) at Rockhampton Zoo in 2014. They're the most intelligent dog I've ever known – but this can make them pretty difficult to teach!

In 2014, I was tasked with training dogs to alert to the presence of the critically endangered Eastern bristlebird (left) without approaching it or making contact, so that rangers could gather eggs and chicks for a captive breeding program and fend off the invasive weeds that overrun the birds' nesting areas.

Right: The bristlebird A-team, with Penny the Wonder Dog front and centre.

In July 2015, I was able to help in the conservation of another critically endangered species, the mala wallaby, by training dogs to detect rabbits.

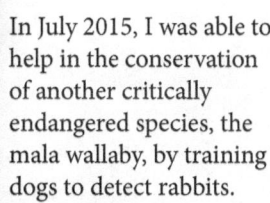

Right: In the field performing rabbit removals – as the mala wallaby's chief food competitor, they pose a severe threat to the species.

With NSW Parks and Wildlife officer Hillary Cherry, working Sally, an English cocker spaniel, in the field in the beautiful Snowy Mountains, April 2015. Sally is being trained to detect hawkweed, a noxious weed that, if left unchecked, can run rampant and choke out other plant species.

Missy showing Sally how it's done.

HUNTING THE WORLD'S UGLIEST TREASURE: TRUFFLE HOUNDS

Diane agreed that it was an opportunity worth taking. If things went really well there could be a seriously big payday at the end of it all. I told Peter and Duncan I was in.

The first step in my training program was to try to find out a bit more about how the French truffle-dog trainers did it. Through their research trips Peter and Duncan had made great contacts with people in all parts of the industry over there, and they arranged for me to phone someone who was said to know all the tricks of the trade. I'm still not sure if this guy figured Australians would be too silly to know better, or if this was really how he trained his animals, but he said to me, 'You get ze truffle, and you put it in ze sock. You throw ze sock, ze dog finds ze sock and brings it back. That's how you train.' '*Merci* for nothing,' I thought, and set about training the dogs using the methods I'd previously refined.

The French trainers might have had spare truffles to chuck around, but I didn't. In the lead-up to (hopefully) producing their own truffles, Peter and Duncan's company had begun importing them from France. However, it could only do that during the northern hemisphere season (December to March) and the season was now over. Even if it had been the right time of year, truffles were too valuable for Duncan and Peter to sling me a whole one, besides which a fresh truffle, or even slivers of one, would degenerate too quickly to be useful for my purposes at this point.

The alternative was truffle oil. This was something that had become very trendy in upmarket restaurants over the previous years. Even though it was considered a gourmet ingredient, it cost a fraction of what real truffles cost. Lots of foodies assume it is made using the real thing. It's not, it's made synthetically (hence the price). But that was what I had to use and, as it turned out, it worked just fine.

Once I'd introduced the dogs to the scent I would train them by putting a drop or two onto a cotton-wool ball and using a screwdriver to push it about 30 centimetres into the ground. Then, with another screwdriver that hadn't had any contact with the oil, I would push unscented cotton balls down at the same depth all around the paddock we were training in. I'd then leave it twenty-four hours before bringing in the dogs and sending them out to find the target. In hardly any time at all they were finding the scent faultlessly on every try. When they found the target the dogs were to indicate it by digging. I trained them in as many different environments as I could — wet ground, dry ground, around farm animals and in areas where there were feral animals, because they were likely to encounter all kinds of animals and would need to ignore them. I started out with quite short training sessions and gradually increased the sessions' duration and level of difficulty to get them fully prepared for long, hard days ahead.

In May 1996 I put the dogs in their travel crates and off we went for our first go at the real thing. I went down to Tasmania fired up and feeling confident that we would soon find this strange buried treasure.

We started what became our regular routine: Pete would pick up the dogs and me from the airport and take us back to the farm at New Norfolk. The next morning we would get up in the freezing dark. Pete and Duncan would have worked out which truffières we would be checking each day.

Their practice was to plant between 500 and 600 trees per hectare, and that first year they'd planted about 50 hectares. So there were a lot of trees to check. And the properties weren't neatly lined up like houses on a suburban street. They were located wherever the company's investors happened to own land that had been judged suitable. Sometimes the next on the list was a mere ten-minute drive away, sometimes it took an hour or two to get there. We always set out for the following truffière thinking, 'Maybe the next tree will be the one.'

We very quickly worked out the most efficient approach and it became our regular pattern for the day. The three of us would walk along the rows of trees. Duncan would be slightly ahead looking at the general health of the trees and watching for a characteristic sign known as brûlé. This is a circle surrounding the tree trunk where the grass has died off. The word means 'burned', as in the dessert crème brûlée – the one for which TV chefs get out the mini-blowtorch. Brûlé certainly isn't a guarantee of finding a truffle, but it does mean the fungus is present and active.

Pete and I would follow behind with the dogs, who were off-lead. Once we'd given them their command to find, the dogs could work a 100-metre row of trees in under ninety seconds. They would run ahead, then circle back to check, then run ahead again, all the time on high alert for their target scent. We'd start two rows in and from there the dogs would check rows one, two and three, criss-crossing in a zigzag between the rows, then we'd turn at the bottom and come back one row over, so each tree would end up being checked two or three times. Truffières often occupy sloping ground, because that's what works best in terms of drainage, so we'd walk up and down the hills, back and forth, over and over and over hundreds and hundreds of rows in the seven or eight hours we were out there each day.

Tasmanian winters aren't just cold, they're bone-chilling. We would be rugged up in boots and thick jackets, with oilskin coat over the top. We'd get some sun here and there, but typically it would be drizzling or raining outright. A few hours in, the effects of the coffee we'd picked up on the drive would have worn off and we'd all be moving a little more slowly. If we were lucky there'd be somewhere we could pick up another coffee on the way through to the next property. The dogs didn't seem to mind the weather at all; they ran around quite happily on even the worst days.

We would work all morning, concentrating hard. I could tell you what the landscape of Tasmania looks like from the roads and from the air much more than from the ground, because for all those hours that we were out there I was looking down at the dogs and the bases of the trees. We'd stop for lunch, and to save time we'd just have it sitting in the field or on the back of the four-wheel drive. Peter and Duncan would have brought thermoses and sandwiches and fruit for three. We'd talk and tell each other stories while we and the dogs rested our weary legs, then we'd get back into it for hours more in the afternoon.

On Saturdays we'd pack up as we started to lose the light. At that latitude in mid-winter the sun sets at about 4.45 pm and the sky is pitch-black thirty minutes later. We'd get into the truck for the ride home, damp and cold, boots soggy, exhausted to the bone. It was a major effort not to fall asleep as soon as the vehicle's heater started up. At least on Saturday evenings I could look forward to being pampered a little. We'd drop Duncan off then head back to Pete's, where Jill would have a roaring fire and homemade soup or something equally warming waiting for us. We'd take care of the dogs, give them a good bellyful of tucker and make them comfortable, then they'd crash for the night. Peter, Jill and I would sit down in front of the fire after dinner and just manage to stay awake long enough for a bourbon or a glass of red before heading to our beds. On those nights I slept more deeply than I ever have, before or since.

On Sunday mornings we'd be up at dawn, ready to start again. The dogs would have a stretch then they'd be as keen as anything to get going. They weren't thinking, 'Oh, yesterday was hard.' Dogs live for today and that makes them eternal optimists. We worked to maintain the same spirit.

We didn't find anything the first weekend, but we told each other that to have done so on our initial try would have been an outrageous stroke of luck, and we'd be successful soon enough if we just stuck with it. So we did. I came back the next weekend and the one after that and the one after that. We looked and looked but we didn't find anything.

That was less than ideal for us humans, but we had all known the difficulty of the task going in. Managing the dogs was a completely different matter. It was crucial that they maintain their enthusiasm for the hunt. So I watched carefully for any signs that they were getting frustrated or losing interest. I knew exactly how each dog behaved when he was fully engaged and he thought there was a target out there, so I could see immediately when they lost momentum. They would start digging up mouse holes, or moving erratically rather than in a systematic way, or they'd stop and stare at the birds. We couldn't afford that because the tree they missed might be the one with the truffle underneath it.

If I saw the warning signs I would drop back to a row we'd previously checked while Duncan, Pete and the dogs kept moving forward. I needed to make sure they had a win to get them back at the top of their game. I'd always have the truffle oil and some cotton-wool balls with me for exactly this purpose. I would put a couple of drops on a cotton ball and push it down into the soil at the base of a tree the dogs had already checked. I would make a mark on the tree that the dogs couldn't see so I knew where the planted scent was.

A little while later we would bring the dogs back over rows they had previously checked. I was careful, though, not to take them only to the 'plant' row, and not to only turn them back when there was a planted scent, because then they would be influenced by expectation, rather than analysing the smell of each row and each tree on its own merits. The use of rows we had previously checked was also a deliberate choice: while it was a long shot, we simply couldn't risk planting the cotton ball on an unchecked tree that just happened to be home to a real truffle. The danger with that scenario was that the dog would respond to the scent, we'd know the 'plant' was there, and we'd assume that was what the dog was responding to, reward the dog and move on, leaving the undiscovered truffle behind!

Every single time I left a plant the dogs successfully found the oil scent, responding just as they had been trained. We would praise them and pat them and reward them with a special mix of cabanossi, devon and chicken – dog ambrosia – and they would get a huge boost in energy and enthusiasm. I might have to do that eight times a day per dog, and each time, having had that all-important win, they couldn't wait to start searching again.

It might seem funny, given that we knew they were staged, but these finds gave Pete, Duncan and me an energy boost too.

HUNTING THE WORLD'S UGLIEST TREASURE: TRUFFLE HOUNDS

Hour after hour, day after day of not finding any truffles can definitely get a man down, no matter how rational he is about it. But the dogs finding the planted cotton balls lifted our spirits because it meant that they weren't missing truffles; we weren't wasting our time searching and we weren't leaving the very thing we'd come for in the ground. We knew that if the real targets had been there the dogs would have found them.

In fact, I'd often plant the scent without letting Peter or Duncan know what I was doing. There were two reasons for this. First, they couldn't inadvertently give the game away with their body language, and second, they would ride a wave of excitement, thinking that this time it might just be the real thing. I'd say, 'What do you reckon, Pete?' And he'd say, 'It looks good, looks good.' Then I'd tell him it was a target I'd planted. That might sound as if it would be more discouraging, but it was the opposite. A little bit of hope and a break in the circuit go a long way.

You had to think to yourself every time, 'Today's the day.' It was like fishing. When you fish, you have to throw in that line expecting the best every time. If you're defeatist when you start you may as well not bother continuing. It was a very different dynamic from working with the quarantine dogs at the airport. There, no finds for a few days in a row can be a kind of win: no-one's trying to bring in anything they shouldn't. Truffle hunting was hard yakka with very delayed gratification. What made it work was the camaraderie.

I'd be lying, though, if I said it wasn't a battle to stay positive as the weeks and then months passed with not a single true find. At various times one or another of us would start to sink a bit. I would begin to question my dogs and then myself, wondering, 'Have I trained them well enough?' I didn't want to let Peter and Duncan down. It's true that I wasn't charging them, but they were spending money flying me over every weekend, and more importantly, they had put their trust in me. For Duncan and Peter the pressure was even greater. Not only was their business's success on the line, but they also had to consider their investors.

As more and more time passed without a find, we had increasingly frequent conversations about whether the trees had been planted on the right side of the hill, or whether the soil was too shallow or too deep. Had the trees been inoculated properly? All of that fell within Duncan's area of expertise, so he worried most about those aspects. Peter had successfully farmed livestock – sheep and cattle – and crops – potatoes, blueberries, even government licensed opium poppies. With all those things you know what to expect at any given point in the year. Nature will have its say, but as long as you put the work in you can expect to see results. This was a whole new ballgame. Peter had to learn to deal with that frustration.

Each of us wanted the others to succeed. We all supported one another and we all backed one another and kept doing so. Peter and Duncan shared my philosophy that you never give in, no matter what. We each felt that it was vital to continue to believe that beneath the next tree was the truffle we were looking for. If we'd gone into the operation seeing the trees as lines and lines of disappointment we'd have been sunk. So we didn't. We stayed strong and kept each other going.

Sunday after Sunday saw Pete dropping me off at Hobart Airport, filthy dirty from the fields. I'd duck into the men's toilets, change into the clothes I'd flown down in and tighten my belt a notch or two, because every weekend I'd have sweated off three to four kilos. I'd stuff my smelly clothes and boots into my bag, drag my weary body onto the plane, land in Sydney, drive home, take care of the dogs, then catch a few hours' sleep before I got up to go to work at Hanrob. Next Friday night I'd be back at the airport ready to do it all again.

By 1999 it was our third winter and we still hadn't found a single truffle. I'd helped Peter train five dogs, both to give him the capacity to look for truffles independently and because when a project goes on that long it's always good to have back-up animals. But I still brought Bobby and Hot Dog with me every time.

Saturday 19 June seemed like all the other days we'd spent hunting. We were on a property near Deloraine, in the central north of the state. It was freezing cold, even with all our layers on. The afternoon was nearly over and we were starting to think about packing up when Pete's dog, Pippa, went to the twelfth tree in the fourth row we were checking and indicated a find. She was quite nonchalant, digging in a relaxed, unhurried way. Pete and Duncan kneeled down to take a look, using the miniature shovels they always had with them.

I was walking over to see what was happening when Pete, unflappable even in a moment like this, held up what looked like a dog turd.

Trying to figure out what he was up to, I asked, 'What's that?'

'It's a truffle,' he said.

Duncan took it and smelled it – checking for, and finding, the telltale pungent odour. He said, 'The science! It works!

The science works!' And then we started jumping around and yelling with the excitement and overwhelming relief of it all.

The truffle itself was about the size of a large strawberry. Its value was measured in hundreds of dollars, not thousands. But it was what it represented that mattered. All the effort had been worthwhile. Duncan and Peter were right: truffles *could* be grown in Australia. And the methods I'd developed could be used to train the dogs that would find them. As for the fact that it was one of Pete's dogs and not mine who made that first find, it didn't even occur to me to worry about that. We were all for one and one for all.

In a state of jubilation, we drove to the home of Tim Terry, who owned the truffière where we'd made the find. He too was delighted, and broke out the good whisky and handed around cigars that looked like they belonged to that rich bloke on the Monopoly box. We celebrated in such style that I didn't fly out until three days later.

A lot of pictures were taken of that first truffle, but we didn't eat it – it would be another couple of months before I had my first taste. The season was still in full swing so I went back down the following weekend; Peter, Duncan and I were walking on air.

If it had been a Hollywood movie we would have continued finding truffles one ugly buried treasure after another, but it wasn't and we didn't. Over the following weeks we found just a few here and there, but we weren't discouraged in the slightest: we knew Duncan's science worked, Peter's farmer's instincts about Tasmania's growing potential had been spot-on, and the dogs I'd trained would find anything that was there to be found.

One weekend before the end of the season we found enough for one of the investors to make a meal for us using truffle. At last, a taste of this thing we'd gone to so much trouble over. I made all the expected noises, of course, but in all honesty the view I formed then is the one I still have: truffles are overrated. It's not that they're bad, just that the mystique surrounding them bears little relation to the ingredient itself. Or maybe the tastebuds of people who swoon over them operate differently from mine. Either way, give me a good steak any day over a truffle.

Still, I did have one very memorable truffle meal during my time in Tassie. One morning when I was staying at Peter's place, we took the dogs out for an early run. It was quail season, so I'd brought my gun with me. The dogs flushed out a couple of quail and I got them. We took them back to the house, where Peter butterflied them in a frypan. Less than an hour from field to plate: you simply cannot beat that experience. With them he fried what must have been $300 worth of truffle. He scrambled some eggs to serve with the quail – eggs that were infused with the scent of truffle after having been stored with them overnight in an airtight jar. Then, for good measure, he grated more truffle over the finished egg.

That season, as the number of finds we made built up, I saw Bobby's cunning side in action. Hot Dog would be out working, working, working, and meanwhile, unless I urged him forward, Bobby would hang behind. I came to realise he was watching Hot Dog, waiting. As soon as Hot Dog caught the scent, which you could tell he had done instantly from the way he lifted his head, Bobby would run over to him, pick up the scent and find the truffle. I would, of course, then reward him, and poor old Hot Dog would get nothing. It took me a good couple of weeks to work that one out!

It was in the following year, the winter of 2000, that the finds became really frequent. On one property every third or fourth tree yielded truffles – bang, bang, bang, one after another. That was fantastic for the dogs, especially the new dogs of Peter's. You can teach dogs using substitute odour in practice simulations, of course, but a couple of real finds in the real environment gives them as much understanding in a few minutes as they would pick up in weeks' worth of training.

Word spread about what was happening and media coverage picked up. We started getting gourmet-food magazine journalists coming out with us. There was a lot of interest from high-end chefs too. Tim Pak Poy had been closely following the endeavour from the beginning. His restaurant, Claude's, was widely acknowledged as Sydney's finest, and was booked out months in advance. But Tim wasn't one to rest on his laurels. He was interested in trying new things and was especially keen on encouraging local growers to develop quality produce he could use. He came down to Tasmania and spent some time out in the truffières with us. His enthusiasm was genuine and he was good company. That season, Peter and Duncan's company was able to supply Tim with Tasmanian truffles for the first time and he created a special celebratory menu at Claude's.

The next season was even better. Tasmania was really coming into its own as a source of the finest-quality ingredients – it was on its way to becoming the foodie destination it has been ever since – and Perigord Truffles of Tasmania won a 2001 Jaguar–*Gourmet Traveller* award for excellence in primary production. In 2006 Perigord realised its ambition to export the delicacies, selling them into Europe and Japan for the first time, and there are now truffières in Western Australia, New South Wales and Victoria, as well as Tasmania. There are now an estimated 160 growers nationally, with about 10 per cent producing a commercial crop. According to the Australian Truffle Growers Association, in 2011 a little over three tonnes of black truffle was harvested nationally, and that rose to 4.5 tonnes in 2014, with two-thirds coming from Manjimup, Western Australia. That makes Australia the world's fourth-largest black-truffle producer behind Spain, France and Italy.

In the end I didn't make any real money from the truffle hunting in Tasmania, but I came away with some far more important things. One was a depth of knowledge about training truffle dogs. Self-praise is no praise, but objectively I'm now among the best truffle-dog trainers in the world. These days if I train a truffle dog it costs $25,000. That might sound like a lot, but a good dog can easily pay for itself within a single season, given a truffle price of around $1500 to $1800 per kilogram. And as I explain to people who initially baulk at the price, that cost reflects the three years I trudged around that Tasmanian countryside in the freezing cold, with the wind whistling at my back, sheer exhaustion flooding over me. They're paying for all that experience without having to go through it themselves.

Some people take a while to get it, though. I took a dog I had trained to Western Australia, accompanying a friend of mine who was trying to get truffle farmers there to understand the benefits of using a properly trained animal. We went to one truffière where the owner was using some dogs he insisted were up to the task. His dogs went around the trees and, sure enough, found truffles. Then the spaniel *we*'d brought went over the same ground and found truffle after truffle that the other dogs had missed. The owner of the property said, 'I'm really glad you came. We made a lot of money today with your dog.' My friend had to point out what was obvious to himself and me but not yet to the farmer: 'It's really not what he found today that counts, it's what the other dogs missed over the last two years. Based on what we've seen today, I reckon you've lost $200,000 in undiscovered truffles.' When the property owner got his colour back he hired the dog, and my mate as handler, on the spot.

By the end of 2002, Peter was all set up with the spaniels I'd helped him train. He'd proved to be a very good dog handler, continuing what we'd started, so I finished my close involvement with Perigord, although I still serve as a consultant to the company.

But our friendship remained strong. Even more precious than the knowledge I got from my time in Tasmania were the two extraordinary friends I gained in Duncan and Peter. Going through those trials and tribulations together in the field had bonded us tightly.

One day Pete rang me up and said, 'What are you up to later on?' I told him I was just doing the usual, training dogs. He said, 'Great, I'm coming to Sydney in a couple of hours to take some truffles to Tim at Claude's. Do you want to have a beer?' Of course I did, so we arranged that I'd pick Pete up at the airport, we'd drive over to Claude's at Woollahra, drop off the truffles, then get a steak and a beer at a pub somewhere.

I collected him and we went to the restaurant. Pete had come straight from his property and was in his farmer's gear of worn boots and jeans. I was no better, in my old dog-training clothes, but it didn't matter because we just needed to stick our head in the kitchen door and then we'd be off. Pete had come to Sydney for similar drop-offs before, but either Tim had met him at the airport, or it had been during the day before restaurant service had started and he had just gone to the front door.

This time, when we got to the restaurant we couldn't see how to get around to the back, but neither could we go in the front looking like we did. So we rang Tim and told him we were outside with the truffles he was expecting. He said, 'Great. What are you blokes doing now?'

I said, 'We're going to get something to eat.'

'Okay, come in,' he said.

'No, we're going to the pub,' I told him. 'You haven't seen how we're dressed.'

But Tim insisted. 'I want to feed you.'

'All right, then,' we said, 'tell us how to get round the back and we'll eat in the kitchen.'

He wasn't having a bar of it. We were eating in his restaurant and that was that.

In we walked, Pete carrying his Styrofoam box of carefully packed truffles. The place was absolutely packed with beautifully dressed people, some of whom had been waiting a long, long time for their very special night out. Not surprisingly, everyone turned to look. Pete and I were both so embarrassed we could have melted into the floor. A waiter started setting up a new table for us. We tried again to thank Tim for his offer and tell him we really had to go.

'*Sit down,*' he said. 'I own the place and you're my guests. Now, we've got some really nice pheasant.' He cracked open a special bottle of wine for us and then the food started coming out.

A reputation like the one Claude's has sets up such huge expectations that they're pretty hard to live up to. But our meal that night surpassed anything I could have dreamed up. It was simply wonderful. When everybody had finished their mains Tim came back out of the kitchen carrying something and said to the restaurant at large, 'Everybody, I'd like your attention for a minute. These are the truffles we have on the menu, this is the farmer who grows them in Tasmania and this is the guy who trains the dogs who find them.'

Next minute we had a circle of people around us. They'd all pulled over their chairs and brought their wine or their dessert with them and were asking us all about truffle hunting. We described what it was like and answered their questions and everyone laughed and joined in. It was quite a night.

My professional life was still firmly focused on quarantine-detection dogs at this point, with AQIS role having led to extra work with the Tasmanian and Western Australian state authorities, which I fitted in around my AQIS responsibilities. But there had been upheaval in my personal life.

Several years earlier I'd had a call out of the blue from someone who said that her name was Vicki Bourke and that she was a dog trainer seeking some advice. I hadn't heard of her or come across her at events, but that wasn't surprising: I was based in southern Sydney, while she was involved with a dog club in the city's north, at Hornsby. She didn't seem very sure of herself and I'll admit that at first I thought, 'Who *is* this woman?' I'd had a few too many calls from people with airy-fairy ideas about becoming dog trainers but no knowledge or understanding of what was involved. So I was initially quite dismissive, saying, 'You know you have to get some experience before you go around calling yourself a trainer.'

She said, 'Well, I have an AOC dog and I'm a qualified Obedience Trial judge.' She had trained a dog to Australian Obedience Champion level? That got my attention.

We ended up talking for over an hour. And when I eventually met her, I couldn't help but notice that she was also a very attractive woman. But we were both married, so nothing could come of that. We became great friends and that was how it stayed for a number of years.

In due course I had to admit to myself that my feelings for Vicki were more than just those I would feel for a friend. But I was very reluctant to do anything about it, for two reasons. First, even though the lack of shared interests between Diane and me meant we had drifted apart, she was a wonderful mother and I felt that it was my duty to be there until the girls finished high school. Second, I didn't know whether Vicki felt the same way about me and I didn't want to risk saying something that might ruin our friendship.

When I finally told her how I felt, she admitted she felt the same way. Eventually, both our marriages broke up and in due course I moved in with Vicki and her daughter, who is called Lauren, like my eldest.

I took my dogs with me – Bobby and a springer spaniel called Sam. I'd got Sam a few years earlier, as Hot Dog was getting older. Hottie had retired from competition and I'd taken Sam up to Field Trial Champion level. He was still in his prime when Hottie passed away – at the good old age of sixteen, he just fell asleep in his kennel one day and didn't wake up. He was a wonderful dog and we'd accomplished so much together. He'd also served as my introduction to the joy of springer spaniels and I've never been without one since.

It was time to consolidate the happiness I had found with Vicki on the home front and shake things up on the work front. I'd been doing the AQIS work for ten years and I was ready for a change. I was becoming jaded, and, thanks to regular exposure at the airport to what we'll call the less desirable side of humanity (the smuggling and bare-faced lying), I was turning into a real cynic when it came to human nature. I was never less than professional while we were running baggage checks, but complacency with some other parts of the job was making me bored, and when I get bored I get up to mischief.

By this stage I'd had a lot of experience doing public talks and I was very comfortable in front of a crowd. Because of this, AQIS used to get me to participate in 'infotainment' sessions they ran – presentations designed to entertain an audience while getting across information about what the quarantine service did and why. One of these events took place at a pet expo held at Sydney's Rosehill Racecourse over a long weekend. We did our show three times a day. I was on stage with a dog called Billy, demonstrating how it all worked, and one of the AQIS PR officers, Linda, was the presenter, talking the audience through what was happening.

I'd have a line of bags set up, some containing targets – fruit, other plants and meat products. The dog would run along the line checking them and indicate when he found a target. Linda would say, 'What has Billy found in the bag, Steve?'

I'd say, 'I don't know, Linda, we should have a look.'

She'd come over and crouch down, and I'd open the bag and pull out the target – 'It's a banana, Linda.'

'Oh, a banana, Steve. Now, we can't have bananas and other fruit coming in because ...' and on she would go.

Linda was a genuinely lovely lady and she was the perfect PR representative: her uniform was perfect, her hair was perfect, her smile was perfect and she spoke perfectly at all times. The shows went like clockwork. But I was bored silly.

By halfway through the third and final day, I was entertaining myself with thoughts of how I could make things a bit livelier. As the final show approached that little devil on my shoulder became irresistible. You know those times when you shouldn't do something, you're very aware that you shouldn't because of how much trouble you might get into, but it's such a good idea you just can't help yourself? This was one of those times.

Kellyville Pets had a display at the expo that included some impressive-looking snakes. I knew the store's boss, John Grima, and I asked him, 'Can I borrow a python?' He asked what for, I told him, he said, 'I'm in', and I was set.

The python he gave me was two metres long and as thick as a firehose. He helped me get it inside a suitcase and then I put the case back in the line-up all ready for the final show. A few minutes later, punctual as ever, Linda came back to the stage. The presentation got underway, all running along the usual scripted lines.

'This is Billy,' said Linda to the audience, which was almost exclusively families. As usual she was speaking through one of those headset-mounted microphones. 'He's a quarantine-detection dog. We use these dogs to check for material that is not allowed to be brought into Australia.' She listed all the things Billy had been trained to find, finishing with '... and reptiles'. She turned to me. 'Now Billy will check the bags.' That was my cue to send him down the line.

I'd shifted the targets around over the course of the weekend to keep Billy on his toes, but it had always been those same items – fruit, plants, meat products. This time he started checking the bags as usual, but when he got to the suitcase in question he pulled up sharply then sat down with unusual slowness. What he could smell inside the bag was making him extremely edgy, but you would have needed to be a dog trainer to recognise that.

'What has Billy found in the bag, Steve?' Linda asked, suspecting nothing.

I gave my usual reply but instead of starting to open the bag when she came over, I said, '*You* should open this one.'

She said brightly, 'That's a good idea', popped open the latches, lifted the lid and came face to face with what, in her fright, must have looked like an anaconda. She didn't scream as such, but she did shout the longest version of the F-word I have ever heard. It seemed to go for about thirty seconds – to the delight of the children in the audience and the shock of their parents. She managed to recover enough to wrap up the show but boy, was she angry with me. Fair enough too.

I got into a lot of trouble over that – deservedly. Looking back, I realise it was a stupid prank to play, no matter how bored I was. I was summoned to Canberra where one of the most senior people in the organisation gave it to me in no uncertain terms: 'I thought you were more professional than that' etc, etc. I took it all on the chin and agreed I would never do anything like that again.

It took a long time for Linda to forgive me and start talking to me again, but in the end, luckily, she did.

Still, it was time for me to look for some new challenges. So early in 2006 I ended my mutually beneficial arrangement with Hanrob – which had been taken over by Bob and Hannie Biggs's sons when they retired and which still has the AQIS contract to this day. I did, however, continue to serve as a consultant to various organisations, including the Japanese, New Caledonian and Tasmanian Governments, for whom I was a consultant on quarantine detection; and the California Narcotic Canine Association, for whom I validated US Government detection dogs (being one of only two non-Americans accredited to do this).

Vicki and I then entered a business relationship with a boarding kennel called Pet Resorts Dural, close to where we were now living in Sydney's north, which offered boarding services for dogs and cats and training for dogs.

On 14 July I took Vicki to a Bastille Day truffle dinner put on by Tim Pak Poy at his new venture, the Wharf Restaurant, where I proposed to her. To my great joy, Vicki said yes, and we had our wedding at Tim's restaurant in January.

It was a very special, memorable occasion in every way. Everything was perfect, including the food. Tim created the most wonderful wedding feast ... with not a truffle in sight.

10

CONSERVATION DETECTIVES

No animal should suffer, even introduced pests.
No matter what the creature is, if it has to be killed
its death must be as humane as possible.

It was in 2006, soon after the move to Pet Resorts, that I made my first foray into what has become my life's work: conservation detection. It started in a small way, with a call from a local council inquiring whether my dogs might be able to find fox dens on beaches. In trying to deal with this problem the council had sought help from the NSW National Parks and Wildlife Service (NPWS) and some of the rangers knew of me from my success in Field Trials. The beach in question was Manly, perhaps Sydney's best known after Bondi. The council knew foxes were living there and wanted to get rid of them because they're feral pests who wreak havoc on native wildlife, including ground-nesting birds. But foxes didn't get their reputation for cunning for nothing, and they were proving elusive.

As well as Sam, by now I had another springer spaniel, Bolt, whom I'd also trained for Field Trial work. What Bolt lacked in the looks department he more than made up for in ability. As required for competition, both dogs had been trained to respond instantly to whistle commands and to follow hand signals. They would repress their own instincts to follow my commands – waiting until I sent them after game, for instance, or stopping mid-stride while they were running flat out – because they knew that something even better awaited, which for them was the reward of ball play. That level of finely honed response was absolutely crucial for the work we were now being asked to do, because the whole idea of a conservation dog is that it must not make contact with any animal, native or feral. That's vital. The dog finds the animal and then authorised people take over and, in the case of a pest, humanely destroy it.

At that time some conservation work using dogs was being done in New Zealand, but in Australia it was something about which people knew very little. There was a huge amount of scepticism among many of those working with wildlife as to whether dogs could be trained not to interfere with native animals or damage habitat. They thought 'hunting dog' and pictured a scary animal grabbing its prey and killing it.

I could understand their fears: if you've never seen these dogs in action it's almost impossible to understand how brilliantly they perform. And I fully agree that if you haven't got full control of a conservation dog you have no right to be there. But I knew that my dogs could change even the most sceptical minds. Talk wouldn't do it; people needed to see them at work.

Manly Beach was a perfect place for that to happen. It's an incredibly busy spot, visited by more than seven million people every year. If rangers flushed out a fox in a national park, shooting it might be the best way to get rid of it quickly and cleanly – but that wasn't an option on busy Manly Beach. And with so many people on the beach and walking dogs along the beachside corso, mass baiting wasn't an option either. Detection dogs were the only safe option.

Detection dogs are a great tool to help you precisely target feral pests. Vixens, for instance, are very, very good at hiding their dens. It's not impossible for humans alone to find them, but it is extremely difficult. Bringing a trained dog onto the scene makes it easy to pinpoint where the pests are, vastly increasing your success rate in eliminating them.

I took the dogs out on that first job and Bolt soon got the scent of the vixen. He tracked it along the beach for 200 or 300 metres, made a sharp left turn, headed straight into the low cover on one of the dunes and stopped, indicating a target. In less than five minutes from go to whoa he had found a den that had been eluding the rangers. It could now be fumigated, getting rid of the foxes without risk to any other beach users. It would also be a quick and humane end for the fox, which was important. No animal should suffer, even introduced pests. I'd like to see every cane toad in Australia eliminated, but the idea of killing them by taking a swing with a golf club is repugnant and wrong. No matter what the creature is, if it has to be killed its death must be as humane as possible. At the same time, people need to be realistic and informed about the damage feral animals do and understand the need to get them out of our environment.

Foxes are terrific in the countries to which they're native, but Australia isn't one of those. Long after all the other Australian states declared the fox an official pest, it was still legal to keep them in New South Wales, albeit under strict conditions, including having them desexed and kept in approved enclosures. In 2014 the government indicated it was going to change this legislation, but there's still a registered fox-rescue charity operating in Sydney. Everyone's entitled to their own view, but to me their efforts are ill-informed and misdirected. Foxes don't need rescuing. The whole point is that they're doing really well at the expense of our native animals. I'd love to see those no doubt well-meaning fox supporters put their energy into a rescue group for bilbies or Bengal tigers or rhinos, or any of the numerous other animals around the world who really need help.

The people from different environmental agencies and other councils who had come along to Manly to watch that first fox hunt were all committed to protecting native wildlife, and even the most sceptical were won over once they saw the dogs at work. That led to more conservation jobs as momentum built through word of mouth. The Australian Wildlife Conservancy (AWC) heard about me and gave me a call, leading to some unforgettable professional highs as well as some personal low blows.

The AWC is a fantastic group that's making a real difference. It was set up in 1991 as a reaction to the fact that Australia has the world's worst mammal extinction rate and many of our surviving animals and plants are currently under threat. It creates sanctuaries both by building partnerships with landholders and by buying land itself. It's now the country's largest private holder of conservation land and it uses science-based practices to maintain the integrity of its sanctuaries.

It looks after twenty-three properties, covering more than three million hectares in some of the wildest, most beautiful and most ecologically important parts of Australia, including Lake Eyre, Cape York and the Kimberley. It was for the last of these that my services were needed. The AWC's Mornington–Marion Downs property covers almost 6000 square kilometres and is home to endangered species that include the Gouldian finch, the purple-crowned fairy-wren and the northern quoll.

The biggest threat to them all is feral cats. In fact, feral cats are the single greatest cause of mammal extinctions and mammal population decline in Australia.

Think I'm exaggerating? Of the twenty-nine native species of mammals that have become extinct here since European settlement, feral cats have been directly responsible for the extinction of twenty-eight. In all, another one hundred species are under threat from them right now. There are around 18 million feral cats in Australia and they kill, on average, more than four native animals every single night. That's 75 million a year.

There's nothing wrong with pet cats. Batman introduced me to the pleasure they can bring. I have two cats now and I love them ... BUT they are desexed and they are indoor cats. I'm all for letting people keep pet cats as long as they take a responsible approach and don't let them out to wreak havoc.

However, the feral cat is something different again. To fit the definition of 'feral' it must be at least the fifth generation to live in the wild. That would take a very long time for humans, but cats can be ready to breed as early as four months old, so five generations can go by in just a few years. Sometimes they look like domestic cats, sometimes they don't. I've seen a feral cat who was the size of a medium dog and weighed close to 15 kilograms, all of it muscle.

Once a feral cat has reached about two years of age he is a formidable opponent – intelligent, wily and absolutely fierce. As a kitten, the feral cat has a predator in the dingo, but by the time the cat has reached adulthood even a dingo is hesitant to take it on. As for the native animals the cats hunt, well, they have no chance. Over eons these creatures have evolved defences against their native predators, including eagles, dingoes and snakes, but they are completely defenceless against introduced stealth hunters like cats.

The person who called me in 2006 was Dr Sarah Legge, then the AWC's chief scientist. She was getting in touch to explore the possibility of my training a dog to find feral cats at Mornington–Marion Downs. Understanding what was at stake, I was keen to help. I acquired a twelve-month-old springer spaniel called Sally and set about training her for a permanent role on the property. As with the truffle dogs, she would have to be trained using the best available scent before encountering the real thing on location. In this case I had several feral-cat tails for scent. I used them to get the odour onto cat-sized dummies and worked at getting Sally used to an animal that climbed trees as well as ran across ground. When she was ready we got onto a plane bound for Western Australia.

The place we were headed to is really remote. Broome is 2200 kilometres north-east of Perth, then the Mornington Wildlife Sanctuary (the porperty's base of operations) is 550 kilometres from Broome, a journey we made in a tiny plane to save the seven hours it would otherwise have taken by four-wheel-drive. Coming in by air was the perfect way to appreciate a landscape that is nothing less than spectacular. That word is used way too often for things that aren't spectacular at all, but here it's barely enough to do the reality justice. This is tropical savannah, with massive steep-sided tablelands, huge sandstone escarpments and gorges, valleys of boab trees, caverns filled with precious, ancient rock art, huge waterfalls and vast green woodlands cut through by rivers. It's genuinely awe-inspiring.

Sally and I were met by Sarah Legge. Sarah was absolutely dedicated to the cause and really hands-on in the field; I liked her immediately. The plan was that I would stay for three to four weeks, during which I would finish off Sally's training and train up the people who would be handling her, including Sarah. Our timetable would be set by the cats' activity, which was in turn determined by the weather. There are two seasons, wet and dry, and two temperatures, very hot and unbearably hot. Nothing moves out there in the full heat of the day. So we'd be getting up at 4 or 4.30 am, well before sunrise, and we'd start driving out in the dark. We'd work with Sally until 10 am at the latest; by then it would be too hot to continue and by early afternoon the temperature would be up in the forties. At that stage everyone would be back in their accommodation, in my case a lovely little three-metre-square wooden shed, where I'd try to catch up on some sleep as best I could given that there was no air conditioning and the humidity was so intense I felt like you could scoop up the air with a spoon. At dusk we'd all head back out again and work until perhaps 9 pm, with the aid of night-vision scopes and spotlights mounted on the four-wheel drives.

Sarah and her team had some frozen cat carcasses waiting for us, and after they were thawed out we used these for the first couple of days, making scent trails by dragging them through the bush and up into trees. That went well, with Sally able to track the scent. On the fourth day she picked up live scent and reacted just as she'd been trained. But she'd never encountered a cat's escape tactics before, and this one was too good for her. Most animals being hunted will run ahead of the predator, but cats are clever enough to loop out wide then backtrack. That was what happened in this case and Sally lost the scent. But she learned from that, and the next time she found a cat and flushed it out, she didn't give up when it took off and she lost the scent. She got better and better as I let her work it out for herself. The next few cats also got away, but it was an increasingly close call each time.

After about a week she was ready. When she lost the scent this time she just went out wider and wider, checking back the way we had come until she found it again. She smelled where the cat had gone up a tree and where it had landed when it jumped out, then where it had gone through a log and come out again. Watching her, I could see the whole picture coming together for her. She was clear and sure now, and the cat could not shake her. In the end it went up into another tree and she was right there at the base, alerting the handler perfectly. The cat was cleanly shot and Sally got lots and lots of praise. I stayed long enough in Mornington for Sally to get another two or three cats and then it was time for me to say goodbye, confident that she would do a great job for Sarah and her team.

Not all the cats are killed. To deal with them effectively it's important to understand their behaviour and movements, and the best way to do that is to fit them with GPS-equipped tracking collars. That's quite the challenge, let me tell you. I stayed in close touch with the AWC and continued to support its work, and in 2011 I went back to Mornington along with a crew from Channel Nine's *60 Minutes* to film a story for the show, as part of which we captured a cat and fitted a collar on it. Sally flushed out this particular cat and tracked it up a tree, but the cat jumped and took off again. With the cat in the lead, Sally hot on its tail and us humans running to catch up, the chase was on. Up another tree it went and Sarah climbed up after it, trying to use a piece of branch to get it to jump down. Some of her team were waiting with a blanket and a large net on a pole so they could catch it as it jumped. But it was too quick for us and took off again. Finally Sally chased it into a third tree. I climbed up this time, using the branch again to encourage it to jump. It did, and got away briefly once more before Sarah and her team finally caught it.

As you'd imagine, cats who are caught like this are not very happy, which makes getting a collar on them a dangerous job. A house tabby can do some pretty impressive damage with its claws if it wants to, but these feral cats are in a whole other class. They carry what are called zoonotic diseases – in other words, diseases that can pass from animals to humans. Both their mouths and their claws are teeming with enough bacteria to make someone extremely sick: a ranger in Canberra had to have three months off work because she became crook from just one feral-cat scratch on the arm.

People don't do this job for glory and they certainly don't do it for the money. Like rangers working for the Parks and Wildlife Services and other conservation organisations all around the country, the AWC workers do it because they are dedicated to protecting this extraordinary land we live in. I regard them as unsung heroes.

I get really annoyed when people take one look at their efforts and say, 'Why bother? It's all too hard and you won't make any difference anyway. There're too many cats, too many rabbits, too many foxes – we'll never get rid of them, it's impossible.' I happen to think nothing is impossible if you set your mind to it. I can't accept the idea of simply giving up; for me that is not an option. If there's something I can do that might make a difference, I'm sure as hell going to have a go. That cat or fox we remove might just represent the tipping point for the native creatures who inhabit that piece of land. The pest animal's absence might leave room for a native bird or animal to survive long enough to breed, producing young who also get to breed, becoming a small but crucial part of pulling a species back from the brink.

There's no kick or thrill for me in killing any animal. As with the quail in Tasmania, I'll hunt to eat, but I'm disgusted by people who 'hunt' elephants or lions or whatever it might be just for the sake of saying they've done it. When I help eradicate feral animals I do it in order to look after this country; I don't take any pleasure in it. But that's not what you'd have thought if you'd read a story that ran in the Sunday papers in early 2012.

I'd been on the board of directors of the Pet Industry Association of Australia (PIAA) for ten years and was in the middle of my second stint as president. The PIAA represents and regulates the businesses that make up the pet industry, including kennels and catteries, pet shops, groomers, trainers and breeders. For some people the very fact that there is a pet *industry* is objectionable. My response to this is that pets play a hugely important role in people's lives. There are tens of millions of pets in this country and we need to ensure their welfare. The best way of doing this is through an organisation that has strict ethical standards, such as the PIAA. 'The childcare industry' is a perfectly common, non-controversial phrase. We accept that people need child care and that much of it is provided on a commercial basis. The important thing is that regulations are met and children's welfare is carefully monitored. Well, it's exactly the same with pets.

Of course there are some people who object to the whole idea of pets. The group Animal Liberation, for instance, which follows what I would describe as the radical theories of philosopher Peter Singer, rejects the word 'pet' in favour of 'companion' because this 'acknowledge[s] animals' independent status' and 'all animals have the right to live free from human intervention'. In my view there's a lot of woolly thinking contained in those few words. Perhaps it's best to leave it at that: we'll need to agree to disagree.

For the PIAA, the way animals are treated is crucially important, and we have worked long and hard over the years to stamp out bad practices and bring in protections for animals handled by our members. Like the RSPCA, we condemn 'puppy farms' and we carefully check and monitor our members to make sure they are meeting our high standards. If we find operators who have slipped through the net we deal with them immediately.

Along with a number of other significant organisations, the PIAA was part of the Companion Animals Taskforce set up by the NSW Government in 2011 to examine the laws around animals and see what updates might be needed. In 2012, with the support of the government, we introduced a new two-part policy. The first part ensures that our pet-shop members sell only dogs bred by PIAA-registered breeders operating to our high standards and independently vet-checked on a regular basis. The second part, on dog rehoming, guarantees that any dog sold by a PIAA member store and later abandoned by its owner and left unclaimed in a pound or shelter will be rehomed. Requisite microchips allow us to trace all dogs sold by PIAA-registered stores.

The PIAA's public profile was fairly high at this time, thanks to these moves, and perhaps that made me, as its president, the target of people who fundamentally disagreed with our approach. That's my best guess as to why a photograph from my time in the Kimberley helping the AWC eliminate feral cats suddenly became a negative story in the media all around the country. The strange thing was that the photograph had been on my business website for the world to see for at least two years before this 'news' story blew up.

The photograph shows me, two AWC researcher–rangers and Sally with a feral cat she had tracked, whom one of the rangers had cleanly shot and killed. In the same way as keeping some cats alive and putting a collar on them provide valuable information, so does finding out what native animals they are targeting. The way this is done is that AWC scientists examine the stomach contents of cats killed in specific areas. So we were taking this particular carcass back to the Mornington lab for analysis.

Because of those high zoonotic disease risks, the policy is that no-one can have direct contact with such an animal. The carcasses are either picked up using plastic body bags designed for animals or, if none is available, rope. This time it was rope. Just as we were about to pack everything up in the truck, one of the AWC staff who was there asked us to pose for a quick shot with the cat. The carcass couldn't be seen in the photo when it was lying on the ground in front of us, so they asked me to hold the rope to get it in the picture. I was happy to oblige: the whole point of the exercise was to remove feral cats. As I automatically do when I'm asked to pose for a snapshot, I smiled.

I woke up one day in March 2012 to learn that this old, perfectly ordinary photo was suddenly in newspapers in Sydney, Melbourne, Adelaide and Perth alongside calls for my resignation as PIAA president 'by animal lovers' who claimed the photo showed how little I cared for animals' welfare. The comment fields below the online versions of the stories were peppered with remarks from people outraged by what they thought the photo represented and completely ignorant of the facts.

A large part of their outrage was that the animal looked like a domestic moggy. They had no understanding of the difference between domestic and feral cats. There were also some wild and outrageous assumptions about the photo, including that I had strangled the feral cat to death(!) and equally ridiculous claims about me, including that I hunted wild game in Africa. It was all so far over the top that I suppose I should have laughed it off, but at the time I was deeply upset by what was being said about me, and even more so, by the damage it might do to the good work of the PIAA.

I immediately offered to step down, but one after another the board members said they wouldn't accept my resignation. Even so, I insisted that they call a meeting, which I would not attend, to discuss the matter. They met, discussed it, and unanimously insisted I stay. Their confidence in me was a great comfort in the face of what became a series of very vicious, personal attacks – many of them by faceless cowards. Somebody searched out our home phone number and posted it online, and Vicki and I got some appalling anonymous calls, including death threats to me and our dogs, and others calling me a paedophile (presumably because it was the worst thing they could think of to say). Someone came into our driveway one night and threw eggs and tomatoes over our car. In itself that was just a stupid nuisance, but the thought that people like that knew where we lived was deeply unpleasant, particularly given how much time I spent away working, leaving Vicki and Lauren there on their own. Poor Vicki was so outraged by it all she leaped to my defence on Facebook, initially trying to educate people, but then perhaps falling into the trap of communicating with some of the keyboard cowards who just wanted to stir up hostility.

As overwhelming as it all seemed at the time, thanks to the twenty-four hour news cycle the majority of the storm had blown over within a week. But the aftermath would surely have irked whoever sent the photo to the media in the first place: via social media, email and phone, conservation experts throughout Australia and overseas, including in London and Los Angeles, contacted me to offer support for the work I'd been doing in the Kimberley. Then parks services in New South Wales and Queensland contacted me saying they'd seen the story, hadn't realised I did feral-cat work, and had some jobs they wanted to talk to me about. Two very solid contracts followed – so I guess I owe whoever started the story a thankyou for all the free publicity!

***

I am completely committed to the conservation work I do. It's an opportunity to make a real difference. It's expanded to take in both sides of the coin: eliminating introduced pests and directly protecting native wildlife.

My dogs have helped guard penguin colonies from predators in New South Wales and Victoria. The first of these jobs took me back to Manly, where there's a secluded cove that little penguins use each year to breed – in fact, this is the only breeding colony on the NSW mainland. Their special status has seen them protected by law. I got a little spaniel called Eco especially for the job and trained her to find penguins as well as foxes and feral cats, which prey on the birds.

As it happens, Manly is just a little way around the harbour from Taronga Zoo, which is home to a number of native penguins. I initially approached the zoo about getting some odour – feathers or poo – but, knowing what I was working on, the keepers thought they could do a lot better than that.

They arranged for me to bring Eco in and train her on their penguins' nesting boxes, which were rich in scent, and as her training progressed they were able to put a live penguin in one of the boxes so she could experience that too. She picked up the training quickly and we were soon down working among the nests at Manly. The rangers who look after the penguins there need to find the wild nesting sites so they can protect the nests and the birds in them, microchipping the penguins to keep track of the population. On her very first day on the job, Eco proved her worth by finding a live penguin nest under a rock, and she continued to do great work for many years until, horribly, she died after eating poisoned fox bait. A conservation dog has two nemeses: snakes and bait. Unfortunately Eco swallowed some bait while she was momentarily out of sight. We've learned from this and put in even stricter protocols for the conservation dogs' bait and snake training to try to prevent it from ever happening again.

Phillip Island in Victoria is home to a much more famous penguin population; indeed, the penguins are a major tourist attraction. I trained two dogs to take with me to the island, both also springer spaniels. Their first task was to find the foxes who were threatening the penguins. Unlike a feral cat, who will kill to eat, foxes get into a kind of frenzy and will simply tear the head off their prey, leave the penguin and move on to the next one. It wasn't uncommon for them to kill several dozen a night. The dogs set to work and soon proved their value in tracking predators. But the island is connected to the mainland by a bridge and there are hundreds of thousands of visitors each year, so the rangers must stay vigilant, which means the dogs are now permanently based there.

I've also trained dogs to find koalas and emus, working for state parks services that need to monitor the populations and, in the case of ground-nesting emus, protect the eggs. My dogs have helped save the turtle population at Mon Repos Beach near Bundaberg, Queensland, by finding the dens of foxes who were digging up and eating the turtle eggs before they could hatch. We've worked for Queensland Parks and Wildlife controlling feral cats at their bilby sanctuary far inland, on the border with New South Wales.

I've also trained them to find cane toads. That will seem a bit odd to anyone in the northern part of Australia where, unfortunately, you only have to step outside at night to see way too many of these introduced pests. But they've been eradicated from the beautiful and ecologically rich Moreton Island near Brisbane, and once a year I take a dog up on behalf of the parks service to check they haven't managed to get back in. Dogs are invaluable for this task. Cane toads are small and easy to miss, but their scent is like a beacon to a well-trained dog.

Even though Tasmania is part of Australia, as an island it has an extra level of quarantine protection and detection dogs are used to check every incoming flight and ferry. I ran the training program for these dogs for seventeen years, right up to 2013 and, just like the AQIS dogs, I trained them to find a range of no-nos, including reptiles. One of the dogs alerted me to a pair of gumboots in a covered camper trailer coming in on the ferry: sure enough, there was a cane toad tucked away in the toe. The driver had been on holiday with his family in Queensland, put his gumboots outside overnight and packed them away for the return journey not realising he had acquired a stowaway.

It would be completely impossible for every possible toad hiding place to be checked by a person, but with a dog on the job you can feel much more secure. They are a remarkable conservation tool.

11

BRISTLEBIRDS, CHEETAHS AND RABBITS, OH MY

If there's a limit to the conservation work dogs can do I have yet to find it.

No matter how many conservation dogs I've trained, there's always something new to learn, and that was certainly the case when it came to finding Eastern bristlebirds. These birds once lived up and down the NSW coast but there are now only about 2000 of them left, in three separate areas. The most precarious population is right on the NSW–Queensland border, about two hours' drive inland, in and around the Border Ranges National Park. Only thirty-five known bristlebirds survive there now; fifteen years ago there were four times that many.

The birds are vulnerable on two fronts. First, their habitat has been hammered by human development. Second, their nesting habits put them at risk from feral cats and foxes. The birds build a domed nest at or just above the ground – right at cat and fox nose and eye level – and generally only lay eggs once a year, producing two eggs each time. It's the same old story: a native animal who has evolved ways to deal with native predators but is completely defenceless against the introduced ones. It's easy to see how the population decline has happened.

The call about the bristlebirds came through from the NSW Office of Environment and Heritage. As with many first-time conservation-dog projects, the idea was to test the viability using one of my existing dogs; if the test was successful I would then train a dedicated dog to work permanently in the area. Dogs were being considered because the birds were scattered in unknown spots in dense, hilly rainforest. Even the most experienced ranger could be standing a metre away from a bird and never know it. In this case the idea wasn't to hunt the predators; instead the dog's job would be to alert rangers to the presence of the bird without approaching or making contact. That would enable them to gather the eggs and chicks for a captive breeding-and-release program and to fend off the lantana, bitou bush and other invasive weeds that threaten to overrun the birds' nesting areas.

My challenge was that there was only a handful of the birds in captivity, and they were so precious that an untrained dog was not allowed near them. But how to train the dog without this access? What the rangers *could* supply, for odour, were droppings, some old nesting materials and any feathers that were shed by the birds in captivity. They had these supplies delivered to me and I started to train Bolt, who was already very good at finding quail. When he was ready we arranged a test at a wildlife sanctuary in Queensland. The bristlebirds were in large room-sized enclosures. One of the keepers would go in and scatter mealworms to draw them close to the wire. With Bolt on a long line outside the enclosure, I was able to demonstrate that he could alert us to the target bird and come within a metre-and-a-half without stressing the creature.

The project got the go-ahead, which meant I needed a new dog to train, one who could remain there. With perfect timing I received a call from Mark, the breeder of two other dogs who had both shown themselves to be excellent at conservation work – Sam, who'd gone to Phillip Island, and Tommy, whom I'd kept as my own dog and used for jobs including fox, rabbit and feral-cat detection. Mark knew about working dogs, having trained them to detect explosives for the British Navy. He also knew just the qualities I look for. He was calling because he had a young dog, the sister of Tommy and Sam, who had been returned to him. 'The owners said they can't handle her,' he told me. 'She's very disobedient. Very naughty. Does things like digs up the garden.' Yep, my type of dog. 'I'll be there in twenty minutes,' I said. Her name was Penny and she turned out to be just as quick at learning tasks as her brothers. That certainly was one talented litter of conservation dogs.

I trained her using droppings and feathers, as I had with Bolt, then we went up north. Though I was working for the NSW Office of Environment and Heritages, Currumbin Wildlife Sanctuary is actually in Queensland; authorities in the two states were cooperating closely. I set to work with three keepers from the sanctuary and three rangers from the Border Ranges National Park, all being trained as potential handlers. Before we headed off into the bush we got Penny used to the proximity of live birds using pigeons from Currumbin – not display birds but ones we'd caught in the sanctuary's kangaroo paddock, where they came by the hundreds to eat the roos' food.

When I was sure Penny would alert us from a short distance away and then stop in position, we headed into the national park. One of the rangers, Dave Charley, has dedicated himself to protecting this wonderful part of the world. He's incredibly knowledgeable about all its flora and fauna and is a real expert on the Eastern bristlebird. He was taking us to the locations within the park where, from long observation, he thought the birds would be found, though for all we knew we'd be out there every day for a week before we encountered one. In fact, it was only two days. We were passing across a slope with particularly heavy cover when Penny stopped dead and whoosh, up flew a bristlebird two metres in front of her. Dave marked the spot using GPS. It wasn't nesting time yet, but the birds stick closely to a small area, and when the time came, this was where the eggs would be.

It was already a good day, but then a few hours later we reached an area where Dave suspected there might be a bristlebird, although he hadn't been able to confirm it. Penny started checking around, and in hardly any time at all stopped and went into her alert posture. I said to Dave, 'I think there's a bird over there. Probably at 15 metres.' Obligingly, the bird then made its call. Dave said, 'I've been looking for that bird for years and your dog found it in less than five minutes!'

Having well and truly proved her worth, Penny stayed in the Border Ranges area to help save the bristlebird. We also expanded her repertoire to koalas and emus, so she's now working to protect them as well.

BRISTLEBIRDS, CHEETAHS AND RABBITS, OH MY

* * *

New challenges continued to arise. Through a friend who was involved in the Buddhist community, I was invited to go to Nepal, where I gave the army some help with their protection dogs and got to see the incredible Himalayas up close and personal.

Next I got a call from a highly experienced dog trainer called Jill McCartney, who had impressed me with her work with fire-ant detection dogs in Queensland. Jill called because she could see an opening for drug-detection dogs in mining camps. The camps draw fly-in fly-out workers many thousands of miles from home. Most of them wouldn't dream of risking their jobs and reputations by bringing drugs into the camps, but others succumb to temptation. In an environment where lives depend on having everyone operating at the top of their game, drug-affected workers are a huge concern. Bringing dogs in to check the accommodation and work sites can be an effective way of dealing with the problem.

I had just the dog for Jill. I'd got Pippa as a two-year-old and she was so withdrawn that Vicki was clearly puzzled by my choice. But I'd seen the little springer spaniel out in the field, finding rabbits on the farm where she was bred, and I knew she was a cracker. I'd also learned that springers, especially females, get very quiet, almost sullen, for about a week in a new environment. I was confident that when she had settled into my place she would come good, and she did – in fact she thrived on the training.

Within five days of starting work intensively one-on-one with me she had gone from a promising dog to a very good one, and by the end of the week she was an excellent detection dog who was so devoted to me she'd have jumped off a cliff if I'd asked her to. Following Jill's call I began training Pippa using what are called pseudo-narcotics – specially produced scent essences of methamphetamine, cocaine, heroin, ecstasy and cannabis.

When she was ready I took her over to Mount Tom Price in Western Australia, where we met up with Jill and arranged to put Pippa to the test of a real-world find. Jill knew a young bloke who lived in a shared house in the area and we asked him to help us. As I'd demonstrated during the quarantine-dog training, it's all too easy for the handler to inadvertently influence the dog. If you're doing a search and you know where the target is, all you have to do is remain in a particular room fractionally too long, or look once too often at the part of the room where the target is hidden. You probably wouldn't even realise you were doing it, but the dog, that master of body language, would pick up the signals. To eliminate the possibility of this we gave a tiny ziplock bag containing pseudo-heroin essence to Jill's friend and had him hide it somewhere in the house. We urged him to try to think like a drug dealer and put it in the trickiest place possible.

We came back the next day armed with the spare key he had given us, and with Pippa. She was in great form, going through that place on a mission. She checked nearly every room with no results, then we got to the laundry and she stopped dead at the doorway, indicating a find. We looked and couldn't see anything, but there was a strip of carpet on one side of the doorway so we figured it must be under there. We eased the carpet up. Nothing. But Pippa was insistent. She would not move from the doorway, sitting right beside the little metal stop that's there to prevent the door from hitting the wall. We pulled up a bit more of the carpet, but still nothing. In the end we figured the young bloke must have accidentally spilled a drop on the carpet and that was what she was reacting to. We took Pippa through the rest of the house again with the same result.

Well and truly stumped by now, we rang our helper and asked where he'd hidden the pseudo-heroin. It turned out that, in a brilliantly devious move, he had unscrewed the doorstop from the floor and hidden the bag inside it! Pippa was spot on; all we'd needed to do was trust her.

Jill trained her dog Voodoo for drug-detection work too, and in due course we got permission to go out to one of the state's big mines to get Pippa and Voodoo accustomed to the noise and dust and machinery. This was still part of the dogs' training; we were guests on the site, not yet doing actual drug detection. Judging from the behaviour of some of the workers, we'd have been successful if we had been. People who didn't know we were going to be on site until they saw us walk in would suddenly excuse themselves and disappear to the toilets or their sleeping quarters. I was reminded of being at the airport, where often we didn't even need the dogs to know something was amiss; the pale faces, sweaty brows and nervous behaviour of passengers waiting in line were dead giveaways.

Those nervy passengers and miners could have learned something from the elderly lady I encountered at one of my service-club talks. Among the things for which I'd trained Bobby was drug detection. It wasn't his specialty, but he did a few little jobs here and there. When I went to do these talks I would often take him with me. I'd arrive early and hide a little synthetic narcotic somewhere in the room with Bobby absent and before everyone else came. Partway through the talk I'd tell the audience about what I'd hidden and send Bobby to find it. On this particular day I'd taped it under a chair in one corner of the room.

It came to the part of proceedings when Bobby had to swing into action. Off he went, around the chairs and tables, checking. Then he stopped and made a beeline for the opposite side of the room from where the target was hidden. He pulled up in front of a little old lady who looked to be in her seventies and, boom, indicated the knitting bag she had sitting on the floor.

I looked at her and she looked at me. I thought, 'Well, Steven, this is a lovely predicament you've got yourself into. What do I do here?' Looking at Bobby, I knew for a fact that there was something in there. If I'd had to guess I'd have said marijuana with which she 'self-medicated'. Somehow I needed to find a smooth way out of this sticky spot while still rewarding Bobby, who had, after all, done what he was trained to do.

I had a flash of inspiration and said to the lady, 'You've probably got a sandwich or some other food in there, haven't you?'

Fortunately she kept her cool and caught on, saying, 'Ah, yes, I might. Yes, yes, I think I do.'

I said to the rest of the audience, 'Oh, he's always hungry, this dog', and took him away from the bag, putting up with jokes about how he'd clearly be no good at the airport. 'If only you knew,' I thought.

The lady discreetly waited to be last out the door at the end of the talk in order to say a quiet but heartfelt 'Thank you' as she went past.

There was a very different response from the dealer at the centre of a drug bust I witnessed while in Los Angeles to give a seminar for the Los Angeles Police Department. As arranged, I was picked up at the airport by a member of the Narcotics Division. Although he was a dog handler he did much of his work undercover. I'll call him Pete. He arrived in an unmarked van with his black labrador in the back. No sooner had we started to drive away than we were pulled up by a uniformed officer from the airport-protection unit. His in-car system, routinely checking the licence plates of nearby vehicles, had thrown up an alert because the van's plates showed up as not being registered in any jurisdiction. For the cop who pulled us over this signalled seriously bad intent, and he wasn't happy when he approached the driver's window.

Pete explained he was an undercover officer on the job and said, 'I'm going to reach very slowly into my jacket pocket and get my ID.' The other cop warily nodded but pulled his gun and pointed it right at Pete's head. The air was vibrating with tension. Sitting three feet away from that gun barrel was like finding myself in a movie, and not in a good way. Finally satisfied the ID was legit, the cop waved us on our way. 'Welcome to LA,' my cool-headed new mate said as we drove off.

The idea had been to deliver me to the hotel, but on the way a call came through: officer and dog were needed on a job that was unfolding nearby. I assumed Pete would drop me on the nearest corner and ask me to get a cab. To my surprise he asked if I'd mind coming along. Mind? Are you kidding? It was an opportunity to go behind the scenes that I'm pretty sure a civilian would never get in Australia.

We pulled into the address given, to see a guy being cuffed at gunpoint. It turned out he lived with his girlfriend and her fourteen-year-old sister. The girlfriend had gone out and come back to find him putting the hard word on the young girl, at which point she'd blown up, called the cops and dobbed him in as a dealer. He was still mouthing off and being read his rights as we went inside the place – I'd offered to stay in the car but Pete had said, 'No, come in and see what we do.'

The labrador was barely through the door before he started alerting us – scales here, one drug stash there, another on the other side of the room, then another. Cocaine, heroin, cannabis: this bloke had it all. There was a record player with a clear hard plastic lid that came down over the turntable, and when all the stashes had been located the dog started alerting us to that. Pete couldn't spot any drugs in the player so he asked what I thought was going on. Crouching down, I could see the lid was lightly scored: it had been used to cut up lines of cocaine. Even though the lines themselves were long gone, the tiny traces that remained were enough for the dog to find.

Pete logged it all quickly and efficiently, and by the time we got back in the van to head to my accommodation I had been in LA less than two hours. City arrivals don't get much more memorable than that one.

The expertise I'd built up in my AQIS days saw me invited to speak about detection dogs at a conference in Dresden, Germany, on the topic of wildlife smuggling. That in turn led, in a roundabout way, to my doing conservation work in Africa, and to an unusual encounter back home between Vicki and a hapless courier.

During the conference I was approached by Brigit Braun, a World Wildlife Fund (WWF) project officer, who asked if dogs could be trained to detect illegal timbers. She explained that rare and protected trees in South America and Asia were being chopped down and their exotic timbers smuggled out hidden in between other, legitimate timbers. I agreed to do a feasibility study, which proved successful – yes, I could train a dog to identify specific timbers. (A couple of years later I did something even more difficult and trained a spaniel called Missy to find a noxious, invasive plant called hawkweed, which is damaging the native flora of Victoria's High Country. Trained volunteers can comb the ground for hours and still not spot it, yet Missy could find it in minutes. If there's a limit to the conservation work dogs can do I have yet to find it.)

My report on the timbers test duly went off, and while nothing came of it immediately, Brigit emailed me to say she knew of a cheetah sanctuary in Namibia that was in need of a dog trainer. Well, she had me at 'cheetah'.

I made contact with the Cheetah Conservation Fund (CCF), run by the remarkable Dr Laurie Marker, and learned that while they had a couple of dogs who had been trained to find cheetah scat, the trainers had moved on and the dogs' performance was slipping. After finding out more about the CCF's work, I volunteered my services free of charge (they supplied the airfares and accommodation). I first flew to Johannesburg, a modern, cosmopolitan city, and from there to the Namibian capital, Windhoek, which was quite a culture shock. Its streets are a fascinating mix of fast-food joints and businessmen in suits next to traditional tribal Africans wearing no clothes at all. All set against a landscape that reminded me of central Australia.

The CCF centre, about three hours' drive north of the city, includes both a research facility and a sanctuary for orphaned and injured animals. Unlike a lot of other animals killed in Africa, cheetahs aren't generally hunted as such; they're shot by the poor farmers of the area, whose livestock they kill. The CCF was set up in response to a crisis in the 1980s, when almost 10,000 cheetahs — about half of the existing population — were killed off this way.

Dogs are part of the solution in two ways. First, the CCF provides farmers with guard dogs — Anatolian shepherds and Kangals — whose presence scares off the cheetahs: a simple but effective solution. Second, there are the scat-detection dogs.

Cheetahs in the sanctuary are brought back to health or raised to an age when they can fend for themselves, then released back into the wild. First they are fitted with GPS-enabled collars so their movements can be tracked. This allows the CCF team to check the health of individuals and make sure they're not moving into farming areas, and also to collect overall population data. But the collars tend to come off eventually, or their batteries die. Scat offers another way to gather the necessary information; it can be DNA-analysed to show where the cheetahs have been and how successfully they are surviving.

The two dogs the CCF was using for scat detection were a border collie cross and one of the Anatolian shepherds. The shepherds are great for guarding livestock, but far from the best choice for a detection dog. During my three weeks or so there I trained them back up as best I could, but I also told Laurie that I would return and bring with me two specially trained springer spaniels and donate them to the CCF.

I had many wonderful experiences at the sanctuary. My bedroom window was just two metres away from a spot at the cheetah enclosure fence where they would gather, allowing me to gaze at them as long as I liked. I got to help raise a baby cheetah, giving it bottle feeds. And I saw the very special moment when three cheetahs who had been brought in as tiny orphan cubs were released into the wild. There was the odd tear around the sanctuary that day, but two days later there was wild whooping and cheering and group hugs because the cheetahs had made their first kill and were feeding on it together: they had the skills needed to survive on their own.

Back home in Australia I found two spaniels who would do nicely for the CCF. The next task was locating cheetah scat. Once again the fantastic Taronga Conservation Society offered to help. The zoo in Sydney has a sister institution at Dubbo, New South Wales, called the Western Plains Zoo, which is home to many African animals. They had a number of cheetahs and offered to supply whatever I needed. I asked them to make me up a 'fruit salad' of the animals' poo, as well as sending individual samples. We arranged that they would send me a fresh batch each fortnight.

Like feral-cat droppings, cheetah scat smells indescribably bad. We're often getting odd bits of equipment and unusual supplies delivered to our place, but the day the first cheetah samples arrived, the courier who came to our door looked distinctly uncomfortable. As Vicki was signing for the box, he seemed like he couldn't quite decide between making the quickest getaway possible and saying something to warn her.

He settled on the latter, saying as he handed it over, 'Look, I'm not sure what's in there but I think someone doesn't like you. I think it's something dead.'

She checked the address and said, 'Oh no, it's fine, it's just cheetah poo.' He couldn't come up with a response to that, so she said, 'Don't worry, we'll ask them to package it up a bit tighter next time.' Poor bloke – he's probably still trying to convince his mates at the pub that he wasn't hallucinating!

The dogs trained up beautifully, but in the end I couldn't take them to Namibia myself as I had planned. Another opportunity had arisen, and this was one I couldn't say no to. It was the most ambitious pest-eradication project ever undertaken anywhere in the world.

I didn't know much about Macquarie Island when I got the first call, in July 2008, asking if I'd potentially like to be part of a government-run program to take the island back to its pristine condition. I was intrigued, and the information kit I received soon afterwards cemented my interest. As I learned, Macquarie is a unique place, a long, thin strip 1500 kilometres south-east of Hobart – in other words, halfway to Antarctica. It is, in fact, a sub-Antarctic landscape, one of the few points of land in that part of the planet where native birds and other wildlife can breed. It's also the only island on the entire planet made wholly of rocks from the earth's mantle, (the hot, semi-solid bit above the earth's core) – something that gets geologists pretty excited.

In today's modern ships it's a rugged three-day trip to get there. I can't even imagine what the journey must have been like for the first people known to have set foot on the island, the seal hunters on the sailing ship *Perseverance* who discovered it in

1810. Within a mere twenty years from 1790 to 1810, sealers had managed to pretty much wipe out the seal population further north in Bass Strait. The crew of *Perseverance* was hoping to find new hunting grounds and amazingly the ship lucked upon Macquarie Island. It might not sound like you'd need luck to spot a landmass 34 kilometres long and three to five kilometres wide — that is, after all, a fifth of the size of the main island of Tasmania — but see it on a map and you'll understand how tiny and remote a speck it is in the vast harshness of the Southern Ocean.

It was that isolation that prevented the island from becoming completely ruined, even though for the next century it was home to an industry that caught fur seals for their skins and elephant seals to extract oil from them. It was also a stop-off for Antarctic explorers. When they'd killed off the vast majority of the seals, the sealers moved on to boiling down penguins for oil. They brought cats with them deliberately, and rats and mice inadvertently, and introduced rabbits to use as food.

No surprise: the cats went feral and the rabbits and rodents multiplied, so even though the island was declared a wildlife sanctuary in 1933 the native flora and fauna were fighting for survival. By 1979 the rabbit population was estimated to be around 150,000. Myxomatosis was introduced, and over the next decade rabbit numbers dropped by 90 per cent. Then in 1985 a feral-cat eradication program commenced.

In 1997 the island got World Heritage listing — a big-deal recognition of how special a place it is. There were two grounds for this honour: first, its geological uniqueness, and second, in the words of UNESCO, which makes the listings, because 'its remote and windswept landscape of steep escarpments, lakes, and dramatic changes in vegetation provides an outstanding spectacle of wild, natural beauty complemented by vast congregations of wildlife including penguins and seals'.

With the rabbit population dropping and the feral-cat program succeeding, things were looking good for all that wildlife. In the summer of 2000 the last feral cat was eliminated. Great, right? There was just one problem: with the feral cats gone the rabbits had free rein. They thrived, breeding like ... well, you know. Myxomatosis always becomes less effective over time, as the rabbit population builds up resistance and the virus itself mutates into less lethal strains, so that wasn't the answer. By 2008, when I first heard about the problem, rabbit numbers were up past the 130,000 mark again.

The rabbits' favourite food – the island's grasses and what are called 'mega-herbs' – aren't just there to give a nice green background to photos of the place. They're a really important part of the ecosystem. Don't forget, this bit of rock is thrashed by some of the strongest winds and wildest weather on the planet. Those plants cover the rocks in a way that prevents them from eroding; they keep the giant hills in one piece; they give seabirds somewhere to build their burrows; and they serve as a home to all the invertebrate creatures like spiders and beetles who will never be pin-ups but are necessary to keep the whole system in check.

Rabbits weren't around when these plants were evolving so the plants didn't build up any defences against the animals. They're really easy pickings and the rabbits are very efficient at finding and eating tiny seedlings, meaning the native shrubs just can't regenerate. By 2008, the effect was simply devastating. Not only had the rabbits changed huge swathes of what should have been diverse wilderness to what one scientist called 'grazing lawns', but their relentless feeding was also a big factor in a couple of major landslips that had happened a couple of years earlier, one of which had wiped out a whole colony of penguins.

Keith Springer was a bloke I would come to know well. A passionate conservationist, he had led the feral-cat eradication program in 2000 and five years later he came back to Macquarie Island as a Tasmanian Parks and Wildlife Service (PWS) ranger. When he left in 2000, rabbit numbers were low and the plant life was doing a good job of getting back into a healthy state. But when he returned he saw a huge change in the landscape. There were bare slopes right around the island and the ground was riddled with burrows. The rabbits were running rife. They had no predators and they were completely unafraid; they were everywhere you looked. The rangers shot 5000 of them in 2005, but Keith told me you couldn't even tell the difference.

It was time for a different approach, so the Tasmanian and Federal Governments got together to fund the new Macquarie Island Pest Eradication Project. Keith was put in charge of implementing a meticulously thought-out plan that involved killing off most of the rabbits and rats using baits dropped across the island from helicopters, then bringing in detection dogs to find the survivors so they too could be eliminated. That was where I came into things. Attempting something on this scale was a first, the challenge of all challenges, and I do love a challenge. But even more than that, I wanted to be part of helping to save this remote little gem of a place.

Once I told them I was interested the project team set up an interview. They were upfront in letting me know they were interviewing the most experienced dog trainers throughout

Australia and New Zealand; those who they felt understood what they were trying to achieve and had the expertise required would be invited to submit a tender.

A little while later I got my invitation. The admin necessary for any job where you'll be paid from public money is rigorous, and rightly so. But this tender was the most difficult I've ever done. Vicki and I worked on it together and it took us six full days.

The project would entail providing seven dogs to detect rabbit scat, tracks and burrows. They would need to be ready to go in two years' time. They could not under any circumstances touch the rabbits, let alone scare or have any contact with any of the native wildlife. They could not damage plant life or do anything else to harm the environment on the island. There would be a painstaking interim assessment partway through the training and then, if the dogs passed this, there would be a final exhaustive assessment before they were certified and permitted to go to work.

We'd get a small initial payment, but essentially we had to cover two years' worth of expenses. If a dog failed the interim test for any reason, including illness on the day, bad luck. If for some catastrophic reason every dog I trained failed, that would be a year's worth of work down the drain. By the time the dogs had completed the two-year training period, they would each be worth $30,000 in terms of the work and care that had gone into them, but if they failed the final assessment, that was that, no payment. So I couldn't train just seven dogs, I had to have back-ups.

And there was one more complication. There is no permanent settlement on Macquarie Island. The Tasmanian Government's

PWS manages the place as a nature reserve but, like the staff at the Australian Antarctic Division (AAD) research station, the PWS officers do limited stints on the island, whose remoteness makes it a hardship posting. So while dogs who did pass certification would be expected to stay down there for four to five years, the PWS officers who would serve as their handlers would only stay for a year, meaning new handlers would need to be trained every twelve months.

I understood the need for the paperwork but that didn't mean I enjoyed doing it. Thank goodness for Vicki's patience! It was all worth it: three trainers were chosen but one pulled out, meaning that two of us would do the job, me from Australia and Guus Knopers from New Zealand. Guus would deliver five dogs, which, with my seven, made for a total of twelve. His would be labradors and I would use springer spaniels, who had already proved what great conservation dogs they could be. Like me, Guus had lots of experience in the field, in his case training dogs to find stoats, weasels and ferrets, along with rabbits.

I went to New Zealand and we sat down together to work out our approach. The signals we used with all the dogs had to be uniform, because they would all be operating in the same place. We couldn't confuse them by having different cues from each trainer for an identical task. That meant not just agreeing on the specifics of each whistle command (how many times you blow, and for how long, to signal 'stop', 'turn left', 'turn right', 'come'), but even what frequency of whistle to use (an Acme 210½, in this case). I hadn't met Guus before, but we worked really well together from the outset and became great friends over the course of the project.

When I arrived back in Sydney my first task was to find enough suitable dogs. I decided I would need to train twenty. Because I wanted springers and needed them in such numbers, they had to come from trusted breeders rather than animal pounds. That didn't just mean puppies, though. Good breeders will always want to rehome a dog they have sold to someone if the person doesn't feel they can look after it any more.

Ash was in that category. Puppies are tiny bundles of limitless promise. Ash was something else again.

He was two when I met him and he seemed the exact opposite of the kind of dog I usually look for. He was timid and quiet; whatever drive he had was well hidden. But I had known his father and grandfather; I'd seen them both in action in my role as a judge at Field Trials. They were impressive and I had faith that this little bloke would be too, once he came out of his shell. I suspected he was unhappy because he had not been given what his breed really needs, just as we humans do: a purpose in life. But taking him was definitely a gamble, and everyone around me thought I was on the losing side.

Vicki shook her head when she saw him and asked if I was sure. The trainers who worked for us at the boarding kennels were far less diplomatic. They spent a few minutes with him then said to me, 'You'll never get this dog up, he's useless. Why did you pick him?' But I could sense the spark in him, and I trusted my instinct that the problem was environmental and could therefore be fixed. I gave him time and positive reinforcement and worked with him patiently, and my faith was rewarded. He turned out to be a real cracker. Not a superstar, but a strong, reliable dog who did his job very, very well.

One of the biggest challenges I had was getting the dogs trained for an environment that I couldn't replicate. I had no wave-tossed ship, no penguins, no elephant seals, no biting wind, no snow. The mountain country of New South Wales and Victoria is far from sub-Antarctic, but it's cold and snowy, so when winter arrived I could at least take the dogs there to give them a taste of what was to come.

The wildlife was a bigger challenge, and it was crucial to get it right. The use of dogs on Macquarie Island was extremely contentious in some quarters. There were people who were sure that they would run wild, killing off native creatures – even though it was a requirement for all the dogs to wear muzzles while working on the island for at least the first month, until they had proved themselves. I knew perfectly well that I could train the dogs properly so no harm would come to any wildlife, but the proof would be in the pudding.

Penguins were the focus of most of the negative talk. On the island, the dogs would have to move around and ignore huge colonies of them. I didn't have any of them available, so I had to be creative. It turned out that the solution was right in my own backyard. Our Mount Colah property was rural acreage and we kept chooks – a lot of chooks. In fact, we had more than a hundred. They would serve as my penguin substitutes. I began getting the dogs used to being amongst the birds. I walked them through the chickens and then fed them in the birds' midst. It worked a treat and they learned to completely ignore the birds, moving through clumps of them without bothering or harming them in any way.

Next came the challenge of big animals. Elephant seals can look after themselves, so the worry there wasn't that the dogs might harm them, more that they might disturb or unsettle them. Again, I knew this wouldn't happen but I did need to get the dogs used to very large animals they didn't encounter in day-to-day life. What animals were accessible who were the right size, mostly placid but potentially dangerous to a dog if they got spooked? Cows, that's what. I found some well-stocked local paddocks and got the owners' permission to regularly take the dogs there and walk them around to get them comfortable around such big creatures.

Using peak training they were soon all performing excellently. Guus and I kept in regular contact and his training was also coming along well. In April 2009 it was time for the interim testing. I'd put the work in and so had the dogs, and I knew they were all up to the job, but it was still nerve-racking because this was such a stringent, exhaustive (and exhausting!) testing process – running for three full days.

The testing was conducted by John Cheyne, a New Zealand dog-training expert with no other involvement in the project, employed as a neutral examiner. Because the days would be long and there was no accommodation within easy reach, John stayed over with us at Mount Colah. We had a very pleasant dinner the night he arrived, but we both knew the rules. The next morning before we started he said, 'Now, Steve, you're a nice fellow but once we get out there all bets are off.' I understood completely. In his examiner role he was hard but fair, and that was just how things needed to be.

He said, 'I will test your dogs one by one. I don't want to know their names, they're not relevant. Each must respond purely to the agreed whistle commands. They must come on command, stop on command, and move in the direction indicated by the whistle. I won't touch them or speak to them.'

That was just the first test. Then John produced fourteen numbered sticks. Two hours earlier each one had been dragged over a dead animal – a rat, a mouse, a type of bird etc. Four of the sticks had been dragged over a dead rabbit. The sticks were laid out in a row and the dogs were brought out one by one to run up and down the row and indicate the four rabbit scents. Over the course of the three days each dog had to perform this task seven times, with different sets of sticks. This being the interim validation, each dog was allowed one mistake during the entire testing period. At full validation no mistakes would be tolerated.

The performance of my twenty potential dogs in the test was a relief and a vindication. I kept the seven who had performed the best, passing with flying colours. The others I rehomed with people who were glad to have them. Guus's five dogs also passed, and in October 2009 it was time for a test voyage to Macquarie Island.

The idea was that I would go and take two of the dogs and prove, in situ, that they could work without disturbing the penguins or anything else. All seven dogs were terrific, but I chose Ash and Gus because I thought the location training would benefit them both the most, especially Ash. In the end the experience would lift him to a new level.

12

MIRACLE ON MACCA: ADVENTURES AT THE WORLD'S END

I firmly believe that our connection with nature is an essential part of our humanity — we need to feel connected to the plants and animals with which we share this planet.

Every time I head off with the dogs on a new job I'm interested to find out what fresh sights I'll see and what I'll learn, but this was on a different scale from anything I'd ever done before. The dogs and I flew to Hobart, where I was kitted out by the AAD. (I'd brought special coats with me for the dogs.) As you'd expect, the high-tech gear was fantastic, from the thermals to the beanies, boots and backpacks. It really brought home the reality of what an unforgiving latitude we were heading for.

We were being taken to the island on the AAD's bright-red supply-and-research flagship *Aurora Australis*. Just under

95 metres long, it can carry 116 passengers plus three helicopters, which take off from the helipad on deck, and it can break through ice if needed. It's no cruise liner, though in dock in Hobart it looked reasonably sized. But it didn't take too many hours of sailing away from Tasmania before the ship started to seem a lot smaller in the midst of all that ocean.

We got some rough seas going down but it wasn't too bad. There was at least one point on each of the three days we spent sailing south when I could train the dogs on deck – always on a long line, of course. No off-leash here; I didn't want them to go overboard.

Finally the island appeared on the horizon. I was just as keen to set foot on it as the dogs were, but down there the weather rules all decisions and conditions were against us. While the ship does carry helicopters, they're very small craft, not designed for transporting the number we needed to get ashore – as well as me and my dogs there was Keith Springer and other members of his PWS team. We needed to be taken in on amphibious vehicles, but the whole first day the sea was just too rough for that.

Though we'd come a long way, there was no guarantee we'd be able to land at all. And in four days' time the ship had to depart for scheduled work elsewhere. The second day dawned with the same unpromising weather, so when things eased up a little the decision was quickly taken: 'Everyone move, we're going now!' The dogs went into the crates, the humans quickly got into life-jackets, we filed into the open-topped craft under leaden skies and we were away.

I'd read all the reports, I'd seen photos and watched videos, but nothing prepared me for the reality of Macquarie Island. It was sheer, wild magnificence. The rocky shore gives way to hills that lead up to huge escarpments running right around the island. The encircle a large central plateau dotted by freshwater lakes and streams that feed waterfalls crashing down over the cliffs. Even in cold, driving rain it was a place of extraordinary beauty.

I let Gus out of his crate. It was the first time he'd put feet on solid land in four days. He was off-leash and about to go for a wee, but he only made it two metres before he stopped, put his nose to a grass tussock and, boom, flushed out a rabbit. The rabbit took off and he went to follow, but I whistled the stop signal and he pulled straight up. That suitably impressed the PWS staff who were assessing us: they saw that a) Gus could find rabbits and b) he was under complete control.

Gus was a good detection dog, but he hadn't needed much skill to flush out a rabbit so quickly: they were absolutely everywhere. You could stand on any spot and look around, and you'd see bare soil with burrows every metre or so and rabbits by the hundreds just hopping about. Other than the tussocks, the vegetation that did exist was stripped almost to the ground and looked scarcely alive — except for one small area, just a few metres square, that caught my eye. It looked like someone had planted a vegie patch out here at the end of the world. As Keith explained, it was the other way round. What I was looking at was the way things would be on the island if the rabbits weren't here. It was a tiny section of land surrounded by a rabbit-proof enclosure in which the native flora was thriving: the tall Macquarie Island cabbage made it look like a lush vegie patch. The contrast with the land around that one little fenced-off section was stark.

There was a lot of work to be done in removing these pests, but that wasn't going to be happening on this trip. Only after the mass extermination using poisoned bait, when a mere handful of rabbits remained, would the hunting begin.

Next came the big test for the dogs in terms of convincing the sceptics once and for all that they would not harm native wildlife. We had to walk right through the middle of a colony of about 5000 penguins – both dogs together, by my side, off-leash. Any flicker, any growl would have been enough for the whole idea to be abandoned, but the dogs were perfect. Despite the intense new sensations all around them (which included the unbelievable stink produced by the colony – penguins look great but the smell of their poo is diabolical!), they did exactly what they'd been trained to do. They walked calmly at heel, then I told them to sit and stay and they did. They kept their eyes on me, ignoring the penguins. When I told them to come, they did. They were faultless, just as unfazed by these weird new birds as if they were still among the chickens back home.

Having performed so beautifully, the dogs got to have a bit of a stretch and a run. Keith's assistant Jeff Woodhouse and I put on our backpacks and set out with them. Gus, whose eventful day had only just begun, was about 10 metres ahead of me when he jumped up on a mound to get a better look around. The ground moved beneath him. Poor old Gus – it wasn't a mound of earth at all, although it looked exactly like one. It was the back of a huge male elephant seal! The seal, who had just been lying there minding his own business until he got the mother of all wake-up calls, rose up with a startled bellow. Gus jumped about three metres into the air and I did the same. He raced back over to my side for reassurance and there were a few deep breaths all round before we were ready to continue on our way.

I stay in pretty good shape — I need to for my job — but Jeff was twenty years younger than I was, a New Zealander who sprang up those steep slopes like a bloody mountain goat. We'd set off to climb one peak, then walk along a connecting ridge to another that we could just about see through the rain. Ash was with Jeff and the two of them were soon out of sight. Gus had been exploring ahead, always where I could see him — he'd circle back to me or wait till I caught up — but then suddenly he disappeared. One minute he was there and the next minute he was gone. I whistled for him. No response. I called his name, but still nothing. I pushed through the tussocks to where I'd last seen him — and there he was, trapped in a seal wallow, desperately fighting to keep himself from going under but losing the battle, without even enough energy to bark.

If you've never encountered a seal wallow, half your luck. They are formed when elephant seals lie packed together in mud during their moulting period. They can be 20 metres across and a couple of metres deep, as this one was. They are a disgusting, fetid mixture of seal faeces, shed fur, mud and the occasional dead seal, and have the consistency of thick custard. The great Australian Antarctic explorer Douglas Mawson described them as 'A hopeless place for a human being to fall into, one could not get out — a quick-mud — and the stench would be injurious.'

That's what Gus was trapped in and in the brief time it had taken me to reach him, no more than a minute or two, he had used almost all his strength struggling. When I spotted him he was going down for what was clearly the last time.

I threw myself down on my stomach, reached back with my left hand to grab a tussock, praying it would be strong enough, and stretched out to grab his collar with my right hand. I was leaning far over the muck, but I managed to get him, closing my fist around that collar with an iron grip, when suddenly my backpack shifted, tilting me so far forward that my face went into the wallow.

I pulled on that tussock with all my might, and with a huge surge of adrenaline yanked Gus up and out onto firm ground, then slithered back to safety myself. I had that disgusting mud in my mouth and all over my face and arm and chest. I checked that Gus was okay, then stood doubled over for a few moments, my heart racing, spitting out mud again and again. I stood up, and Gus and I set off again.

A few minutes later the light of Jeff's headlamp appeared through the rain up ahead. He'd come back to see if everything was all right. He took one look at me and said, 'What happened to you?'

'Long story,' I replied, still trying to get the taste out of my mouth.

The rest of the day was fortunately devoid of disasters, though I'd gained an even more intense appreciation of how unforgiving this environment was. It began to snow as we climbed. We reached the top of the second peak. The island's raised plateau was at our backs, and in front of us sheer cliffs fell down to the thrashing ocean. The wind howled. Thousands of miles away in one direction was South America, and thousands in the other was Africa. There was nothing else in between but this piece of rock. If something happened to you up here you were done for. There were medical facilities on the ship, but getting you there would require huge effort, with no guarantee of success. This was true, merciless, majestic, wild nature.

We made our way back down to the others and headed for our allocated shelters. Known as huts, these are actually converted water tanks. They're orange and look like alien spaceships from a 1950s sci-fi movie: egg-shaped, with oval windows. They sit a metre-and-a-half or so off the ground, cradled in tubular metal frames. You get into them via a ramp leading from the ground to an enclosed wooden platform that opens into the 'hut'. Each one has its own water tank and uses wind-generated power. It's not the Hilton, but it felt like pure luxury to me to be able to get into a hot shower at the end of that first day, although no matter how I scrubbed and scrubbed I couldn't get rid of the stink from the seal wallow. In fact, I was still catching the whiff of it weeks later.

The dogs passed every test that they were given, and two days later we got back onto the ship to go home. Gus and Ash were housed in one of the helicopter hangars at the rear of the ship. They were cosy in there and safe in their dog crates. To reach them you had to go outside the main cabin and along a kind of gangplank-style passageway for about 15 metres, then in through a door that led to the tool-bay area, which opened onto the hangar. I would go down to see them four times a day, taking them out for exercise on deck where possible or just letting them have a bit of a run around inside the hangar area and giving them their food and drink.

But then we hit what the ship's captain, Scott Laughlin, described as some very bad weather. On the Great Southern Ocean scale, 'very bad' is what most of us would call 'horrendous'. Twice the entire ship was underwater. It was made to withstand that kind of thing and Scott was extremely experienced, so, as hairy as it all felt, I knew we were in safe hands. Like all the other enclosed parts of the ship, the hangars were, of course, watertight, so the dogs were safe too. But they did need to be fed and watered. Even so-called anti-spill bowls weren't meant to deal with this kind of weather. Whatever water the bowls had in them would have been spilled as the little ship climbed the mountainous seas and fell back down again, over and over.

I'd seen to the dogs before the weather turned and I completely understood when the captain said, 'No-one's going out. It's too dangerous.' So I just sat tight. But twenty hours later, with the sea still raging, I went to him and said, 'Scotty, I've got those two dogs down there, I have to give them water and food. I have to get there.'

He said, 'Well, you're not going down, mate. Will they live?'

'Yes, they'll live,' I told him. 'They won't be dehydrated yet, but I can't just leave them with no water.'

'Sorry, but the risk is too great,' he said firmly.

On a ship the captain's word is law, so I went away and tried to be patient, hoping the storm would die down. Two hours later it was still just as bad, but I didn't have a choice – I had to take care of my animals.

I went back to him and said, 'Scotty, I've really got to go to them.'

He wasn't happy about it but he understood and said, 'All right, well, get into the gear and harnesses. The first mate will go with you and you'll have to hook yourselves up as you go.'

The ship has railings running right around the superstructure as well as on other connection points. We hooked ourselves to one another and then made our way to the deck door. We opened it into the gale and worked to keep our footing as we took turns hooking ourselves onto the railing. Every few metres there was a join where the railing was riveted on, and we had to unhook on one side of the join and hook back up on the other. Meanwhile, the waves were smashing over us so hard it was like being hit in the head with cricket bats, and the heaving deck was awash. After what felt like an hour we reached the door into the tool bay safely.

The dogs were coping with this whole experience extraordinarily well. They weren't distressed, but they were certainly pleased to see us. We let them out and they relieved themselves then had a good drink and feed and stretched their legs within the safety of the hangar. We stayed with them for about two hours, making sure they had plenty to drink and eat and cleaning up after them. Then it was time to put them back into their crates, where I knew they would be fine for a minimum of twelve hours. The prospect of leaving them there for that long certainly wasn't ideal, but there was no other choice until the weather changed.

We hooked ourselves up to one another and went back out. If anything, it was worse out there now. We inched along and made it almost all the way back when suddenly the first mate went down. His feet had been washed from under him. He was rolled over by the force of the wave, which smacked his head into the metal deck. I picked him up and managed to get us both inside the door and someone helped us get to the doctor. The doc took one look at us in our drenched wet-weather gear, blood pouring from my new friend's head, and said, 'What were you bastards doing out there?' I explained about the dogs while he stitched up the wound.

Needless to say, we learned a lot from that. It was the first time anyone had taken dogs on the ship, and now we knew that when we came back with the full contingent for the actual eradication they needed to be housed somewhere we could reach them safely no matter what the weather.

The program had started to get some publicity, and over the following months, back home in Sydney and as I travelled around Australia doing other work, people who were critical of the project made free with their opinions.

They fell into two main camps. From within Australia there was rubbishing of the likelihood of success. Plenty of self-appointed experts declared we had no chance, from talkback radio hosts to people who would come up to me at an event or even just at the local shops and say, 'You'll never get rid of the rabbits there. I've been trying to get 'em off my place for years. It's just a waste of government money.'

Then there were the people overseas who were worried we *would* succeed. These animal-welfare activists sent emails and even called to say things along the lines of, 'What you're doing with rabbits is disgraceful. They should all be desexed and left to live a free and wonderful life.' It was pointless trying to explain to them that rabbits weren't native to Australia like they were to America and Europe. Here they were feral pests that endangered the whole ecosystem. These people simply refused to hear it.

The plan had been that the baiting would take place in the middle of 2010 and the dogs, the handlers, Guus and I would return a few months later. Baits would be dropped over the entire island using special hoppers slung beneath helicopters that released the poisoned baits at a controlled rate. Computer mapping would be used to make sure the entire island was covered. Winter was chosen as the best time to do this, because while it meant dealing with much less favourable weather, its also brought several advantages. It was the time when the fewest native creatures were on the island: many of the birds, for instance, migrated to warmer climes; plus the rabbit (and rat) numbers were at their lowest, since breeding rates drop over winter. It was the season when the vegetation was also at its least abundant, meaning that the rabbits would have less other food and so would be more likely to eat the baits.

The bait drops began on 5 June that year, but weather conditions were so bad that the chopper pilots only got in five days' worth over the next three weeks, and only 10 per cent of the island was covered. The wildlife experts who had been part of drawing up the plans had expected that there would be a small number of bird casualties from the baiting, but the numbers were higher than expected. Eighty per cent of the island's bird species were not affected, but those who were included the southern giant petrel, which is an endangered species, and the northern giant petrel, which is a vulnerable species. While the recorded numbers of deaths for each (10 and 276 respectively) were not large in context, they were of enough concern for those involved to take a step back and see what could be done differently.

Giant petrels are scavengers, and they died as a result of feeding on dead rabbits and rats. Other birds, such as kelp gulls, died because they ate the baits directly. Two solutions were implemented. The first was to control the potential damage by collecting the carcasses of the poisoned animals so they couldn't be scavenged. The second was to try a different method to get rid of the majority of the rabbits. This was calicivirus, an infectious disease that was fatal to rabbits but would not harm birds who might scavenge them. It hadn't been used as a first step because evidence had suggested that the virus would not do well in such a cold, wet climate. But in February 2011 it was tried and it proved to be a great adapter to the environment, racing through the rabbit population and killing off between 80 and 90 per cent. Three months later baiting was recommenced, this time running as planned and with the safeguard of carcass collection afterwards. Now everything was set for the dogs to get to work, and they were well and truly ready.

Guus and I ran a ten-day training camp for the handlers and dogs in Hobart. This covered both theory and lots of hands-on practice. It was such an interesting exercise for us to match the dogs with the handlers best suited to them. It was even more important than usual to get it right, because they would be living together for the next twelve months. The handlers' mix of personality traits was intriguing. The nature of the job dictated that they be very independent people, yet it was vital that they could work in a team environment. They were a great bunch. We shared an understanding of the importance of the job at hand and worked hard to prepare for it.

In late July I set out again on the *Aurora Australis* for Macquarie Island, but this time I had one labrador and six springer spaniels with me, including Katie, a brilliant little female spaniel and one of the best dogs I've ever trained. She hunted rabbits like a demon but she was easy-going and affectionate. She loved a pat, and almost every afternoon after training in Sydney I would have a beer and sit in the sun with her and talk about the world and its problems. Surprisingly, she had an answer for every one of them.

Guus was also aboard with his five labradors, as were the six handlers who would stay and work with the dogs after we left (they would each run two dogs). It was much smoother sailing this time, fortunately. In fact, conditions were so good we were able to run the dogs on deck every day, taking them and the handlers through their paces in what was undoubtedly the first ever canine-obedience class to have been conducted on the Great Southern Ocean.

As with the previous visit, to get ashore the dogs had to be loaded into their crates, which were then enclosed in cargo nets and lowered by crane into the amphibious vehicles. The fact that the ship's crew were experts at this and that I'd seen it done before didn't make it any easier to watch – after all, one slip sideways and the crate would have been in the water, giving the dog inside no chance of survival. As the last one was safely settled on land, I let out the breath I hadn't realised I'd been holding.

We knew from aerial and ground surveys conducted by the rangers after the baiting that there was only a small number of rabbits left, but we didn't know how many. Why was it important to get rid of those last few? The answer lies in the rate at which rabbits can reproduce. As the CSIRO notes, rabbits can start breeding at five months old and if conditions are suitable a female can be pregnant with litter after litter for between six and eight months of the year, producing a total of thirty to forty young in twelve months. In theory, if none of the offspring died, a single breeding pair could produce 350,000 descendants in just five years. Of course, in the real world there will be some mortality, but still it's common for rabbit populations to increase eight or ten times in a breeding season. Even two rabbits were too many to leave on the island if they happened to be a fertile male and female.

Guus and I had three weeks in which to make sure all the training we had given both dogs and handlers was followed through on the island with solid work. Once we left, the handlers would stay there for a twelve-month stint, during which they would cover every square metre of that island. The dogs would wear GPS trackers on their collars so that this could be done on systematic grids; nothing was to be left to chance. When they caught a rabbit they wouldn't know if it was the last one or not — only time would tell.

The dogs had been trained to find rabbit urine, rabbit droppings, live rabbits and rabbit carcasses. While Guus and I were there, they found evidence of rabbits. When the dog indicated urine or fresh droppings the protocol was for the handler to radio it in. The rabbit would then be humanely killed, either by being shot; by having its burrow fumigated; or by being captured in what's called a soft-jaw trap (which prevents the animal from getting away but does not harm it), then cleanly shot.

The ethical standards were set very high, and quite rightly so. The pests who were killed must never suffer; kills had to be quick and clean, as humane as possible. When it came to the native wildlife the ethical standard to which everyone on the island had to adhere was to cause as little disruption as possible. This meant not interfering with any native creature — not even a gull who'd had a wing bitten off by a shark, or a seal who was dying. Nature had to take its course as if we weren't there: the whole purpose of the project was to undo the damage that had followed humans' arrival on the island. There was no taking home a pebble or even a leaf as a souvenir. Human waste was treated on site and dog waste was collected as part of the island's rubbish-collection program. We truly left nothing but footprints and took nothing but photographs.

The dogs were required not to come within 10 metres of the native wildlife – but of course the wildlife didn't know that. So we'd be kneeling down at the edge of a rabbit hole as one of the dogs checked it out to see if it was still being used and we'd turn around to find eight penguins behind us, peering over our shoulders to see what we were looking at. The dogs would just look at them as if to say 'Can't you see I'm busy here?' and go about their business.

Each night we all met up in the large common room, which was a mess hall and bar combined. These were truly great nights. The food was freshly cooked and delicious, much appreciated after a long day in the field. The company was excellent and the conversational wheels were greased by home-brewed beer, some of which was good and some of which wasn't, though after a few glasses the taste seemed to improve. Sometimes the walk back to the bunks was a little wild and woolly, but we never had to call out the dogs to find a lost soul.

At the end of the three weeks Guus and I said goodbye to the dogs we had worked so closely with for so long, and the handlers with whom they would now have the closest of bonds, and sailed away knowing we had done all we could to set them up for success.

It turned out that only thirteen rabbits had survived the double hit of calicivirus and bait, a far lower number than even the most optimistic projection. The last of these was gone by that November, just four months after the dogs arrived: an amazing result considering the difficulty of scouring those peaks on foot. For the handlers, month after month with no rabbits found was a great result, but it did make it tricky to keep up the dogs' motivation. We'd thought about this, of course, and there were frozen rabbit carcasses on the island that were judiciously employed as the months went by to drag across the ground as 'plants', as were tennis balls soaked with rabbit urine. The other challenge that was a direct consequence of success was the landscape itself. Not being ravaged by rabbits, the ground cover thickened, making getting around and finding any survivors even more demanding.

With the rabbits all gone, three New Zealand rodent-detection dogs were brought in during March 2013 to ensure that the rats and mice had also been eliminated by the baiting program, as seemed to have been the case. This was confirmed, and finally, in April 2014, the project was declared complete, with all its aims achieved. At last the island was free of the pests who had been harming it and its wildlife. Three years earlier it had been struggling under the demands of 150,000 rabbits and an untold number of rats and mice; thanks to the pest-eradication program it was once again pristine.

Now when visitors come they can rest assured that, thanks to the efforts of Tasmania's PWS and the AAD, their presence won't cause future problems. Like all cargo that comes to the island, the clothes and footwear of visitors are screened before they land to make sure they're not accidentally bringing in any pests or pathogens.

In all, the teams of dogs and handlers had walked a total of 92,000 kilometres, capping off an incredible effort from so many people – everybody from the electricians and plumbers who maintained the huts without which people couldn't survive on the island, to the crews of the AAD ships who provided transport, the helicopter pilots who did the baiting, the administration staff who organised the provisioning and all the other crucial logistics, and on and on. The steering committee that oversaw the project and fought for its integrity in the face of the scepticism was outstanding, as were Keith Springer and his deputy, Jeff. It was a great privilege to be part of the dedicated team that finished this world-first project more than one year early and $5 million under its $25.6-million budget.

I was there in Hobart on 7 April 2014 along with Keith and Guus and many of the other project participants to welcome the return of the final group of dogs and handlers on the ship *L'Astrolabe*. It was an atmosphere of jubilation. The scale of what we had collectively achieved was recognised by the state's governor, Peter Underwood, who held a reception for us all at Government House a few days later, and by the opening up of the lawns of Parliament House for the public to join the celebrations in an event named 'Miracle on Macca'.

The dogs all went on either to other important jobs or to well-earned rests. Tama, one of Guus's dogs, was the oldest of the crew, being about four when we set to work in 2014. He went to work in Hobart checking cargo bound for Macquarie Island before retiring to go and live with Dr Sally Bryant from the Tasmanian Land Conservancy. Keith Springer and his wife, Emma, took Hamish, one of the springer spaniels I'd trained (well, with Keith's surname it was always going to be a spaniel he took, not a labrador, wasn't it!). The dog still does some work here and there with Keith for the PWS.

Having survived elephant seals and their wallows and done a great job on Macquarie, Gus retired and is having a lovely time living in the much warmer climes of the NSW north coast with former AAD station leader Narelle Campbell. Brilliant Katie is still working, doing fox-scat detection to protect Tasmania's wildlife. My hope is that when she retires I'll be able to arrange for her to come back to me. I hope to continue the in-depth discussions we used to have back when I was training her.

In September 2015 the work of the dogs and their handlers was recognised via the huge honour of a special Australia Post stamp issue, 'The Dogs that Saved Macquarie Island'. There were four stamps, one of which showed Katie and handler Nancye Williams. Nancye expressed it perfectly when she described it as 'a lovely and worthy tribute' to what was achieved by those incredible dogs.

Yet even now there are still people who can't understand why saving Macca matters. Well, I'm lucky enough to have seen some spectacular places on this planet, from the Himalayas and the Grand Canyon to sub-Saharan Africa, but without question Macquarie Island is the best place I have ever been to. I firmly believe that our connection to nature is an essential part of our humanity. Think about it – why else would we have indoor plants? Why else would we have fish tanks? As humans we need to feel connected to the plants and animals with which we share this planet. If you're deprived of that connection something warps in the brain. Macquarie Island and places like it feed our souls, even if we only see them via pictures or videos, or check in via a webcam.

There's another huge benefit to what was done on Macca, and that's in showing us it's never too late. In just a couple of hundred years, because we didn't know any better, human beings nearly wrecked the place. Our presence led the native plants and animals to struggle for survival and damaged the landscape itself. But we learned from our mistakes and we figured out how to fix them. And that's crucial for us as a species. We were able to restore Macquarie Island's wild beauty, making this one of the world's best conservation stories and without doubt the highlight of my career so far.

13

DANGEROUS DOGS AND A SCARY SEA LION

The more aggressive you are with a dangerous dog, the more likely you are to be attacked. Protect your vital parts while you are walking away quietly to minimise the chance of being hurt.

I've owned and loved many wonderful dogs and they have enriched my emotional life almost beyond description. There have been lots of highs but there have been lows, too, because we humans outlive our dogs. If an animal becomes so frail or ill it has no quality of life you have to make a call about its death. That's wrenching, but it's the best thing for the dog and so it has to be done. The way I see it, letting a pet suffer because the owners can't bear to say goodbye is truly cruel.

If you get really lucky, a dog you love will have a peaceful, easy passing in ripe old age, as happened with Hot Dog. If you get unlucky there is a sudden and unexpected death that comes far too early, which was what happened with King, the best dog I ever owned.

A working-line Rottweiler, he came to the Dural kennel as a fourteen-month-old in 2007. He was compactly built, small but very powerful. He'd been with the police or army, but they'd only partially trained him and then, for some reason, decided they didn't have a place for him. He'd come to us to be rehomed. I wasn't actively looking for another dog of my own at that point, but right from our first encounter I felt there was something special about King. He had the lively, curious attitude I seek, but there was an extra, indefinable spark too. I decided there and then that he'd be coming home with me.

Rottweilers often intimidate strangers, but King was completely lovable. Everywhere he went he was adored. He really enjoyed being around other people, and he certainly loved Vicki, but he and I had a unique bond. It was unlike anything I'd experienced with a dog before, even Sunny and Hottie. I set about training him and he was quick to learn. He was exceptionally eager to please me without ever being what you might call wussy about it. We deeply enjoyed each other's company: he wanted to be around me, and when I was off somewhere working I used to look forward to coming home to see him. He was strong, he wasn't afraid of anything, and he was loyal. He was, in fact, the epitome of all the qualities I sought out in other people and strived for in myself.

I didn't go into competitions with him the way I had with previous dogs, in large part because I was now so busy, but I did use him for dangerous-dog training because he was trained in what's called bite work. I'd started doing bite work back when I had Sunny. It was what I'd demonstrated with Bobby at

DANGEROUS DOGS AND A SCARY SEA LION

the Movie World show. The trainer wears safety gear, typically a specially built, densely padded slip-on sleeve that looks a bit like a section of a crash-mat. On command the dog attacks and bites — but only on the sleeve — and on command it instantly stops. The attack is very specific and controlled.

There are plenty of so-called experts who claim that just playing tug-of-war with a dog will make it nasty and aggressive — as for bite work, that creates monsters. I'm here to tell you that's a load of rubbish. Tug-of-war is great. It cleans dogs' teeth, builds up their strength and is interactive, so it generates a nice rapport between you and the dog. It's an excellent reward alternative to food. Done properly, bite work is also very, very good for dogs. They can release their frustrations within safe limitations and, just like any other trick, they love getting it right and being rewarded. It's an enjoyable game to them.

Formalised bite work is part of a dog sport called IPO Schutzhund. The IPO part translates from German as 'International Testing Regulations', while Schutzhund means 'protection dog'. Schutzhund competition has three elements: obedience, tracking and protection (also known as 'man work'; this is what bite work trains for). The sport was originally designed for German shepherds, and while they still dominate, other breeds do take part.

I'd participated in it for many years before I got King. Back in my days as head trainer at the Sutherland dog club, I'd been approached by the local council for advice on handling dangerous dogs. My interest in IPO Schutzhund had built at the same time and I'd gradually acquired more and more of the specialist protective gear used for dealing with dangerous dogs.

By the time I got King in 2007, dangerous-dog training was an established part of my business. (It's still a significant part of the mix.) King was the ideal dog to use in seminars and demonstrations. These are typically run for people whose jobs might bring them into contact with aggressive dogs – posties, meter readers, council rangers and so on. The idea is to teach them how to read a dog's body language to help reduce the chance of being attacked and, if that doesn't work, educate them on how to minimise injuries.

Theory is important, but the best way for them to really get what I'm talking about is by experiencing an attack. Obviously, I'm not about to sic an actual dangerous dog on anyone, so what I use is a nice, well-trained dog who can act the part of a dangerous, aggressive animal. King was perfect for the task. He could hit that sleeve like a steam train, looking the full hair-raising part. If I'd told him to, he could have taken anyone down and they would not have got up again. But he controlled his attacks flawlessly and stopped instantly on command. One minute he'd look like the fiercest thing you'd ever seen, the next he'd be gently playing ball with a five-year-old.

The most effective way of demonstrating his temperament involved a bucket, his favourite toy ball and some of our chickens from home. I'd put the ball in the bottom of the bucket, then put in some chicken feed and a live chicken. The chicken would be busily pecking away and King would put his head in, gently nudge the bird off the ball, then lift the ball out without harming even a feather. I could place a chicken on his back and even add some seed for the bird to peck at and he wouldn't bat an eye. He was magnificent.

He was just six when he died. Each morning I would go out first thing to see the dogs in their enclosure and he would always, without fail, hear me coming and be waiting at the gate. When he wasn't there one morning I knew instantly something was wrong. I called his name but there was no answer. Then I saw him lying on the ground, and even without touching him I could see he was dead. I feed my dogs about 75 per cent high-quality kibble and 25 per cent raw meaty bone (never cooked). King had been eating that with no problems since the day he first came home with me, but running my hands over him in my distress, trying to understand what had happened, I could feel something hard lodged at the bottom of his throat. He had choked on a piece of bone: a terrible accident.

I was devastated and so was Vicki, who adored King almost as much as she did her own beloved dog, border collie Chilli. In fact, there was a remarkable outpouring of sorrow from people who had known him. I grieved for weeks, months. Even now, three years later, driving along I'll catch a glimpse of a man throwing a ball to his dog and there will be something painfully familiar about the way the dog moves, or I'll be sitting out on our porch swing having a bourbon and Coke as I did so often with King sitting beside me, and the ache of his loss will wash over me again.

It was twelve months before I was ready to get another large dog in his place. Maybe one day I'll be able to choose another Rottweiler but it certainly won't be anytime soon. Instead, I got a German shepherd, whom I named Django, and he and Chilli now help when I'm educating people on dangerous dogs.

* * *

I bring Chilli and Django out at the start of the course and explain how the day will unfold, then we get into a bit of the theory. After that I say, 'Okay, who wants to have a go with the dogs?'

Generally the women and older men are still a bit hesitant at this point; the ones who are volunteer are the macho 21-year-old blokes who think they know everything. I understand them because I used to be one of them. They're only there because their employers require it of them. They're young and strong, six feet tall and bulletproof, as the saying goes, and they're sure they can handle anything. 'Oh I'm not worried about dogs,' they say. My job is to get them to stop being so gung-ho and listen long enough to pick up something useful.

I fit the sleeve on the bloke who's volunteered and get Chilli up. They look at him as he sits there all calm and handsome, looking like the gentlest dog in the world. I say, 'You ready? He's going to hit you on the arm.'

'Yeah, yeah, I'm right,' they say, very sure of themselves.

I send the dog and less than a second later the bloke is down on the ground, helpless as Chilli savages the padded sleeve. I call the dog off and say, 'Righto, now I'll get the shepherd out.'

'No, no, hang on ...' is the usual response. They've learned the first lesson: don't *ever* underestimate a dog. It's a lesson even the most experienced of us, me included, need to be reminded of again and again. I was at a pound in Gladstone, Queensland, recently giving a dangerous-dogs seminar to council rangers. Standing in the run with a medium-sized cross-breed who had formally been declared a dangerous animal, I had just finished telling the rangers never to take their attention off a dog whenever they were within attack range. Then I did just that. I turned away for a mere moment but that was enough for the dog to launch at me. He got me pretty good, too, biting me on the arm and both hands hard enough for me to require a couple of stitches. (Well, there would have been stitches if I'd gone to hospital. Instead I did what I do when I'm out in the bush, far from an emergency department: I stopped the bleeding then superglued the wounds. But kids, don't try this at home!)

What I know on the topic of dangerous dogs I've learned the hard way, by facing down such dogs for real. If a dog is loose on the street or has already attacked someone, council rangers and police will be involved in subduing and removing it. But there are other times when private individuals, or businesses such as real-estate agents, or organisations like the RSPCA need to get a threatening dog out of a situation. As a licensed dangerous-dog expert (formally, a Department of Local Government Temperament Assessor) I'm one of the people they call for help.

I've been asked why the dogs can't just be sedated using tranquilliser guns. The answer is that, unlike in the movies and on TV, tranquilliser guns are difficult weapons to use and not particularly accurate. And as with any other gun, there are lots of things that can go wrong if they're used when there are people or other animals around. The hands-on solution is far better and more effective as long as you know what you're doing and have the right protection. A sleeve is for practice bite work; for the real-life jobs I wear specially made full-body padding, including gloves.

I've had to get dogs out of houses that have been used as meth labs, and animals who have been sitting under a table while meth is being made are crazy – there's no other word for it. But at least in those places you know what to expect going in. Years ago I went to a house for an estate agent where a lovely old widowed gentleman had lived. He'd been quiet and never had people into the house, but the neighbours thought he was fine, because even though he was over ninety he would go out in his car every day to the local shops to buy bread and whatever else he needed. Then one day he had a car crash and was taken to hospital, where it became clear he had quite severe Alzheimer's and wasn't capable of living alone.

Someone came to check on his house and opened the door, to find the floor completely covered in food and other waste – most of what he had bought each day from the shops had gone straight into the pile unopened, creating a haven for vermin. It was more than a metre high throughout the whole house. Heartbreakingly, there was a picture of him and his wife on their wedding day on one wall and his World War I medals were mounted underneath it in a presentation case. Picture and case were spotless, lovingly polished every day. They were the only clean things in the house.

He was known to have had a dog and the RSPCA was brought in. But the dog was proving tricky to get out and the state of the house made the task harder, so they called me. I dressed in all the gear, pushing my way through the mess, when the dog suddenly appeared and charged at me. I was ready for it, with my metal catching pole and slip lead. I got the loop around the dog's neck and started to lead it outside, but the next thing I knew something slammed into me so hard it put me clean through the plaster wall. It was a second dog we hadn't even known was there. I tried to stand up and my foot went straight through the floor, down into vermin central. Rats were running up my legs and mice were fleeing across the top of the rubbish. The dogs – big, black German shepherd crosses – saw their chance and started attacking me simultaneously. I kept my head and managed to get control of both of them, but it was a hairy few minutes. I sure earned my money that day.

Then there was the time I got a 7.30 am call from a stranger who said, 'I need your services urgently. I don't care what it costs.' It turned out that he and his wife were the owners of a property under construction, a multi-storey mansion overlooking Sydney Harbour. They'd had an altercation with their builder. Each party thought the other was in the wrong and the builder was refusing to let them onto the site until they paid him. To keep them out he had hired two guard dogs, Rottweilers, and locked them inside the fenced-off site.

I met the owners at the place, got into my gear, entered the site and started looking for the dogs, whistling for them and calling out. I shone my torch into the dark under a partially built level, saw a pair of eyes and heard the angry growl. There was nothing for it but to crawl in and position myself in such a way that the dog latched onto the bite sleeve. He did, good and hard, enabling me to crawl out backwards, dragging him along with me. I'd just got us both out from under there and put the lead on him when the other dog flew at me from behind. She came in hard but I managed to get a lead on her, too. I spoke to them with authority: 'Sit! Stay!' They'd obviously had some kind of training because they calmed down pretty quickly. I wish I could say the same for the rest of the situation: as I was getting the gear off and preparing to leave, all hell broke loose. The builder and a bunch of his burly crew turned up, completely outmatching the security guard whom the owners had hired. Bolt-cutters were produced, punches were thrown and both police and the owners' solicitor arrived. I left them to it. Sometimes a dangerous dog is actually the easiest part of the problem.

But as hairy as things can get with a dangerous dog, they don't even come close to my most alarming animal showdown. That honour goes to Orson, a sea lion at Taronga Zoo. Over the years various zoos have brought me in to give workshops for their keepers and animal trainers, and it's something I always enjoy doing. Afterwards they often take me back behind the scenes, to the parts the public never gets to see, showing me their techniques and allowing me to get up close to gorillas and other awe-inspiring creatures. I'm the proud owner of one painting done by a gorilla and another by an elephant as mementos of these privileged experiences.

Zoos also sometimes bring me in to interact directly with the animals, including a recent trip to Rockhampton where I worked with the keepers who look after the big saltwater crocodiles, using positive reinforcement and operant conditioning to get the crocs to come out of the water and into their enclosure on cue. Crocodiles have a primeval power that is pretty intimidating, even when you're on the right side of a safety fence, but even that pales next to facing off with Orson.

I met him when I was brought in to do some experiments on sea lions' odour-detection abilities. It was thought that there might be an application for the findings when it came to mothers' detection of babies following oil-slick contamination. I worked with a keeper called Andrew, who cared for the animals and guided them through the regular sea-lion shows put on for zoo visitors. As one of the show's stars, adult male Orson was already very well trained to respond to rewards and so he was chosen as our focus. We assessed his ability using lemon scent (not something a sea lion would normally encounter), placing containers in various parts of the enclosure, some with the target scent and others without, and rewarding him when he found the targets.

It was fascinating being around him and watching him get better and better at the task over the weeks. It all went beautifully, until one day when Andrew and I and the postgraduate uni student who was observing our work were in the enclosure with him. The testing started as usual, but at a certain point Orson, who weighed well over 200 kilograms, stopped what he was doing, turned directly to me, reared up to his full imposing height and produced a bellow from deep in his gut that turned my blood to ice-water. It was easily the most threatening sound I'd ever heard, and even though there were two other humans present it was most definitely directed at me.

The student, who was in my eyeline, froze and turned grey with fear. I had the sense not to move, just saying out of the corner of my mouth to Andrew, 'What's going on?' Andrew replied, 'Whatever you do don't move a muscle. He's getting ready to either charge you here or pull you into the water and try to drown you. I'll try to get his attention and you go through the safety door I showed you.'

As part of the daily show Orson had a particular spot he needed to get into and the command to get him there was Place. Moving slowly and making his body language as unthreatening as possible, Andrew went near the spot and said, 'Orson, Place!' Despite everything else that was going through his brain, the sea lion was so well trained that he turned and went to his accustomed position, allowing us all to get out of there safely.

It turned out that one or more of the female sea lions who were nearby had come on heat. The student was female and therefore not perceived as a threat, and Andrew, though male, was so known and trusted that he too was judged unthreatening. That left me, a possible competitor for Orson's harem.

Having a huge sea lion poised to launch his full fury right at me was absolutely terrifying, and nothing I've experienced with any dog before or since has come close to it. Yes, in case you're wondering, we did resume the experiment – but only weeks later when we were absolutely certain that all Orson's lady friends were back off heat!

The word 'dominant' is over-used in the dog-training world. People often talk about the 'top dog', who maintains control through aggressive dominance. I reject that. I often have eight or ten or twelve dogs housed together, three of whom are my own dogs, the others being dogs who are with me temporarily for training before they go off to wherever they'll be working. There's no 'top dog' and no fighting for position. There has to be a leader, someone the dogs respect, and that's me. I'm consistent and calm with them no matter what. I'm their benevolent dictator. I decide who sleeps where, who goes out for training or exercise and when, and all the rest of it, and I do it in a very clear manner. The dogs understand that I'm in control and they feel safe with that. So if a new dog comes in, they don't have to worry about trying to establish control over it; they know if there's a problem I will take care of it.

Genuinely dominant dogs are rare indeed. In fact, in thirty years of dog training I have met three of them, and they're the only dogs who have ever truly scared me. One was a malamute who was being boarded during my time at Hanrob. I went to get him out of his enclosure for training one day but his female companion in the adjoining run was on heat and he just lost it. I brought him out into the central area of the shed. He looked at me and his eyes went back up into his head. I didn't stop to think, I scrambled up the wire frame on the inside of those kennel walls like a possum going up a tree. I was only wearing shorts and a t-shirt, and there was no doubt he would have killed me if he'd been able to get to me. He kept me up there for an hour and a half and his aggression didn't lessen even a tiny bit. I was clinging on right up inside the roof, yelling for help. But every time I yelled he barked louder, and that set off all the other dogs who were still in their runs. Finally, someone came to look for me and they were eventually able to get him into the run with his female dog. After that he was as good as gold, but when he'd felt she was threatened he was absolutely terrifying.

The second dominant dog was a Rottweiler, and as I discovered, he had been raised in the very anthropomorphic, indulgent way that ruins many dogs. He belonged to a childless couple who regarded him as their 'fur child', and in their eyes he did no wrong, ever. If he growled threateningly at a neighbourhood child they'd say it was the kid's fault. If he growled threateningly at the woman owner she would say, 'It was my fault, I walked too close to his bed.'

I knew none of this at the time, only that she wanted to show the dog, who was a four-year-old 'entire' (i.e. not desexed) male. She asked me to come and take a look with an eye to training him. I went into the yard and the dog backed itself into me then turned his head over his shoulder to stare at me in a challenge pose typical of the breed. They get themselves into that position, wait for the other dog to make the first move then turn and attack. I quietly moved away, saying softly to the woman, 'Put the lead on the dog, will you, please?' When she'd done so I told her, 'This is a very dangerous dog. He's had his own way the whole time and as a consequence he thinks he's King Farouk. He is going to cause you a lot of trouble.' Unfortunately, she simply refused to accept it at the time, although I heard she saw things differently when she had a baby a couple of years later.

No-one was in denial about the third dominant – and truly scary – dog I met: he had the runs on the board for all to see. I encountered him in my role as a judge at the European Championship of Customs Drug Searching Dogs in Prague. This role was another unforeseen but excellent offshoot of my participation in the Dresden wildlife-smuggling conference. The championship is a huge deal, with participants from customs and police agencies in more than thirty countries, including France, Britain, Germany, the Netherlands and Russia. It takes place on a train carriage supplied by the Czech Government in which the judges have secreted drugs somewhere – in the seats, the roof, the walls, the floor, anywhere. The dogs must find the drugs within specific constraints, which include no more than five minutes to search the entire carriage and instant disqualification if they go past the hidden article by more than one metre. The championships are held at irregular intervals and 2015 marked my fourth time as a judge.

DANGEROUS DOGS AND A SCARY SEA LION

I met this third scary dog on day two of my first championship, back in 2005. I'd learned to expect the unexpected the day before when, amid the labradors and shepherds and golden retrievers and spaniels – all the usual drug-detection breeds – a Belgian officer had walked in with a poodle. Not a standard poodle, but a toy one, handbag-sized. Human participants wear their uniforms, including side-arms, and this officer was in black combat gear, complete with pistol, looking very serious and macho, leading this tiny dog.

I figured it was a welcome joke for the new Aussie judge and I decided just to play along. If he could keep a straight face, so could I. I said good morning and ran through the rules, as required. I was curious to see when he would crack, but no, he kept up the act. So be it. I told him to start whenever he was ready. I had hidden 10 grams of cocaine inside the metal tubing of a fold-up guard's seat at the other end of the carriage. The handler gave his toy dog the Find command, and the dog ran confidently along, got the scent 15 metres back from the seat and went straight to the drugs, all in a matter of seconds. As I learned afterwards, that poodle was famed as one of the best drug dogs in Europe.

So by day two I was trying not to make any assumptions about anything. A seriously big Czech Customs officer came in, limping, with a malinois, sometimes known as a Belgian shepherd – they're similar to German shepherds but with a squarer frame and a smooth coat. Just to make conversation, I gestured to the bloke's leg and said, 'What happened to you?'

In heavily accented English he said, 'I get shot.'

'Oh, that's no good. How?' I asked.

'I was on Poland border. Stopped a car, sent dog to the boot. He alert, I open boot: two kilo of heroin.'

'What happened then?'

'Driver get out, he shoot me.'

'What did you do?' I asked.

'I shoot him, boom. Kill him dead. But the other one, the passenger, he run away.'

'Did you get him?'

'I could not run but I send my dog. He caught the man but I was slow because I got the bullet and I am bleeding.'

I said, 'So did you and the dog get the man in the end?'

He said what sounded like, 'He ee tim.' I was trying to match this up with the few little bits of Czech I'd tried to learn for the trip, but to no avail. Was it a word for capture? Arrest? Escape? I couldn't figure it out. 'Sorry,' I said, 'what is *ee tim*?'

He said, 'The dog, he eat the man. When I get there, he was eating him. Eat his stomach, his kidney, eat his lung. Eat him. The man, he died.'

I took a minute to take this in, then asked, 'What happened to the dog?', thinking he was sure to say he had been put down.

He said, 'Dog's fine. This is him here.'

I looked down at the dog. The dog looked up at me. I thought to myself with a shiver, 'I'm inches from a man who fatally shot someone without hesitation and a dog who killed someone with his teeth. Please let them do well. I really do *not* want to have to fail this pair.'

To my enormous relief, the malinois made the find easily and dog and handler walked away happy.

Each time I've been to Prague there has been at least one memorable moment or one good lesson. TYD (Trust Your Dog) was the theme for the championship at which a young female officer came in with her labrador. We ran through all the usual protocols and confirmed that the target was cocaine, then the handler, another Czech as it happened, sent her dog off. It went only five seats along, stopped, turned and indicated an air vent near the carriage floor. The handler raised her hand to show they had made the find. I said, 'Sorry, it's not there, that's a false response.' But the dog was insistent and so was she. She started speaking urgently in her own language, pointing her finger at me for emphasis. I said to her, via my bilingual assistant, 'Don't point at me, just relax, I'm telling you that's not where the target is – I should know, I'm the one who hid it.'

She absolutely would not back down; in fact, just the opposite. To avoid an international incident I asked my assistant to go and find a screwdriver so we could show her she was wrong. He located one and we unscrewed the vent – only to find a needle and burned foil from some previous passenger who'd had a hit of heroin and then shoved the evidence there to hide it.

I didn't need my translator to know that her response was: 'Ha! Told you so!'

I said, 'But I told you to find cocaine and this is heroin, so who was right?'

Via the translator she said with a twinkle, 'I think we were both right', and we all laughed. Then her dog went off and found the cocaine in no time flat.

I think of her every time I am teaching handlers the cardinal rule of Trust Your Dog. She knew that dog back to front and trusted it completely, and she was absolutely right to do so.

There was another valuable lesson in there too: from that day onwards we ran a detection dog through the carriage before we planted the target drugs, just in case.

How to deal with a dog attack

I often meet resistance when I tell the people in my courses what to do if worst comes to worst and they can't avoid being attacked: curl up as tightly as possible with your least important body part – your bum – towards the dog and take the bite. By this point in the day the young blokes have often got their swagger back and they'll say, 'No, that's wrong, you've got to get in there and kick the dog hard.' A lot of people would agree with that, but they'd be wrong. Without question, the more you fight, the more the dog will bite. The more aggression you show, the more aggression you will receive back.

There *are* exceptions to the rule about curling up. If you're large and fit and wearing steel-capped boots, and the dog isn't too big, perhaps you can get away with kicking the dog then outrunning it. Perhaps. But for 99 people out of 100, or maybe 999 out of 1000, returning the dog's attack will only make things much, much worse. A predator's instinct is to bring down prey. Once the prey is down and in shock, the predator's need to continue to attack diminishes. If the attack does continue, try to remain as calm as possible and continue to protect your most vulnerable parts – there is not much else you can do.

Fear aggression

It's really important to learn how to avoid getting to the attack stage, if you possibly can. The first step is recognising whether a dog poses a threat. Most dogs whom people see as aggressive are actually terrified. They're in a state called 'fear aggression'. You can recognise this because the dog is barking with very loud, constant yaps. It has its hackles up, its tail is down between its legs, its ears are flat and its eyes are moving from left to right – these are all signs of fear. A dog like this is dangerous because it feels threatened. It will bite if you make it feel cornered by entering its 'critical zone'. This might be the area around its food bowl or favourite toy, or near its owner's vehicle or something else it feels it has to defend.

Unfortunately, because the critical zone is arbitrary and invisible, you can stray into it unwittingly. The good news is that if you leave fearful dogs alone and get out of their area as calmly as possible, most of the time they won't touch you. Regrettably, in many cases where children are mauled by dogs, it's because the child has been left around a dog unsupervised and has come into the dog's critical zone. Never, ever leave children around dogs without adult supervision.

If you are confronted by a dog like this you need to turn around and walk away very slowly out of the dog's zone. This takes incredible self-control because your body is likely to be flooded with adrenaline, giving you a strong urge to run. If you give in to this urge, in the dog's eyes you become prey that is escaping and must be stopped. Don't try to give the dog commands or mollify it; don't talk, just walk. Adopt a submissive posture with your head down and your shoulders stooped. Don't make eye contact – in fact, pretend to be focused on something in the opposite direction to the dog. If the dog is 100 metres away and you are two metres from a gate you're sure you can open, or a car you're sure is unlocked, or a tree you're sure you can climb, then, yes, run like hell to get to safety. But you must be 100 per cent certain you can make it. If you're not, don't risk it.

Offensive aggression

Far more dangerous than a fearful dog is one who's in prey drive already: his aggression is offensive rather than defensive. Picture a lioness about to attack a zebra; that's the state these dogs are in. They are quiet, not barking, standing very steadily and looking right at you. They're not afraid of you at all. Dogs like this are very, very rare, but they are very, very dangerous.

If you're walking along the street and you're not sure if a dog is a threat to you, turn around and walk in the opposite direction. Don't continue to approach the dog while you mentally debate whether you're being silly or not. It's simply not worth taking the chance. If there's any doubt in your mind at all, anything that is making you concerned about that dog, turn around, keeping as quiet and calm as possible.

If you have your own dog with you, do all of this while keeping your dog on a short leash. If this tactic doesn't work and the aggressive dog starts fighting yours, do not attempt to separate them by trying to grab the other dog by its collar or by kicking it or screaming. These actions will only increase the dog's drive. Instead, grab the aggressive dog by its hocks (the middle joints in the back legs), lift it up and drag or swing it away. If you do this you have to be able to follow through. The dog will try to bite you, but as long as you have a firm hold of it and swing it by his hocks, it cannot reach you. You might be able to swing it away over a nearby fence or even onto a roadway. If you panic and drop it, or simply aren't strong enough to hold it, you're in a lot of danger.

If a child is present

If you have a child with you and a dangerous dog attacks, don't pick the child up. Instead, curl your body over as described earlier, but first put the child under you to protect him or her. If you have a child and a dog with you when an aggressive dog threatens, get the child to safety first. Never try to intervene in a dogfight while the child is still there and at risk. If you are in a situation where you are witness to an attack on a child, act immediately. An aggressive dog can kill a small child in seconds. If picking the dog up by the hocks and swinging it won't work because its jaws are clamped onto the child and it won't let go, jam something in its anus – a stick, a hose, your thumb, anything available. The dog will then try to turn its attack towards you, but at least it will have let the child go.

As experienced and confident as I am, I don't take any chances. I'm an accredited expert witness on dog matters in New South Wales courts and I've seen first-hand far too many examples of the terrible consequences of dog attacks. If a dog is off-leash, with its owner or without, I don't let that dog come near me. I walk away and keep going. I apply the same caution to my dogs' interactions. I never allow them to have contact with another dog in the street unless it's on a lead, and even then I assess its demeanour first.

14

LIFE-CHANGING DOGS: THE YOUNG DIGGERS AND MORE

Dogs can work miracles, saving lives just by being there.

I've learned so much from dogs about how to live a good life. At a very young age I discovered that you get out of animals what you put into them: if you want the results, you have to do the work. It wasn't much of a stretch to understand that didn't only apply to teaching tricks to goldfish or a puppy, it applied to everything else too. If you're persistent and patient and you learn from your mistakes you can achieve anything; I firmly believe that. We all feel tired or frustrated or downhearted at times, and at those moments it's tempting just to quit. But it's so important not to. If I had to boil my entire life philosophy down to one phrase it would be: never, ever give up. It doesn't matter how many times you fall down, what counts is how many times you get back up again.

LIFE-CHANGING DOGS: THE YOUNG DIGGERS AND MORE

Don't give up on animals, don't give up on people and don't give up on yourself.

That was strongly in my mind when I met Josie, a girl at risk of slipping between the cracks. She came into my life when she was nineteen. She was homeless and living in her car with her two dogs. One of the dogs had bitten a passer-by and the local council had put a dangerous dog control order on it. Josie had thought that was unfair, that her dog wasn't really dangerous and had only reacted out of fear, and she'd asked the council ranger how the order could be removed. He'd told her that she needed to have a professional temperament assessment done, and had given her my name as someone who might be able to help.

She came to see me and when she outlined her situation I was tempted to start lecturing her about how crazy it was to have dogs, and large dogs at that, living in a car. But something told me to shut up and listen. She didn't reveal too much on that visit or the following one, but she had a depth and sincerity that made me want to help her. I offered to take the dogs into our Dural kennels and give them vet care and the training they needed. She offered to pay off the cost of the services a little at a time, but instead I asked her to help out at the kennels regularly and she agreed.

After a time I had to tell her that the best thing she could do for her dogs was to rehome them. It took her a while to accept this. She was very reluctant to let them go, but she was intelligent and caring enough to see it was what they needed, as hard as it was for her. Because I'd listened and offered practical help rather than lecturing her, she trusted me enough to open up. The reason she was homeless was because she was pregnant and when she'd told her parents they had kicked her out.

My mother would have been just the same. Her view would have been, 'You've made a stupid mistake, now you can live with it, don't expect any help from me.' I had vowed never to be that kind of person.

Vicki and I made some calls to people who might be able to help and Josie was offered a place in Salvation Army accommodation. We gave her a bit of money to set herself up and bought her food and supplies, including baby clothes. She got settled, in due course had the baby and a while later she called us and said she'd decided to go to TAFE and get her vet-nurse qualifications. We made sure she had what she needed, and she worked hard and gained the skills for a good job. Now she's a happy, successful young woman with a beautiful child, a good partner and a stable home. It was a privilege to have played a part in her story. Who'd have thought all that would come from a dog bite?

The way I see it, reaching out and helping people, giving them a second chance or lifting them back up when circumstances have knocked them down is a really important part of life. Sometimes, as in Josie's case, you stumble on the chance to help an individual. But sometimes you can do it on a much bigger, better-organised scale, and that's what has happened with the Young Diggers Dog Squad project.

Young Diggers is a brilliant volunteer-run organisation founded by army veteran John Jarrett and run by him and fellow veteran Peter Walters. Its purpose is to help serving and former Australian military personnel who are dealing with post-traumatic stress disorder (PTSD), many as a result of tours in Iraq or Afghanistan. It provides various kinds of practical and emotional support, including companion dogs, which is where I come into things.

LIFE-CHANGING DOGS: THE YOUNG DIGGERS AND MORE

The Dog Squad, of which I am director, provides companion dogs to these diggers. Not just pet dogs but specially trained, accredited companions who wear identifying jackets and have the same status as other assistance dogs, meaning they are allowed in shopping centres and on public transport. The difference these dogs make to the mental health of suffering people is amazing. On its own that would be enough to make the whole program worthwhile, but what's really incredible is that it also helps another deeply scarred group, prisoners, and on top of that, the dogs we take into the program come from pounds and animal shelters where they might otherwise have been put down. It's win-win-win.

Prison inmates around the country have been training dogs for a number of years, either as part of the individual prison's rehabilitation program or, more commonly, for Assistance Dogs Australia. Thanks to a prison officer nicknamed Scotty, Bathurst Correctional Centre (commonly known as Bathurst Gaol) in the NSW Central Tablelands was one of the places where dog training was already taking place, and it had been a real success, with a very positive effect on prisoners' behaviour. The people there heard about the Young Diggers Dog Squad and approached us at the beginning of 2014 to see if we'd like to work with them.

Before we start the training we have to find the right dogs for the task. Unlike the high-drive dogs I use for detection work, here what we need is for the dog to be relaxed, friendly and easy around people. That's very important, because many of the diggers we'll be helping are so debilitated by PTSD or the depression that can accompany it that they're unable to leave the house. The dogs are key to helping them get out into the world again. Those of us who volunteer for the project go out to pounds and shelters and animal-rescue organisations looking for dogs who might be suitable. Breed doesn't matter but we don't tend to work with puppies, preferring young adult dogs. Volunteers take potential candidates home and spend a couple of days observing them and assessing their temperament. Our hope is to build the program to the point where we can have a dedicated kennel–training centre.

Any dogs who don't quite fit at this stage or later on during the training are rehomed. The rest are sent for an eight-week training period in Bathurst. Their prison-inmate trainers are all in the minimum-security wing, where they sleep one to a room. Being selected to take part in the training program is a privilege and the inmates have to maintain a clean behavioural sheet or they lose that privilege. Their allocated dog is with them twenty-four hours a day, and inmates who are doing really well are given two dogs to look after. I go out there several times during the training period to work with them, and we have a Bathurst-based trainer, Tenika, who is there five days a week and keeps me closely updated on progress. The inmates do daily training exercises with the dogs, and when they're ready the animals pass through three levels of obedience testing. The final one confirms them as fully qualified assistance dogs. (Some diggers already have their own dogs and wish to use them as companion dogs, which is fine as long as the diggers go through the training program with them and the dogs pass the accreditation.)

A lot of us look at people in prison and think with a bit of a shrug, 'Oh, well, they've got what they deserve.' But having spent time at Bathurst (an all-male prison) getting to know some of the blokes' stories, my stance has softened. I made some good choices when I was younger, but I made some very, very stupid ones too. I got off pretty lightly after my mistakes, but a lot of the people in prison weren't that lucky. There's no doubt that some of them have made dozens of bad choices, one after the other, without learning from their mistakes. But others did one really stupid thing when they were young and now they're paying for it big-time. I reckon every fourteen-year-old boy should be taken through a prison. Girls too, but particularly boys. They should be shown the reality so they do everything possible to avoid going down that path.

Then there are the people who have the odds stacked so high against them from the beginning that it would be a miracle if they *didn't* end up in prison. I can congratulate myself as much as I like on my good choices, but I wasn't in a car crash at thirteen in which my sister was killed next to me and my mother and her boyfriend, both meth addicts, climbed out and ran away, leaving me trapped there. A young bloke I met in Bathurst was. We'll call him Sam. He was nineteen years old and in jail on a drugs charge. Thanks to Scotty, he had been given a chance in the Young Diggers program, in the hope it might help him change his path.

The first time I met Sam he couldn't look anyone in the eye and he was slouched over, wearing an untucked, bedraggled uniform. Everything about him told the world he didn't care about himself or anything else. I had him very much in mind when I spoke to the group at the start of the program, saying, 'Remember one thing: your dog is going to be a direct reflection of yourself. If you want a good, happy, strong dog who's upright, who's proud and who will do what he's told with vigour and with honesty, you've got to be the same way. That includes the way you speak, the way you dress, the way you act – to your mates in here, to me and to everyone else. If you don't give a shit, the dog won't give a shit.'

That message must have struck some kind of nerve, because when I came back a month later Sam had changed. He was standing tall and communicating so well with people that he was chosen to go out on a visit to a local special school. He sat and explained clearly and patiently to the kids how the training worked and what kinds of 'tricks' the dog was capable of. It was remarkable.

For some of the inmates, like Sam, being part of the program is the first thing that has ever brought them positive attention. I'm not exaggerating. I gave some well-earned praise one day to a prisoner who looked to be in his early forties. As I was walking away one of the officers tapped me on the shoulder and asked curiously, 'What did you say to him?'

I said, 'I told him he should be proud of himself, because he's done a really good job with his dog. Why do you ask?'

He replied, 'Because I've known him for a very long time and I've never seen him smile. Until now.'

At the end of the eight-week training program the diggers come to Bathurst for two or three days for a handover, spending time with the dog earmarked for them and the prisoner who has trained it. They work together, one man teaching the other the commands, and the dog and its new owner getting to know each other.

You might think that the diggers would come in judgmentally, with an attitude of 'I've been serving my country while you've been doing all this bad stuff', but they don't. There's a kind of unspoken communion in the fact that both sides are damaged in some way. The diggers are genuinely respectful and appreciative of the work the inmates have put in, and they tell them so. It gives those men who are locked up a sense of worth that stays with them long after diggers and dogs have gone.

When the diggers get back home the training continues. Each dog learns to do specific tasks, depending on what its veteran needs. If they're an amputee or someone with mobility problems the dog will be taught specialist skills to help with that particular need. In other cases the problems aren't physical, but they're every bit as real. Nightmares plague many, distressing the diggers and their families. We teach the dogs to wake them when the nightmare begins, which seems to help a lot. You train for this by mimicking it: having someone lie in bed and after a time start to thrash about and moan, at which point the trainer urges the dog up onto the bed to lick the person's face or paw at them, then reinforces the behaviour with a reward. There are psychologists and therapists involved with each digger, aiming to stop them having nightmares at all, but that's easier said than done when some of these young men and women have seen hell. Being woken and reassured by your companion dog before the dream gets to its full intensity is a pretty good interim solution.

The difference the dogs have made in the lives of some of these veterans and their families can't be overstated. I've seen people go from intensely suicidal to positive and motivated and feeling part of the world again. More than one has said to me that if it weren't for the dog they wouldn't be here. These are people with wives or husbands and young children who are in soul-deep anguish about the thought of leaving them, yet can't see any other way out. But a companion dog, with its uncomplicated loyalty, compassion and devotion, helps them start to heal. It's not a fairy story, though; these people are on a long, long road to recovery. I've had diggers call me at 2.30 am, ostensibly about a problem with their dog, but really because they just needed to hear an understanding voice.

One of our Young Diggers, Josh, says this about how his dog, Lucky, has completely changed his life: 'A mental-health assistance dog like Lucky, their primary role is just to be by your side twenty-four hours a day. Lucky understands my body language. I've worked hard with him to help me get out of a depressed state. He will come and lick my face and bark and try to calm me down, and we'll go outside and throw the ball. It helps change my mindset and get me away from the negative thoughts that come in all the time … Having him by my side has given me the opportunity to step back out into the community again and be involved in the community, which has given me a sense of self-worth.'

Josh even takes Lucky to local schools and gives talks about their experience together. I've seen first-hand that by helping change things for Josh, Lucky has changed things for his whole family. The lives of his wife and children have been transformed by seeing the man they love find a way through the darkness. That one little dog has made a very big difference.

Michelle is another Young Digger who is very different from the person I first met less than two years ago. Back then she could not get out of the house. She described what it was like, saying to me, 'I wake up and a dark veil comes over me. I go from the bedroom to the living room and I sit in front of the TV at 9 am. I stay there until 9 pm hardly moving and I go

LIFE-CHANGING DOGS: THE YOUNG DIGGERS AND MORE

to bed. I get up and the same thing happens, day after day'. She had been prescribed various medicines but nothing worked. She wasn't living, she was just surviving hour to hour. It had been that way for more than a decade.

But Michelle found out about the Dog Squad and something inside her told her to give it a go. She decided she wanted a Maltese and got one from a breeder, named him Bobby and they entered the program together. As dogs do, Bobby made demands on Michelle: she had to clean up after him and exercise him, which meant going out into the world. The Dog Squad training was also demanding. Within twelve months her life was unrecognisable. Not only had she re-engaged with other people, she had even found the strength to try for her pilot's licence. She said to me one day, 'I always wanted to fly a plane.' I said, 'Why don't you, then?' The old Michelle would have recoiled at the very idea. The new one said, 'Yeah, why don't I?'

One Monday I got a call. It was Michelle and her voice was shaking, but the news was wonderful. She said, 'Steve I've just got off the plane. You're the first person I've rung. I did it. I've just got my pilot's licence.' I got emotional myself that day, let me tell you. If that isn't a story about the power of dogs to transform lives I'll walk naked backwards to Canberra!

And those are just two of the more than 200 Young Diggers we've helped. As I said, the dogs can't and don't fix everything, but they do make a huge difference.

We're keen to expand the program and we need more volunteers for that to happen. If you'd like to know more, go to www.youngdiggers.com.au.

Epilogue

GIFTS BEYOND MEASURE

I've often been asked whether dogs love us. In fact, not too long ago I took part in a TV program entirely devoted to that question. My view is that we'll never know for sure what dogs are feeling or thinking, or how nuanced their emotions are compared with ours – and that doesn't matter one bit. I know I love my dogs. The love I feel for them is different from the love I feel for my wife, but that love is different from the love I feel for my daughters, and that's different again from the love I feel for my friends, and so on. I don't need to analyse the differences; I just love each of them and that's all I need to know. My dogs act in a happy way when they're around me and they show loyalty to me. That's enough for me, whatever label we put on it.

I can't imagine my life without dogs in it. Living on a semi-rural property, Vicki and I are lucky enough to have plenty of room for plenty of animals. We have two large tanks and seven ponds for fish; another pond for frogs; four ferrets; many birds; two cats; and our dogs – not counting those who are with me for training at any given time, we have Chilli, Tommy, Sally and Django, plus a little Jack Russell called Tony. But if it came down to it and I had to choose between having the rest of the menagerie and having a single dog, it would be the dog every time. If I were to become physically incapable of taking a dog out for exercise, I'd hire someone else to do it. Whatever solutions had to be found to keep a dog in my life, I'd find them. I can manage without all the rest as long as I have my family and my dogs.

While we were in the process of finalising this book my trusty, irreplaceable Bolt died suddenly of a brain aneurysm. He was only six years old and I grieve his loss deeply. There is comfort, though, in knowing how much he enjoyed the time he had.

He was named after a white lightning-shaped mark that was particularly pronounced when he was a puppy, but he could have just as well been named to honour runner Usain Bolt, because that little dog had only two speeds: faster than fast and asleep.

I worked with him in every state of Australia. He saved native wildlife, he hunted, he played, he ran, he jumped and he slept beside me under the stars. Even though it was cut short, he lived a life other dogs can only dream about. Vale Bolt.

What I've gained from the dogs in my life has been beyond measure. They've given me loyalty, companionship and affection when I've been starved of it. They've led me to a career I didn't even know existed. My work with them has taken me all around the world, putting me into unique and privileged positions, including giving me the chance to provide a service for my country and do my bit to help save this incredible planet of ours. Dogs even brought my wonderful wife Vicki to me.

I can't wait to see where they take me next.

APPENDIX

MY TOP TIPS FOR DOG OWNERS

Over the years there are some questions that I have been asked again and again about choosing, owning and training dogs. Here are my top tips for those most frequently asked.

Should I get a purebred or crossbred dog?

First, a note on terminology: you might have noticed that throughout the book I've described dogs with mixed ancestry as 'crossbreeds', not 'mongrels'. Whether it's applied to people or dogs, mongrel tends to be a derogatory term; I choose to use the factually accurate neutral alternative instead. Crossbred and purebred dogs are equally good; the choice just depends on your individual circumstances.

The only way to be sure a dog is purebred is to buy one who has come from a breeder. People often have good reasons for wanting purebred dogs, including the purpose they'll be used for and their temperament. Some people just love a particular breed. That's fine too. It's easy to make fun of the 'designer oodle' dogs that have become so popular – Cavoodles, Labradoodles, etc. But all the breeds we have today were crossbred at some point in their history. German shepherds, Jack Russells, border collies, springer spaniels and all the rest started out as a combination of many dogs before their breeding was focused on certain desired characteristics.

So the kind of crossbreeding that has gone into the 'oodles' is nothing new. Labradoodles were particularly bred not to shed much hair, which makes them good for people who love dogs but have a problem with dog hair. I think that's absolutely fine. What I do have a problem with is where the breeding has resulted in a poor outcome for the dog: for example, a female dog who needs to be manually inseminated because she can't mate naturally, and when she has puppies they have to be delivered by caesarean section. That's exactly what's happened with the bulldog and I think that kind of over-breeding is very wrong.

Pound dogs are much cheaper than purebreds, because what you pay doesn't really even cover the organisation's costs when you factor in vaccinations, desexing, care and overheads. There is an unbeatable satisfaction in rescuing a dog from an animal shelter, saving it from potentially being euthanased – sadly there are always more animals in shelters than there are people who want to take them and the ones who aren't taken have to be put down. There are many, many wonderful dogs waiting in shelters for a loving new owner to take them. But there are others whom the shelters have identified as unsuited to becoming family pets. That's when they turn to me.

Recently, for example, I got a call from an Animal Welfare League Australia (AWLA) shelter in Sydney. The AWLA operates in a similar way to the RSPCA, caring for unwanted animals and attempting to rehome as many as possible. In this case they had a crossbred female (Staffordshire terrier–labrador was the best guess), around four years old. She was black, which reduces a dog's chance of being selected for adoption – many people seem to find black dogs threatening on principle, no matter what their personality. In this case she really was a textbook boisterous 'hard to handle' animal, full of energy, jumping all over the place. They'd named her Vader. I went to the shelter and ran some tests, playing with her using a tennis ball to test her prey drive, and testing her hunt drive by doing retrieves with increasingly long gaps between throwing the ball and letting her go and find it. She had both drives in spades, making her a perfect candidate as a working dog. Without that option this beautiful, vital dog would almost certainly have been put down. That's been true of many of the hundreds of unwanted dogs I've trained.

If you're getting a dog from a shelter is it best to get a puppy or an adult dog?

You don't need a puppy to have a great dog. Adult dogs are terrific and if you train it the same way as you would an eight-week-old puppy, you'll be fine. The good thing about adult dogs is that you know their temperament, you know their physicality and you know their size. The breed of puppies in pounds is often just a best guess. They might tell you a puppy is a little border collie cross, not realising it's been crossed with a mastiff and will grow up to be enormous. Or vice versa – you imagine yourself with a largish dog and it turns out to have been crossed with a pug.

If I go for a purebred what breeds are best?

I don't think there is a 'best'; again it depends on you and your lifestyle. Whatever dog you plan on getting, be realistic about it. If you love the look of long-haired coats, great, get a collie or a Komondor – but only if you're prepared to brush it every day. Don't get a working-dog breed and expect it to behave like a lapdog. If you're interested in training the dog to an advanced level, choose with that in mind. Golden retrievers and border collies and German shepherds are generally easier to train than Afghans, Rhodesian ridgebacks and other hounds, who tend to be more aloof, to put it in human terms. Dalmatians are always a little bit loopy, in my experience. But the biggest factor that determines an individual dog's behaviour is not its breed, it's the owner.

What's the most intelligent breed?

It depends on how you define intelligence. You often hear it said that border collies are the most intelligent breed. Sunny and Bobby were great examples of how highly you can train a border collie, but you could argue that a standard poodle is far more intelligent because if you throw a ball on a cold afternoon and it goes into the water a border collie will be in there before the ball has even hit the surface. The standard poodle will just give you a look as if to say, 'You threw it, you get it.' The most intelligent dog I've ever known is the dingo, and they are almost completely untrainable.

Are specific breeds naturally aggressive – pit bulls, for instance?

No. Any dog can be made to be nasty, and any dog can be made to be good. It's all about the environment it's brought up in. I'll go on the record saying that pit bulls make excellent family dogs. It's the people who tend to own them who muck them up. What does a typical pit bull owner look like? He's nineteen or twenty, he wears a singlet, he's got tattoos all over him and he wants to project toughness and aggression. Now, that's obviously a huge generalisation. But if a guy who fits that description is going to get a dog, a pit bull or something similar is the kind of dog he's going to choose. It's all about fashions and trends. When I was that age the desired image was long blond hair, a Kombi van with a surfboard on top and an Afghan hound to complete the picture. Now it's the 'tough guy with pit bull' look. In ten years' time it will be another dog altogether. If pit bulls were only the preferred breed of grandmothers over sixty-five they'd have a far different image.

Is it okay just to have one dog or are they pack animals who need other dogs as company?

It's fine to have more than one dog if you want to and if you have room, but you definitely don't need to do it for your dog's sake. Instead, make sure you not only give your dog an hour of exercise a day but also spend quality time with it – throw a ball, play tug-of-war, have the dog by your side when you're watching TV in the evening, whatever it might be. If you are contemplating multiple dogs, be prepared to put in the extra work that will entail, and never choose two dogs from the same litter. I train working dogs from the same litter but I would never keep them together long-term. It's a real no-no, because the dogs have never been apart and they become so dependent on one another that when they are separated, whether it's because one has to be rehomed or through death, the other usually goes completely to pieces.

How important is it to socialise a puppy?

There are a couple of big myths about socialising dogs that need to be busted. People often think socialising a dog purely means getting it used to being around other dogs. That's only part of the picture; it's a big mistake to think socialising begins and ends there. Dogs need to be socialised to all the things they're going to encounter in the world: kids, adults, cars, planes, footy balls, skateboards … You name it, they should be exposed to it. The walk up the street to the park is every bit as important as the time your dog spends *in* the park.

When you get your puppy vaccinated, the vet will generally advise you not to let your dog mingle with others until its vaccinations are complete, at twelve weeks. Now, that's good advice if you understand it to mean 'Don't put them around a whole lot of other dogs'. But there is a window when puppies are between eight and sixteen weeks old in which they need to be 'socialised' to the wider world, and if they miss that it is very, very hard to make up that ground.

If I'm driving along with my dogs and I come upon a circus that has animals, I stop downwind and let my dogs have a smell of the lions and the elephants and the monkeys. I try to give them as many experiences as possible. That's true 'socialisation'.

Is it true that you're not a fan of dog parks? Why on earth not?

Lots of councils, especially in cities, have designated areas where people can exercise their dogs off-leash. Many dog owners love them and they're shocked when I tell them that I will never allow my dogs in one. Dog parks are great in theory, and the vast majority of people and dogs who use them are fine. The problem is the tiny minority of irresponsible owners who take dangerous dogs to these parks. It's possible that you could go months without crossing paths with one of these dogs, but sooner or later you'll be there when there's an incident and the best you can hope for is that it doesn't involve your dog. Every week dogs are critically injured and sometimes killed in dogfights at off-leash parks around Australia. (Some coastal councils have off-leash beach areas and at least here a dog can find an escape route if threatened, unlike in an enclosed dog park.)

The aggressive dogs generally belong to problem owners of the kind I come across in my role as a licensed dangerous-dog expert. A typical example is a bloke I met who had a big malamute who had killed another dog and consequently had a dangerous dog order put on it. I did its temperament assessment. If a dog fails the test – in other words, if I think it genuinely poses a danger to people and other animals – the owner must have it desexed and then go through a training program with it, and they can't take it out in public until those things have been done. This dog failed the test, no question, and the owner said straight to my face: 'I don't care, I'm not doing any of that. I'm a rate-payer, I'm taking my dog down to the park tomorrow.' I said, 'But it kills other dogs.' His answer was, 'That's not my problem.' Yes, rangers can be on the lookout for people who break these orders and the council can take action, but in the meantime that dog is a time-bomb and when it's in the dog park every other dog who's there is at risk. My dogs are far too precious for me to expose them to that. If you visit one of these parks with your dog, I urge you to be careful and keep a close eye on what's happening around you.

Is there a place for electric stimulus collars?

First, it's important to note these collars are illegal in some states, controlled in others and unrestricted in the rest, and anyone who is considering their use needs to check the laws that apply where they live. I don't advocate them as a training device, but they can be incredibly effective in saving dogs' lives in certain situations.

I would never use something on a dog without trying it on myself first, so I can report first-hand that the stimulus the dog receives isn't the 'electric shock' you might imagine, it's a brief, uncomfortable buzz that reminded me of physiotherapy treatment I've had in the past. With the help of the handlers, I use this kind of collar to 'snake-proof' the Phillip Island penguin-protection dogs; the use of the collars is legal in Victoria with specific veterinary approval. We borrow a large pet python and put it in a secure, grassy area. We start the dog off a couple of hundred metres away, and when it approaches the snake – as it inevitably will, being curious – we send a charge through the collar. The dog associates the snake with the unpleasant sensation and generalises that to all snakes, which means from then on it avoids snakes, venomous or otherwise, when it encounters them in the wild while working. That keeps it safe.

I don't agree with the collars' use as a general tool to stop barking, but in very specific situations they can be effective. I was brought in by a woman (in a state where the collars are legal) who was on the point of a nervous breakdown because of the problem she was having with her dog. It was well trained and she took excellent care of it, giving it an hour's walk both morning and night. But it was barking so loudly and long when she and her husband were out at work that she was getting hate mail from people in the neighbourhood, and the council's rangers had told her they were on the point of issuing a nuisance order. She'd tried everything to stop the dog from barking but nothing had worked.

As I saw when I went there, the dog wasn't barking out of boredom or aggression, it was having a ball. There were two large trees in the backyard and a flock of sparrows would land in one. The dog would race to that tree and bark. The birds would fly to the other tree and the dog would race over there and bark. This went on for hours every day. It took just two corrections using the collar – one for each tree – and the dog stopped barking at the birds for good. You definitely have to know what you're doing, though, and the timing of the correction is crucial, otherwise the dog won't make the right association. So I encourage anyone who is contemplating using a collar to seek the advice of a reputable dog trainer.

Traumatised dogs

When you meet a person who has been damaged in some way, they can at least tell you what happened, if they trust you enough. Dogs can't do that. Over the years I've taken more than 500 dogs from pounds and shelters and given them a new life. It's an incredibly satisfying thing to do, but you have to be realistic about the fact that the animal brings unknown baggage with it. These days, with all that experience behind me, I can get a really good feel for a dog's temperament in just a couple of minutes, though I know what I'm seeing might not be the whole story. Some of those dogs have been deliberately mistreated, others have been traumatised while they were running wild, and you'll only find out about it when a trigger sets them off and they lose it completely, becoming scared and aggressive.

Because you don't get a warning light just before this happens, it's often really hard to figure out what the trigger was. Was it a particular movement someone made? A noise? Did the dog just catch sight of someone wearing a certain style of hat? It can be like trying to find a needle in a haystack, but if you're patient and observant the picture eventually becomes clear. I had an example of this back in my AQIS days when a dog I was training would intermittently try to bite people. I couldn't spot the trigger for the longest time; he seemed like an equal-opportunity offender, going after men, women, short people, tall people, ladies in dresses and in pants, blokes with hats, blokes without hats. One day he went for one of the guys who was working with me at the kennels. I stopped the dog in time, but it got me thinking. This guy was a heavy smoker ... hmm, I wondered. I set up a couple of situations in which the dog encountered similar people, some of whom didn't smell of cigarette smoke and some of whom did. Bingo, that was it: he wanted to bite anyone who smelled strongly of cigarette smoke.

I don't know what had happened to that dog to make him react that way. The temptation is to think he was treated cruelly by someone who stank of smoke, and that might well be true.

A trigger can certainly have a direct relationship to the dog's fear and anxiety. But it can also be an association that exists only in the dog's mind. Let's say a dog is afraid of motorbikes. Yes, the dog might have been hit by a motorbike at some point, but she might just as easily have been walking along a footpath and trod on a nail, really hurting herself, just as a motorbike passed by. The dog thinks the bike caused the pain, so every time she hears a motorbike engine she associates it with being hurt and panics.

It's generally possible to cure dogs of these associations. You do it by desensitising them a little at a time. In the case of cigarette smoke, you would have someone smoking at a distance and every time the dog got a whiff of the smoke you'd bring him to you, calm him and reward him. Gradually you would bring the smoker closer and closer. But it's a very slow process, and when it comes to working dogs it's often better to rehome the dog and start again, which was what happened with the dog whose trigger was smoke. Even if the training schedule had allowed time to desensitise him, it would have been too risky to have him in a busy airport environment where he would have been frequently exposed to that trigger.

Anxious dogs

But sometimes there isn't a particular trigger. Instead, you're dealing with a generally traumatised, anxious dog. Unfortunately, there are some people who try to make themselves feel tough by laying into an animal, and others who neglect them horribly. The way to help these dogs heal is to do what I do with every single dog I take charge of: treat it like an eight-week-old puppy and give it every bit of kindness and patience you would show that puppy. It doesn't matter if I get a dog at six months or four years old, I always give it the latitude to make the mistakes an eight-week-old would make. If that dog does a wee where it shouldn't, no big deal; for today it's eight weeks old. If it pulls the dinner off the table, that's okay, it's eight weeks old and doesn't know better. Don't get me wrong, I don't want those behaviours, but I know I can train the dog not to do them.

If the dog starts to wee inside I'll say, 'That's okay, buddy, but come outside and do it.' When you continue to apply that calm, consistent, patient approach, the dog is never afraid of you and the speed at which it learns would amaze you. The progress is telescoped. So it might take you a week to make the first breakthroughs, but in the following three weeks a dog will absorb three months' worth of learning, and so on. If a dog has a genetic problem, let's say mild hip dysplasia, the best you can do is to manage it, through exercising it in a specific way and avoiding certain activities. But environmental problems can actually be solved if you're prepared to put the work in.

Sadly, there is a lot of misinformation about behaviour management, perpetuated by self-appointed experts who have built a high profile despite the fact that they don't train dogs and never have. The nonsense they peddle puts the canine-training industry back decades. I've seen one of these know-nothing 'experts' on TV taking on a dog who was being very guarded around its food bowl, growling at anyone who came near. The 'expert's' approach was straight from the bad old days: walk up to the dog and threaten it using a hostile face and a hostile tone, basically saying, 'You touch that food and you'll cop it.' The dog felt threatened and responded by biting him, which was completely understandable.

Why is the dog behaving like that in the first place? Because it's highly anxious. Responding in the way described above makes the situation a thousand times worse. What I would have done is to get another (empty) food bowl, put a tiny bit of food in the dog's original bowl, and place them about two metres apart. I would call the dog over to the first one: 'Here, buddy, here's some food.' As it was eating it I would go over to the other bowl and put a little food in there. When it had finished at the first bowl I'd say, 'Here, here's some more!' And I'd keep repeating that process so the dog comes to view the presence of people around the bowl in a positive light: 'I like it because you give me more food.' Over time you decrease the distance between the two bowls. You make sure the process is always about giving the dog something, never about taking it away, and you can see the animal's anxiety level dropping right down.

I've heard people brag about the control they have over their animals by saying, 'I can take food out of my dog's mouth.' What a stupid thing to do! Try to take food out of *my* mouth and you'll be lucky not to get a fork in your hand. By all means require your dog to sit and stay and wait for a command before eating, but putting your fingers into the dog's mouth while he's eating is just ridiculous.

Don't rub his nose in it!

While we're setting things straight, don't ever let anyone tell you to use the 'rub his nose in it' approach to correcting dogs' behaviour. This is not just pointless, it's also counterproductive. Unless the correction you give for undesirable behaviour is instantaneous it's not going to work. If a puppy does a wee and you find it half an hour later and rub her nose in it, she has no idea why you've done that. None at all. Which means she can't learn what you want her to do instead. Seeing the puppy start to wee inside and yelling at her for it is just as bad. The message the dog takes is not that she's getting in trouble for weeing, but that she's getting in trouble for weeing in front of you. 'Next time,' she thinks, 'I'll go behind the sofa and do it, that way I won't get yelled at.' Use *positive* reinforcement by taking her outside and praising her lavishly when she wees out there and she'll soon get the right message.

If you're one of those people who says, 'When I come home and my dog's made a mess, he knows he's done something wrong, I don't even have to speak', I'll give you a friendly tip: don't ever play poker. When you open that door and see paper or clothes strewn across the living room, your dog isn't looking guilty over what he's done. He hasn't been dreading your arrival and wondering how he's going to break the news. He's purely reacting to your reaction. Dogs are masterful at reading human body language. Long before you've opened your mouth, your dog knows when you're angry. Without even realising it, you ball up your fists and your face hardens and your posture changes. The dog instantly picks up on all this and he knows what follows those signals: he gets yelled at. That's why he looks unhappy or fearful; it's got nothing to do with guilt.

Exercise is essential

Dogs aren't people and we shouldn't try to treat them as if they are. Don't anthropomorphise them and don't ignore their essential nature. I don't have anything against little fluffy dogs or Chihuahuas, but I think the way they're often treated is cruel.

They might be small but they're still dogs. If you wouldn't carry a Doberman everywhere, don't carry the Chihuahua. Let it roll in the mud and run on the grass and feel the rain and the sun. Let it be a dog.

All dogs need an hour of exercise a day. For big dogs that generally means one or two sizeable walks, but little breeds need it just as much, although for them it might mean playing with a ball in the backyard. Either way, if you can't commit to that minimum requirement, you're not ready to have a dog. The importance of exercise can't be overstated. Ninety-nine per cent of behavioural problems can be dealt with by increasing the amount of exercise the dog gets. You can keep a Doberman in a tiny little apartment and still have a healthy, happy dog if you give it exercise and keep it interested – I see it often in big cities in the United States. (Another little tip: this doesn't just apply to dogs. When my three girls were growing up they did dance classes several times a week and practised at home in between. We had no boy problems because healthily tired teenage girls don't focus on the opposite sex the way girls who haven't burned off their energy do.)

If a dog is getting enough exercise and still exhibits behavioural problems, the first thing to consider is whether it's a physical issue: has it got a sore tooth, has it been hurt in some way, is it ill? Once that's been ruled out you have to look at the home situation. Dogs are very sensitive to changes in their owners' emotional state. It's all about those unspoken signals – the way people in the house speak, the way they walk around, the way they throw their keys onto the bed. The dog is reading body language the whole time and when things become abnormal it becomes anxious, which can manifest as aggression. I can walk into a house and tell you what your children are like before I see them just by looking at the dog, and vice versa. If the couple of the house is getting divorced or the seventeen-year-old is on drugs or someone has lost their job, their behaviour changes and the dog picks up on it and its behaviour changes too. People can't avoid major life changes, but there are strategies you can put in place to make the animal calmer.

Beware the rigid routine

Funnily enough, while change can unsettle dogs, too rigid a routine can also hurt them. The quality of the time you spend with your dog is all-important, not the quantity. In fact, if you spend every minute of the day in close contact with a dog it becomes over-dependent on you and gets anxious about even brief separations. Mixing things up is good for dogs. It makes them flexible and able to adapt to all sorts of different situations.

Vicki and I very deliberately don't let our dogs sleep in the same place all the time. Chilli mostly sleeps inside, but sometimes he'll sleep outside in his crate and sometimes in the dog yard with the other dogs. If it's a nice summer night my dogs might sleep in the yard itself rather than on their bedding, or on a cold night in their crates in the truck. My dogs are as happy as Larry wherever they are.

That's particularly important for me because they are working dogs, travelling with me to jobs all around the country, but I think variety is important for every dog. I've seen dogs get urine infections because they had such a rigid routine they would only urinate in their own yards, and when they had to be taken somewhere else they simply held on long past the point when their bladder was full. In the case of one woman who called me for help, the family had almost become slaves to their dog when they tried to vary the habit of having it constantly with them. If they attempted to leave it alone in the yard, it barked and howled incessantly the whole time they were out. If they left it inside, it urinated and defecated all over the house (something it never did if they were present). Holidays were out of the question and things had got so bad they didn't even go out to dinner all together; one person always had to stay home with the dog.

When a situation has got that far out of hand there will be a bumpy period of adjustment as the dog is retrained, although the short-term pain will be worth the long-term gain. But it's important to face up to the problem.

I once had a lady ask me, 'How do I stop the dog from urinating on my bed?'

I said, 'Is there a door to your bedroom?'

'Yes,' she replied.

'Well, shut it. Problem solved.'

She said, 'Oh, but my dog wouldn't like that! He'd get upset.'

That may well be true but it would be a short-term pain. If you don't want to live with urine-scented sheets or chewed-up shoes or constant barking or whatever the issue might be, you have to face the problem and put in the work to deal with it.

Some words of advice on dogs' behavioural problems

Don't over-think it. Some problems need addressing at the behavioural level but others are a matter of practical management by the owner. Here's a good example of the latter: Vicki and I brought home a little pound puppy called Lenny. He was nine

MY TOP TIPS FOR DOG OWNERS

weeks old when he came to us and we'd had him for three or four weeks when we couldn't find him one morning. The usual routine was for me to let him out of his enclosure first thing. He would then have a little run around and he'd come and sit on the verandah with Chilli. The first part went as usual, but when we looked for him a little while later there was no sign of him and he didn't come when we called.

Living where we do, and having the birds we have, we get foxes. The night before I had put out a 1.5-metre-long fox trap – a humane one, of course – and I'd used some beautiful fresh sausages as bait, with pieces leading up to the trap and others inside where eating them would trigger the door mechanism. It took a few minutes before we thought to look in the trap, and sure enough, there was young Leonard, unable to get out but completely unperturbed about it, happy with his nice big tummy-full of sausages.

Now, I could have done a whole training program with him to get rid of his happy association between the trap and an extra feed, but there was a far simpler solution: shut the gate. Lenny had got out through a gate that was meant to be locked but had been left ajar. If we made sure that gate stayed shut his fox-trap days would be over.

If your dog escapes from the yard, fix your fence or build a pen. If he did it once and you got him back, you got lucky. Next time he might get hit by a car or crawl into a drainpipe and take four days to die. That should never happen, but it does. Management of your animals' situation is just as important as training and caring for them in other ways.

Treat your animals well and they will give you companionship that will enrich your life immeasurably.

Acknowledgements

Many people – and animals – have helped me get where I am today. In particular: my wife, Vicki, who is always there; my three daughters, Lauren, Rochelle and Claire, who put my feet on the ground; and my stepdaughter, Lauren Bourke, who makes sure they stay there.

I'd also like to make a special thanks to Peter Chasak, a true friend and mentor; to Peter Cooper, who never lost faith in the dogs; and to the entire team behind the Macquarie Island success – proving that nothing is impossible.

To Robyn Stark, my PA and friend, thank you for doing the work and letting me receive the credit.

Thank you Hazel Flynn, for helping me find the words and relive the adventures. And thanks to the ABC Books/HarperCollins team, in particular Katie Stackhouse who wanted to hear the stories and Rachel Dennis who kept everything running smoothly, and to the eagle-eyed Alex Nahlous.

And to Sunny and King, the best dogs any person could ever own, thanks for giving me the skills I needed more effectively than all the books, videos and seminars in the world could have done.

About the Co-author

Hazel Flynn is an author, editor, features writer and columnist and a former publisher. This is her seventh book. She specialises in bringing history to life and helping people like Steve tell their fascinating stories.